Modern Critical Interpretations

Modern Critical Interpretations

Toni Morrison's
Sula

Edited and with an introduction by
Harold Bloom
Sterling Professor of the Humanities
Yale University

CHELSEA HOUSE PUBLISHERS
Philadelphia

Library of Congress Cataloging-in-Publication Data

Toni Morrison's Sula / edited and with an introduction
by Harold Bloom.
        cm.—(Modern critical interpretations)
    Includes bibliographical references and index.
    ISBN 0-7910-5194-3
    1. Morrison, Toni. Sula.   2. Afro-American women
in literature.
    3. Ohio—In literature.   I. Bloom, Harold.   II. Series.
PS3563.O8749S838   1999
813'.54—dc21   98-50188
                                                   CIP

Contributing Editor: Henna Remstein

Contents

Editor's Note

My Introduction dissents from all socio-political and ideological interpretations of Sula Peace.

Rita Bergenholtz sees *Sula* as Toni Morrison's satire on clichéd thinking, while Marie Nigro examines the characters who live in Medallion, Ohio. Barbara Christian reads Sula as a paradoxical fable, at once a critique of the community's failure to live, and yet a celebration of survival, after which Hortense J. Spillers traces the changes in black female characterization in the transition from Zora Neale Hurston and Margaret Walker to Toni Morrison.

Stephanie A. Dematrakopoulos emphasizes the primacy of the relationship between Nel and Sula, while Melvin Dixon traces Morrison's symbolic geography. Trudier Harris refreshingly comments upon the ironies of *Sula*, which subvert morality and ideology, while Carolyn M. Jones contrasts Sula's status as unredeemed outcast to what she judges to be the self-redemption of Sethe in *Beloved*.

In a useful analysis, Karen Carmean suggests that *Sula*'s aim is to help us give up a simplistic dualism, after which Patricia Hunt returns us to a dualistic politics, even as she decries white political dualism. Philip Page accurately shows that *Sula* incarnates a series of unresolved opportunities, while Biman Basu praises Morrison for catching "the Black voice."

This volume concludes with Jan Furman's judgment that Sula is "unthinking and childlike," and so destructive. We come back full circle to my Introduction, which intimates that such judgments are foreign to this tale, if not to its teller.

Introduction

Political interpretation has been all the rage, academic and journalistic, during the last thirty years. No contemporary novelist of anything like Toni Morrison's eminence is so insistent that she desires political interpretation by her exegetes. She certainly has received what she calls for: an entire sect of cheerleaders crowd in her wake. Very little can be done against such a fashion at this time. If the United States achieves a larger measure of social justice in a generation or so, then Morrison yet may be esteemed more for her narrative art, invention, and style than for her exemplary political correctness. Myself an archaic survival, a dinosaur still lurching about the halls of Yale and New York University, I go on reading for aesthetic experience only. This brief Introduction therefore will consider *Sula* only as an artistic achievement, and not as a weapon wielded against indubitable societal oppression by a celebrated African-American feminist Marxist. The essays reprinted in this volume are more than sufficient to meet Morrison's expressed ideological standards for her academic followers.

Sula herself is a total rebel against all society, all conventions, and nearly all moralities. A "demon" in the eyes of the black community, Sula is a kind of Lilith, taking sexual satisfaction where she will. Not evil but doom-eager, Sula quests desperately for freedom, but she necessarily is self-victimized, as Morrison makes clear:

> In a way, her strangeness, her naiveté, her craving for the other half of her equation was the consequence of an idle imagination. Had she paints, or clay, or knew the discipline of the dance, or strings; had she anything to engage her tremendous curiosity and her gift for metaphor, she might have exchanged the restlessness and preoccupation with whim for an activity that provided her with all she longed for. And like any artist with no art form, she became dangerous.

Trust the tale and not the teller: is Sula an artist without an art form, or is she a Zora Neale Hurston–like vitalist who has wandered into the wrong novel? Morrison brooks no rivals: Ralph Ellison is a hidden target in *The Bluest Eye* and *Song of Solomon*, while Hurston's heroic egoism is parodied in *Sula*. Aesthetically, this is all to the good; Morrison is at her best when she is most agonistic. Sula Peace bears a name itself ironic, since her mode of individualism can achieve no peace whatsoever. Her mother Hannah, the freest of all erotic beings, dies in an accidental fire that can be interpreted as a punishment only if you are morally diseased. Sula, like Hannah, is a natural seductress, a witch if again you have it so. But ideological readings of her pathos seem to me as irrelevant as moral judgments; Sula floats free of interpretative designs, including Morrison's own. She remains Morrison's most memorable character, largely because she resists categorization. Her challenge to the community is both ancient and original; doom-eagerness cannot be confined. Her intensity and fatedness are alike Faulknerian; she would give another dimension to *Sanctuary*, without disturbing the violent cosmos of that now underrated novel. As a vivid figure, she is curiously unique in Morrison's fiction, and we allegorize or moralize Sula to our own loss. No program of Liberation would have saved her from herself, or from the individuality of her familial past.

RITA A. BERGENHOLTZ

Toni Morrison's Sula: *A Satire on Binary Thinking*

Attempts to define Toni Morrison's novel *Sula* are as numerous as they are diverse. The text has been read as a "black woman's epic," a study of "female friendship," an "antiwar novel," a "fable," an exploration of the "feminine psyche," and "a prime postmodernist text."! If one were to single out one particular interpretation and argue that it were somehow superior, somehow right while the others were wrong, that person would fall into the trap of binary thinking which is also what Morrison's text is "about." Deborah E. McDowell explains further:

> The narrative [*Sula*] insistently blurs and confuses . . . binary oppositions. It glories in paradox and ambiguity beginning with the prologue that describes the setting, the Bottom, situated spatially in the top. We enter a new world here, a world where we never get to the "bottom" of things, a world that demands a shift from an either/or orientation to one that is both/and, full of shifts and contradictions.

In my own attempt to describe *Sula*, I will expand upon McDowell's thesis and argue that the novel may also be read as an extended satire on binary (reductive, clichéd) thinking. Because satire is a notoriously imprecise term, a clarification of its usage in this essay is appropriate.

From *African American Review* 30, no. 1 (Spring 1996). © 1996 by Rita Bergenholtz.

The traditional definition of satire as a didactic art form was articulated by Horace in the first century B.C., restated and amplified by Dryden at the close of the seventeenth century, and upheld by several prominent theorists in the first half of the twentieth century. In fact, as recently as 1985 Linda Hutcheon argued that parody should not be confused with satire, "which is extra-mural (social, moral) in its ameliorative aim to hold up to ridicule the vices and follies of mankind, with an eye to their correction." Dryden's "Discourse concerning the Origin and Progress of Satire" (1693) has largely been responsible for this view of satire. As Dustin Griffin explains, "Our reigning notion of satire as a moral art and as a carefully constructed and unified contrast between vice and virtue finds its fullest and most influential presentation in Dryden's essay." According to Dryden, "Satire is a kind of Poetry . . . invented for the purging of our Minds; in which Humane Vices, Ignorance, and Errors, and all things besides . . . are severely Reprehended." This definition highlights two related points which deserve attention. First, Dryden's theory of satire as correction and reformation clearly fails to describe his own satiric practice; and, second, it is intended to describe only formal verse (or Roman) satire and not Menippean (or Varronian) satire.

Regarding the first point, Edgar Johnson aptly notes that "it is hard to detect any reformatory zeal in Mac Flecknoe and the booby-trap denouement of its coronation scene." The same may be said about the satires of Horace, who argues that his goal is to laugh men out of their follies—thus drawing attention to the moral aspect of his satire—but, as Griffin notes, "Satire, as Horace practices it, is considerably more diverse than laughter at folly." In fact, contrary to what the satirist may claim in defense of his or her work, the satirist's primary aim has generally been to upset our conventional literary and moral expectations—not to validate them. Moreover, as John R. Clark argues, rather than attacking folly and vice, "Satiric plots regularly dramatize the triumph of folly or vice." We need only recall the end of *Gulliver's Travels*—where Gulliver converses with his horses—or the conclusion of Pope's "Epilogue to the Satires: Dialogue I"—where Vice triumphs with great pageantry—to recognize the validity of this statement.

Furthermore, it is significant that Dryden's theory is intended to describe only formal verse satire (as practiced by Horace, Juvenal, and Persius), and not Menippean satire. Like Quintillian before him and many theorists after him, Dryden draws a clear distinction between the two satiric traditions—privileging the Roman tradition of verse satire established by Lucilius (second century B.C.) and disregarding the older, more complex Menippean tradition, named after its founder Menippus of Gadara (third century B.C.). In the twentieth century, such prominent theorists as Northrop Frye (*Anatomy of Criticism*, 1957) and Mikhail Bakhtin (*Problems of*

Dostoevsky's Poetics, 1929) have attempted to rectify this imbalance. However, Bakhtin's theory—which reverses the traditional hierarchy and privileges "dialogic" Menippean satire instead—also maintains a distinction between satiric traditions. Building upon Bakhtin's theory, Frank Palmeri's *Satire in Narrative* (1990) likewise favors narrative satire:

> . . . verse satire does function conservatively to enforce an established cultural code by ridiculing deviations from it. However, narrative satire parodies both the official voice of established beliefs and the discourse of its opponents. In doing so, it interrogates any claims to a systematic understanding of the world. Narrative satire is . . . potentially more subversive.

In *Satire: A Critical Reintroduction* (1994), Dustin Griffin develops a more comprehensive approach to the two major traditions of satire, privileging neither. Indeed, Griffin suggests that "to read Menippean works alongside those of Horace, Donne, or Pope is to see poetic satire, even formal verse satire, in new light. The moral design is but one of several elements. Neither tradition, in Bakhtin's terms, is 'monological.'" Furthermore, instead of viewing satire merely as a rhetoric of persuasion, Griffin argues that "we may arrive at a fuller understanding of the way satire works if we think of a rhetoric of inquiry, a rhetoric of provocation, a rhetoric of display, a rhetoric of play." Satire as Griffin describes it may be found in either verse or narrative; however, since the novel's "rise" in the eighteenth century, this genre has proved to be the satirist's preferred form. As numerous theorists and critics have now recognized, the satirist attacks, indirectly, all kinds of unexamined and clichéd thinking. In short, the satirist's primary goal is not to "teach" us moral lessons or to reform us, but to entertain us and give us food for thought.

This contemporary view of satire underscores one of Toni Morrison's acknowledged goals as a writer. In an interview with Nellie McKay, Morrison remarks, "I don't want to give my readers something to swallow. I want to give them something to feel and think about. . . ." Moreover, this broader view of satire aligns itself closely with the poststructuralist project of inverting and then leveling hierarchies, whether they be moral, philosophical, or linguistic. A closer look at the "nigger joke" in the first chapter of *Sula* will allow us to recognize how Morrison consistently frustrates any attempt to think in strictly binary terms, impelling us to contrast the valley with the Bottom, the Bottom with the suburbs. Opposition engenders competition, hierarchy, and taxonomy. Morrison's view of this process is clear from *Sula*'s concluding sentence: "It was a fine cry—loud and long—but it had no bottom and it had no top, just circles and circles of sorrow."

Morrison employs and undermines binary opposition with the agricultural imagery which she evokes at the outset of *Sula*. The slave in Morrison's "nigger joke" knows what bottom land is, but he is fooled by a "good white farmer" who convinces him that the fertile bottom land is actually up in the hills, which he describes as "'the bottom of heaven—the best land there is.'" The credulous "nigger," therefore, appears to be the butt (or "bottom") of the good white farmer's joke. But is he really? If the Bottom's hilly terrain is unyielding, then why do the white hunters wonder "in private if maybe the white farmer was right after all. Maybe it *was* the bottom of heaven"? And why do the white folks later change their minds, move to the Bottom, and rename it the "suburbs"? Perhaps the knavish farmer is really the fool? In any case, the joke does amuse, for the guileless slave believes—literally—that heaven has a top and a bottom. This brief look at the "nigger joke" which introduces *Sula*—and serves as an emblem for it—highlights a number of binary oppositions that are interrogated throughout the text: black/white, good/evil, tragic/comic, spiritual/material, literal/metaphoric, real/fantastic, and free/enslaved.

Although the introductory joke hinges, in part, upon a black/white opposition, white people remain peripheral figures in this text. Apparently Morrison, like Sula, is not merely concerned with surface differences like color. Plainly, Morrison wants us to understand how reductive and destructive it is to affix antithetical labels such as good and evil to entire races of people, although many of the characters in the novel do just that. For instance, according to the white bargeman who finds Chicken Little's body, black people are simply "animals, fit for nothing but substitutes for mules, only mules didn't kill each other the way niggers did." Similarly, according to most of the residents of the Bottom, the worst thing a black woman like Sula can do is to sleep with a white man: "They insisted that all unions between white men and black women be rape; for a black woman to be willing was literally unthinkable. In that way, they regarded integration with precisely the same venom that white people did." The trenchant irony is not just that both blacks and whites employ binary thinking, but that black women attempt to look more like white women (with all of their nose pulling and hair straightening) and black men yearn to do the white man's work, while both white men and white women, according to *Sula*, secretly lust after black men and their legendary penises. The distinction between black and white is further blurred by the marginal character Tar Baby, a man who may be white or may just be an undefinable mixture of black and white.

Binary thinking operates on the notion that one term of an opposing pair will be privileged. In the following excerpt from an interview, Morrison suggests a weakness in binary perspectives which she explores in *Sula*: "I was interested . . . in doing a very old, worn-out idea, which was to do something with good and evil, but putting it in different terms." Morrison continues: "I started out by thinking that one can never really define good and evil. Sometimes good looks like evil; sometimes evil looks like good—you never really know what it is. It depends on what uses you put it to." Eva, the matriarch of the Peace family and a symbol of black folk wisdom, presents a number of interpretive problems in this area. How, for example, are we to respond to her abandonment of her children, her loss of a limb, and her torching of Plum? Should we admire her stoutheartedness and her ability to survive, or should we be horrified by her actions? What about the deweys? Should we praise Eva's generosity for housing these stray boys or censure her absent-minded treatment of them? Joanne V. Gabbin offers one possible answer when she remarks that Morrison "avoids the pitfalls of attributing all that is good to the tradition. In *Sula* proverbial wisdom of the folk is held up to Morrison's spotlight and collective ignorance often appears." Specifically, Eva follows the folk wisdom which urges a mother to treat her children the same. Consequently, the deweys are "bludgeoned into insipid sameness by folk love and indifference."

Like her grandmother, Sula Peace presents a problem for people who think in binary terms, people who insist that a character be discreet, consistent, and thus confinable. Should we admire Sula's courage, her determination to be free to "make herself"? Or should we loathe her for engaging in casual sex with her best friend's husband? Our initial response to Sula's act of betrayal is to side with the people of the Bottom and label Nel the "good" woman and Sula the "evil" one. After all, Nel behaves properly; she fits nicely "into the scheme of things," into her society's hierarchical structure which has a clear moral top and a definite moral bottom. Indeed, Nel admirably performs all of the obligatory roles: dutiful friend, respectful daughter, loyal wife, and nurturing mother. Later, she acts the wronged wife and the forgiving Christian woman. In contrast, Sula disregards social conventions, following only her own heart and conscience. Sula doesn't care that the definition of a black woman is one who makes other people. Sula doesn't care that the men she sleeps with are married. And Sula especially doesn't care that a "good" woman, like Nel, would never be on top of her man during sexual intercourse but beneath him, not unlike the hem of his garments.

Traditional definitions of satire tend to reduce it to a form of "romance" which, in its broadest sense, may include any narrative which has a well-defined "good guy" who triumphs over a well-defined "bad guy" in order to produce the expected resolution: a happy ending (which is also the moral). Such absolutes, however, are uncommon in satiric novels. In fact, Morrison clearly wants us to recognize that although Nel and Sula appear to be quite different—one the epitome of goodness and the other the embodiment of evil—they are also quite similar. That is, if Sula is evil for watching Hannah dance in pain as flames melt her lovely skin, then Nel is also evil for experiencing a sense of pleasure and tranquility when Chicken Little disappears beneath the water. The "Wright" approach to morality judges an action evil only if it is witnessed by others. In contrast, Morrison suggests that the distinction between good and evil is rarely so clear-cut as Helen and Nel suppose; consequently there is some good and some evil in both Sula and in Nel. The most significant difference between the women might be that Sula accepts the fuzziness of moral categories with her usual good humor, whereas Nel refuses to look at the unacceptable aspects of herself, aspects which confound her clichéd thinking. In fact, Sula's ability to laugh at herself may be her most redeeming quality.

Like the "niggers" who tell the "nigger joke" on themselves, Sula understands that in life ". . . the laughter [i]s part of the pain." So when Nel asks her if she "'still expect[s] folks to love'" her after all "'the dirt [she] did in this town,'" Sula's creative reply is painfully funny. Instead of responding with a clichéd remark like the townspeople will love her "when hell freezes over," Sula imagines new ways of inverting the world of the Bottom, new metaphors for describing what "never" feels like:

> "Oh, they'll love me all right. It will take time, but they'll love me. . . . After all the old women have lain with the teen-agers; when all the young girls have slept with their old drunken uncles; after all the black men fuck all the white ones; when all the white women kiss all the black ones; when the guards have raped all the jailbirds and after all the whores make love to their grannies; after all the faggots get their mothers' trim; when Lindbergh sleeps with Bessie Smith and Norma Shearer makes it with Stepin Fetchit; after all the dogs have fucked all the cats and every weathervane on every barn flies off the roof to mount the hogs . . . then there'll be a little love left over for me."

The tone of this passage, like the tone of the "nigger joke," may be described as tragicomic. Indeed, tragicomedy has much in common with the Negro blues. As Ralph Ellison explains, "The blues is an impulse to keep the painful details and episodes of a brutal experience alive in one's aching consciousness, to finger its jagged grain, and to transcend it, not by consolation of philosophy but by squeezing from it a near-tragic, near-comic lyricism." In fact, the satirist has always been fond of grotesque combinations which confound the ridiculous and the terrifying, the fantastic and the real, the human and the bestial. In an oft-quoted remark, Thomas Mann predicted, correctly, that the grotesque would prove to be the dominant artistic style of the twentieth century: "The striking feature of modern art is that . . . it sees life as tragicomedy, with the result that the grotesque is its most genuine style."

Grotesque images are provocative, for they create "a clash between incompatible reactions—laughter on the one hand and horror or disgust on the other." Such imagery pervades Morrison's text. How else could we characterize the image of Eva swinging and swooping around her house on crutches, or the image of Hannah "bobbing like a sprung jack-in-the-box," or the three deweys, who play chain-gang in the intolerable heat and who dance "a little jig around the befuddled Shadrack" before they lead the people of the Bottom on a macabre dance of death? In fact, throughout *Sula* death is repeatedly treated in a tragicomic manner. A salient example is Sula's demise, which "was the best news folks up in the Bottom had had since the promise of work at the tunnel." As the narrator informs us, some people came to the funeral simply to verify Sula's death:

> Others came to see that nothing went awry, that the shallow-minded and small-hearted kept their meanness at bay, and that the entire event be characterized by that abiding gentleness of spirit to which they themselves had arrived by the simple determination not to let anything—anything at all: not failed crops, not rednecks, lost jobs, sick children, rotten potatoes, broken pipes, bug-ridden flour, third-class coal, educated social workers, thieving insurance men, garlic-ridden hunkies, corrupt Catholics, racist Protestants, cowardly Jews, slaveholding Moslems, jack-leg nigger preachers, squeamish Chinamen, cholera, dropsy or the Black Plague, let alone a strange woman—keep them from their God.

Although death permeates this novel, egregious lists like this one provide a "sense of joy" which invigorates Morrison's writing and animates Sula's thoughts, a sense that is absent from the lives of most of the women up in the Bottom, especially "the church women who frowned on any bodily expression of joy (except when the hand of God commanded it)." Morrison's satire criticizes these ostensibly good women who are preoccupied with appearing religious. In truth, these women are more concerned that "their straightened hair [will] beat them home" than they are about Sula. Moreover, from their distorted perspective, nearly everything and everyone is an obstacle on their righteous path to God. The end result is that they diminish the spiritual element of life to the material, just as the slave in the "nigger joke" reduces heaven to some hills overlooking Medallion, Ohio. As Alvin B. Kernan explains, pseudo-religious people often substitute "some objective thing for an subjective reality: a pious expression . . . folded hands, and frequent references to the Deity for true religion."

This is a rather accurate description of Helene (or Helen) Wright, a woman who grew up in a "somber house that held four Virgin Marys," a woman whose "dark eyes" are "arched in a perpetual query about other people's manners. . . . It was Helene who never turned her head in church when latecomers arrived; . . . Helene who introduced the giving of banquets of welcome to returning Negro veterans." In the following monologue, Morrison exquisitely captures the essence of Helene's superficial, automatic religion:

> Lord, I've never been so glad to see this place. But look at the dust. Get the rags, Nel. Oh, never mind. Let's breathe awhile first. Lord, I never thought I'd get back here safe and sound. Whoo. Well, it's over. Good and over. Praise His name. Look at that. I told that old fool not to deliver any milk and there's the can curdled to beat all. What gets into people? I told him not to. Well, I got other things to worry 'bout. Got to get a fire started. I left it ready so I wouldn't have to do nothin' but light it. Lord, it's cold. Don't just sit there, honey. You could be pulling your nose . . .

The juxtaposition of religious terminology—"Praise His name"—with dust, rags, curdled milk, and nose pulling tends to diminish the sacred. (Or, to look at it another way, the comparison magnifies the secular, thus transforming nose pulling into a kind of religious ceremony.)

Confirming Kernan's point above, Palmeri explains that "the plot and rhetoric of narrative satire cohere in accomplishing the same movement of lowering or leveling." He continues:

> Narrative satire reduced the spiritual and abstract to the same level as the physical and material, concentrating for this purpose on the natural functions of the body. . . . With this focus, narrative satire reduces all that might be heroic and noble to a common level of physical experience which it openly acknowledges, if it does not always joyously celebrate.

Sula is a novel which does indeed acknowledge all of the natural functions of the human body, what Bernard McElroy refers to as "the four irreducibles of human life . . . birth, food, sex, and death." In fact, McElroy suggests that the "closest link" between such writers as Rabelais and Joyce may be "their depiction of the grotesque body. . . . The celebration of copulation, birth, devouring, and elimination that Bakhtin finds in Rabelais is everywhere in Joyce, culminating in Molly's ruminations in the final chapter." Morrison belongs to this long satiric tradition, which includes writers as diverse as Swift and Sterne in the eighteenth century and Barth and Nabokov in the twentieth. Unlike romance or tragedy, satire is a genre in which characters find the time to eat and to secrete. By developing such scatological themes, the satirist is able "to rivet the attention, to shock, and to move [her] audience."

The satirist also entertains. Part of *Sula*'s absurd humor resides in the fact that the initial joke about the "bottom of heaven" is carried on throughout the novel. That is to say, in nearly every chapter, a "bottom"— or, if you prefer, an ass, rear-end, derriere, or buttocks—makes a literal or metaphoric appearance. Such a preposterous number of bottoms suggests that Morrison—a black woman—is able to laugh at one of the physical features with which black people (especially black women) have often been pejoratively associated. First there are a number of literal bottoms to be observed. There is Nel's "wet buttocks" being soaped by her mother in Cecile Sabat's house; poor Plum's exposed buttocks in the frigid outhouse; Nel's and Sula's "behinds" strolling down the street to Edna Finch's Mellow House—a "view" which men both young and old watch "with interest"; Hannah's "behind," which "she made men aware of"; and Sula's rear-end "gliding, with just a hint of a strut, down the path toward the road. . . . Even from the rear Nel could tell that it was Sula and that she was smiling. . .".

Even more significant is the way in which blacks and whites use the "bottom" synecdochically to represent the whole person. For instance, when Helene Wright boards the wrong car of a train, the white conductor barks, "'We don't 'low no mistakes on this train. Now git your butt on in there.'" The narrator employs similar imagery to describe Nel and Sula as twelve-year-old girls: They were "wishbone thin and easy-assed." Further-more, when Hannah inquires whether or not Eva ever loved her, Eva replies, "'You settin' here with you healthy-ass self and ax me did I love you? Them big old eyes in your head would a been two holes full of maggots if I hadn't.'" And when Sula returns from her ten-year odyssey, Eva warns, "'. . . don't let your mouth start nothing that your ass can't stand.'" One final bottom deserves mention. As the narrator explains, ". . . if a valley man happened to have business up in those hills—collecting rent or insurance payments—he might see a dark woman in a flowered dress doing a bit of cakewalk, a bit of black bottom . . . ".

Like the "nigger joke," however, the identification of the self—here, the black self—with the "bottom" or behind is both comic and tragic.

Focusing on the "bottom" instead of the whole person results in a demeaning, fragmented perspective, a way of seeing people which may degenerate into the white policeman's view that, if Tar Baby "didn't like to live in shit, he should come down out of those hills, and live like a decent white man." This is not to say that there is anything wrong with looking at or talking about "bottoms." The problem arises, however, when one particular body part becomes a metaphor for a whole person. Morrison seems to underscore this by populating her novel with fragmented characters, characters like Nel, whose sexuality is represented by "empty," "old thighs"; Shadrack, whose monstrous hands are a metaphor for his inability to reach out and touch other people; and the deweys, whose "magnificent teeth" signal their animal rapacity.

Perhaps the most memorable fragmented character in *Sula* is the one-legged matriarch, Eva Peace. Apparently she gives up a leg in order to survive, in order that her children may survive. The sacrifice is, of course, heroic. Survival, it seems, is quite expensive. Nevertheless, Eva's tragedy recalls the cliché "it cost an arm and a leg," which is, according to *A Dictionary of Catch Phrases*, a variant of an earlier expression, "even at the cost of a leg." The dark humor encircling this absent limb becomes plain once we realize that Eva's condition is a literalization of a metaphorical expression. Palmeri explains that "the reduction of the spiritual to physical in satiric narrative corresponds to the rhetorical reduction of metaphor to literal meanings . . . [which] often operates on idioms and clichés . . . [and] works to satirize hidebound characters . . . who live within the confines of clichés and received ideas." In fact, this technique of reducing the metaphorical to the literal is a pervasive source of ironic humor in numerous satiric works, from Jonathan Swift's *A Tale of a Tub* to Gabriel Garcia Marquez's *One Hundred Years of Solitude*.

Similarly, much of *Sula*'s dark humor results from this same strategy: Distorting the responsibilities of motherhood, Eva murders her son because she fears that he literally wants "'to crawl back in [her] womb,'" yet she literally takes a free fall in an attempt to save her daughter; exceeding the bounds of curiosity, Sula concludes that "it's just as well [Ajax] left. Soon I would have torn the flesh from his face just to see if I was right about the gold . . . '"; parodying all of the boy/men in the novel, the three deweys decide to remain literally as children in body as well as in mind; spoofing the Trojan myth, Ajax (or A. Jacks) is (almost) literally a Greek "bearing gifts"; mocking the conventions of marriage and the white world, Jude literally abandons his tie; and undermining the dignity of Nel's grief and bitterness, a gray ball literally forms "just to the right of her, in the air, just out of view."

This final example of Nel's gray ball is especially significant because it exemplifies Tzvetan "Todorov's notion of the supernatural as literalized trope." We can believe—perhaps with some difficulty—that Eva could ignite her own son or that the deweys could stop growing; however, the idea of a gray ball's defying the laws of gravity and following Nel for some twenty-eight years introduces us to the realm of the fantastic. We no longer ask what the ball means, but whether such a ball—and such a world—is possible. Brian McHale explains that "the 'bottom,' the deep structure of the fantastic, is . . . ontological rather than epistemological. . . . The fantastic, in other words, involves a face-to-face confrontation between the possible (the 'real') and the impossible, the normal and the paranormal." Moreover, Morrison's use of the fantastic links her with such celebrated satirists as Lucian, Rabelais, Swift, and Garcia Marquez. According to Bakhtin, "We could not find a genre more free than the menippea in its invention and use of the fantastic." He continues: "We emphasize that the fantastic here serves not for the positive embodiment of truth, but as a mode for searching after truth, provoking it, and, most important, testing it."

The satiric strategy of literalizing language also reminds us that language is conventional. As Catherine Belsey explains, language "comes into being at the same time as society." The members of a society implicitly agree "to attach a specific signified to a specific signifier." Through time and habit, however, we tend to forget that language is not "a simple process of naming preexisting objects and states but a system through which we give meaning to the world." In short, the nomenclator has the power. In many mythologies, God gives the right to name to a privileged individual. In *Sula* Morrison bestows this power on Eva. Karen Stein explains:

> Eva takes on an important task which the Biblical Adam performed, that of giving names. However, these labels hinder rather than promote the development of the people she names. The nicknames she gives to neighbors and to her real and adopted children become the ones they are known by. When she calls each of three very different adopted children Dewey the similar names create an identical fate for all of them.

Beginning with the "nigger joke," Morrison reminds us that there is no proper meaning inherent in words or names—just as there is no correct meaning for Sula's birthmark or for the plague of robins—only meanings we assign to people and events in our attempts to establish the limits—the top and the bottom, so to speak—of reality. More so than Eva, the "good white farmer" uses and abuses his power to name. Maliciously inverting the truth, he calls the top of the valley the Bottom to maintain control over the black slave as well as the fertile bottom land. But if the "good white farmer" controls the language and the people, then how are we to account for this most remarkable sentence tucked up in the "nigger joke":

> A good white farmer promised freedom and a piece of bottom land to his slave if he would perform some very difficult chores. When the slave completed the work, he asked the farmer to keep his end of the bargain. Freedom was easy . . . the farmer had no objection to that. But he didn't want to give up any land.

"Freedom was easy . . ."? If there is a message in this novel, it seems to me that it is precisely the opposite: Freedom is never easy. However, Morrison is more concerned with posing questions than with delivering messages. What, we might ask, does freedom really mean. Like all of the black women up in the Bottom, Nel is free. Yet for forty-three years she labors under the burden of assuming that she must be the good girl and Sula the evil one. Is this freedom? Nel's husband Jude is also free. Yet Jude wastes his adult life telling "whiney tale[s]," mostly about how "a Negro man ha[s] a hard row to hoe in this world" and other such comforting clichés. Is that freedom? Morrison provides no answers; her goal, like that of many a satirist, is to provoke thought. For only by frequently inquiring what it means to be free, to be in love, to be human, to be black or white, to be good or evil can we truly be alive.

MARIE NIGRO

In Search of Self: Frustration and Denial in Toni Morrison's Sula

Although Toni Morrison may not have intentionally created a novel to celebrate the working class or to explore the consequences of work among African Americans, she has, in *Sula*, celebrated the lives of ordinary people who daily must work and provide. *Sula* celebrates many lives: It is the story of the friendship of two African American women; it is the story of growing up Black and female; but most of all, it is the story of a community. Events that befall the denizens of the Bottom, a segregated community of mythical Medallion, Ohio, can be seen as those that might befall residents of any Black community in any town during the years of this narrative, 1919 to 1965.

Historically, great literature has concerned itself with nature, death, and love. Writers have been literary professionals whose primary occupation was writing and whose experiences were far removed from those who must work for a living. Critics such as Nicholas Coles, Terry Eagleton, Louis Kampf and Paul Lauter, and John Wayman have objected to a historical canon that is irrelevant to "everyman." Eagleton observes that literature has been created for the cultural elite, and the rest of us have come to consider literature as a reflection of an elitist lifestyle to which the ordinary person cannot hope to relate. He suggests that the literary establishment embrace works that celebrate the lives of ordinary people and acknowledge the struggles of real people, for example, working-class writing.

From *Journal of Black Studies* 28, no. 6 (July 1998) pp. 724–738. © 1998 by Sage Publications Inc. Reprinted by permission of Sage Publications, Inc.

Coles defines working-class literature as that written by working-class persons or professional writers from working-class backgrounds. He stresses the importance of creating and reading texts for most people, including minorities, women, and working-class students.

Kampf and Lauter also see literature and literary criticism as separated from life—as a self-serving ideology that is related to the lives of the literary establishment but offers nothing to readers who may be from ordinary families or working-class backgrounds. Wayman decries the irrelevancy of contemporary imaginative writing, which has nothing to offer working-class men and women. He finds it wrong that a national literature does not deal with "problems, aspirations, failures, and successes of the majority of men and women who inhabit the country." He notes that our culture, by ignoring real people and real problems, is saying that "we and our problems are not significant." He sees work as a "major shaping experience in our lives," an experience that deserves to be celebrated in literature. If, as Wayman suggests, work is the major shaping factor in our lives, what are the consequences of having no work, of enduring a demeaning job, or of having no outlet for one's creative energies?

In an interview with Claudia Tate, Toni Morrison notes that

> It would be interesting to do a piece of work on the kinds of work women do in novels written by women. What kinds of jobs they do, not just the paying jobs, but how they perceive work . . . . It's not just a question of being in the labor force and doing domestic kinds of things; it's about how one perceives work, how it fits into one's life.

She adds, "Aggression is not as new to Black women as it is to white women. Black women seem able to combine the nest and the adventure. . . . We don't find these places, these roles, mutually exclusive."

In the tightly knit community of the Bottom, survival is serious business, and each person must determine a means of existing in a world that is alien—White and male. Residents manage as best they can, working menial jobs, scrimping, and helping each other but always remaining within the understood boundaries prescribed by the hostile White world.

Although Morrison's novel is "imbedded in the context of the Black experience in America," the author of *Sula* succeeds in bringing to the reader of any race the joys, the suffering, and the pain of Eva, Hannah, Sula, Jude, and Shadrack.

Morrison carefully delineates Sula's family tree, allowing the reader to better understand the remarkable young woman that is Sula Peace. Before we ever meet Miss Peace, we meet her grandmother, Eva, who after five years of marriage to Boy-Boy, finds herself abandoned with three children and no idea of what to do next. Neighbors bring what food they can spare, but Eva realizes that she will soon wear out her welcome, so she asks a neighbor to watch her children and promises to be back in a few days. Eighteen months later, she returns on crutches with a shiny new purse and one leg. A check begins arriving monthly, and Eva starts building a house on Carpenter Road.

Eva's daughter, Hannah, is widowed when her only child Sula is age three. Mother and daughter move in with Eva where Hannah settles in to assume a life of caring for her daughter and her mother. Eva and Hannah create their own unconventional household. With the exception of Eva's husband Boy-Boy, mother and daughter love all men. Eva expresses her love for maleness by laughing, playing checkers, talking with her faithful men callers, and displaying her remaining one leg, which is "stockinged and shod at all times."

For Hannah, love of men and maleness is physical but without guile. She enjoys the company of men and leads the men of the Bottom to her bed. Her loving is described as "sweet, low and guileless . . . nobody, but nobody could say 'Hey sugar' like Hannah."

The business of survival is an everyday concern for Eva and Hannah, but because they are Black women in the 1920s, the only paid work available in Medallion is as domestics for ungrateful White families or as prostitutes. And even the prostitutes have fallen on hard times. So mother and daughter devise their own means of coping. During the summer, they join their neighbors in canning the harvest of fruits and vegetables in preparation for the hard winter ahead. The mysterious loss of Eva's leg provides a much-awaited monthly check. In addition, Eva takes in an array of boarders and stray people, some of whom pay and some of whom do not. It is in this unconventional and often chaotic household, filled with boarders, adopted children, and gentlemen callers, that Sula Mae Peace grows up.

In another part of the Bottom, in a house of suffocating order and real lace curtains, Nel Wright is growing up under the careful eye of Helene Wright. Sula and Nel meet in school and become friends who find in each other what each lacks in herself. Coming from an oppressively neat household, Nel relishes the casual disorder of Sula's household, where people drop in unannounced, chat, and laugh and where dirty dishes or stacked newspapers pile up. On the other hand, Sula enjoys going to Nel's house where she can sit on the red velvet sofa in the quiet of an afternoon for ten to twenty minutes—"still as dawn." The girls grow into womanhood clinging to each other, each providing what the other lacks in herself. Morrison explains to the reader that the two girls met and immediately "felt the ease and comfort of old friends. Because each had discovered years before that they were neither white nor male, and that all freedom and triumph was forbidden to them, they had set about creating something else to be." Together they create a single complete individual: Sula the impulsive, emotional one; Nel the practical one.

After graduating from general school, Sula goes to college and Nel marries Jude Greene. Under her mother's watchful eye, Nel and Jude have a "real" wedding in a church followed by a reception that Helene Wright has spent days preparing. Jude is a handsome young man who sings regularly in the church. He is 20 years old and works as a waiter in the Hotel Medallion. Jude knows his job could never support a wife, but he has plans to move on to something more lucrative. He has his eye on the New River Road.

Medallion has needed a bridge that would span the river and replace the raft presently used to take residents across to the next town. Although the plans are later changed to the construction of a tunnel, the project is still called the New River Road. Work has begun when Jude, along with a few other young Black men, go down to the hiring shack. Jude desperately wants to be part of building something that would last, something he could point to with pride. He longed for real work, not carrying trays and other people's dirty dishes. "More than anything he wanted the camaraderie of road men . . . that in the end produced something real, something that he could point to. . . . 'I built that road,' he could say."

Jude stands in line for six days and sees the gang bosses pick out southern White boys, Greeks, and Italians but never the young men from the Bottom. His masculinity is offended; his job at the hotel not only pays poorly, but it is demeaning to carry trays and pick up after other people when he wants so desperately the self-affirming job of building something where nothing had existed before. It was then that he considers marriage to Nel. He determines that she will be his anchor. She would always be there, whatever his fortune. She would be someone to whom he could always come home; he could care for her. With Nel, he could be complete. Together, Jude and Nel could make a complete person. So Nel joins with Jude to once again merge herself with another. She recognizes her role and performs the expected functions: She supports her husband, raises their children, and joins the church.

During an era in which the role of Black woman is clearly and stiflingly defined, Sula, unlike Nel, is determined to be herself. She refuses to accept the conventional boundaries of her race and gender, and by rejecting the mores of the outside world as well as those of her own community, Sula stands alone. When she returns to Medallion after ten years, looking fine and wearing city clothes, she appears much younger than her Medallion counterparts. When she confronts her grandmother, Eva scowls at her, suggesting that she needs to get married and have some babies.

Sula replies, "I don't want to make somebody else. I want to make myself." Eva retorts that a woman has no business "floatin'" around without a man. Shortly after that conversation, Sula places Eva in Sunnydale, a home for the elderly. The community quietly notes this as Sula's first aberrant act.

Sula returns to the Bottom with absolutely nothing to do; the town watches her every unconventional move. All the town knows that she has been to college and lived in big cities. It is even whispered that she has done the unforgivable and slept with White men. Morrison explains Sula's dilemma:

> Had she paints, or clay, . . . had she anything to engage her tremendous curiosity and her gift for metaphor, she might have exchanged the restlessness and preoccupation with whim for an activity that provided her with all she longed for. And like any artist with no art form, she became dangerous.

Dangerous indeed. Yet she never realizes how dangerous she really is because her sins are never intentional. During an afternoon visit, while Nel is sprinkling diapers, she asks Sula about life in the big city. Sula replies that the rest of the world is just a bigger version of Medallion. Later, when Nel walks in on Sula and Jude, they are down on all fours, naked. Jude, still waiting tables at the hotel, and Sula, with nothing else to do, each needing to fill up space in their lives, have found each other for that moment, and in that one moment, Nel's carefully ordered domestic life ceases to exist. Jude packs up and leaves on a bus for Detroit, and Nel is left with only his yellow necktie and a gray fuzzy ball that follows her wherever she goes.

Reliving that dreadful moment of discovery, Nel wonders: How could Sula have done that? How could Jude leave? The two most important people in her life have betrayed her. Nothing is left but that gray fuzzy ball hovering about her head and the pressing need to carry on for herself and her children. She takes a job as a chambermaid at the Hotel Medallion. And Sula, surprised at Nel's reaction, discovers that Nel is one of "them." Now Nel belongs to the town. It surprises her that Nel is so offended and acts as she does. Her friend is one of the reasons Sula has returned to Medallion, and now Nel is lost. Sula's refusal to conform or reform has cost her the only relationship she ever craved. Sula cannot understand that she has caused Nel intense pain, and that by a single act, Nel's life is changed forever. Sula, however, is not contrite as she stands alone, outside the boundaries of the community.

To fill up the emptiness in her life, Sula uses men much as her mother (now deceased) had done but with a different spirit. Whereas Hannah had been sweet and without guile and had respected the ways of the community, Sula goes to bed with men as often as she can but then carelessly tosses them aside. Unlike Hannah, for whom lovemaking was comforting, Sula regards lovemaking as wicked. The community of the Bottom now has even more reason to despise Sula, yet they tolerate her presence in their midst.

Should the reader consider Sula amoral, a monster, a devil? Here is a woman who has ruined the life of her only friend and then cannot understand Nel's pain. Here is a woman who beds the men of the town with bitterness, who appears to have no purpose in her life but that of self-gratification.

Renita Weems observes that in the characters of Sula, Eva, and Hannah,

> Morrison pays tribute to those women who are doing everything in life but what they are supposed to be doing: creative women—like so many of us and our mamas—without outlets for our creativity. An "artist with no art form" is how Sula Peace is described.

And with no art form, no outlet for her energies and her creativity, Sula, in her quest to "make herself," self-destructs.

To the little community in the Bottom, Sula has become a pariah. Sula is different from anyone the townspeople have ever known, and because she is not seeking money or material gain, she feels she has no obligation to explain her actions.

Barbara Smith observes that Sula is a frightening character because she refuses to settle for the "colored woman's" lot. Smith recalls her own experience:

> Having grown up in a family of talented women who worked as teachers in the segregated schools of the South and as domestics in the white kitchens of the North, I saw first hand the demoralizing effects of stymied intelligence and creativity.

Smith adds that folks in the Bottom hate Sula because she is a "living criticism of their dreadful lives of resignation."

When Nel visits Sula on her sickbed, she tries to understand her friend's insistence on living her life as she chooses:

> "You can't have it all, Sula."
> "Why? I can do it all, why can't I have it all?"

"You can't do it all. You a woman and a colored woman at that. You can't act like a man. You can't be walking around all independent-like, doing whatever you like, taking what you want, leaving what you don't."

Nel reminds Sula of her isolation from the community as the price of her independence. Sula replies that her loneliness is her own making. Nel's, she points out, is "somebody else's. . . . A secondhand lonely."

Sula Mae Peace dies before her thirty-first year. When she realizes that the dying is without pain, she smiles. "'Well, I'll be damned,' she thought, 'it didn't even hurt. Wait'll I tell Nel.'" Sula dies in 1941.

Life in the Bottom goes on. Each year, on January 3, Shadrack, a crazed army veteran who lives outside of town, marches through the community celebrating his own holiday, National Suicide Day. Shadrack began this morbid custom many years earlier as a means of coping with his own fear of death. A victim of World War I shell shock, he returned to the Bottom, but he could never forget the smell of death that had been all around him, frightening him out of his mind. He neither sought nor received companionship on his return, although he had formed a mysterious bond with a very young Sula. When the people of the Bottom realize that he is harmless, they leave him alone, tolerating his ranting, drinking, and his celebration of National Suicide Day. Shadrack's idea behind the holiday is that death is frightful, and if he could set aside one day a year for death, people could "get it out of the way" and not have to think about it for the rest of the year. And so, he began his own celebration of National Suicide Day, walking through town carrying a hangman's rope and ringing a bell. A few other outcasts follow him, but usually Shadrack marches alone as people hustle their children off the street and watch from behind their windows.

The march of 1942 (the year following the death of Sula) is different and will be remembered for years to come. This year, Shadrack's tribute to National Suicide Day comes during an especially cruel and bitter winter; folks are shivering in their poorly heated homes; children are sick; and adults are weary. Shadrack is grieving the loss of his only visitor, Sula, and has lost his zeal for the holiday. He thinks about calling off the march, but the brilliant sunlight on a winter's day encourages him to go on. To his surprise, he finds he is being followed by laughing children. No one has ever laughed during his marches. Soon adults join the march, laughing and dancing. Beckoned by the sunshine, the laughter, and the dancing, the crowd grows larger and larger as they "strutted, skipped, marched, and shuffled down the road." They continue through the White part of town and head for the New River Road. As they gaze at the excavation site, the bricks, the timber, and the iron girders, they see the broken promises, and they remember the words "no work today." As they gaze on the site in the bright winter sun, the dancing turns to rage; the laughter ceases. Without realizing what is happening, the marchers, men and women, jump over the gate and pick up the steel rails, smashing the bricks and timber, killing the tunnel they were not permitted to build.

What happens next is talked about for years to come. The earth shifts, shorings slip, and the marchers are lost in a wall of water. Many die on that National Suicide Day as Shadrack stands there watching, ringing his bell.

Morrison's narrative shifts from that awful day in 1942 to a day in 1965. A mature Nel observes that things are better now, or at least they seem better. Colored people are working in the shops in town, some even handling money and wearing cash register keys. Karla F. C. Holloway believes that the novel finally belongs to Nel, the survivor, who is still picking up the pieces of her life, still working, and still doing the "right thing." As part of her charitable work, she visits the aged Eva in Sunnydale. As Nel introduces herself to Eva, the old woman, barely rational, rants about a long buried childhood incident involving Nel and Sula. She mumbles a question, asking Nel how she killed the little boy so many years ago. Nel is quick to say that it was Sula who threw the boy into the river.

"You. Sula. What's the difference?"

Nel leaves hurriedly. This is not the visit she intended. Holding her coat tight against the winter wind, she begins her long walk home. Suddenly she stops. The soft gray ball that has been following her for so long begins to break and scatter. It is not until now that the gray fuzzy ball, which has covered Nel's heart since Jude's departure, begins to break up. It is only then that Nel realizes that it is not Jude she is missing but Sula.

> "All that time I thought I was missing Jude. . . . O Lord, Sula,"
> she cried "girl, girl, girlgirlgirl." It was a fine cry—loud and
> long—but it had no bottom and it had no top, just circles and
> circles of sorrow.

So perhaps, as Holloway has suggested, in the end the novel is Nel's—Nel Wright, the righteous one, Nel the conforming one. She is, as Holloway points out, "everywoman": "She carries the additional burden of shadow that white culture projects onto black people. But she is still typical of most women in Western culture." Holloway continues that no matter how sympathetic one may be about Jude's plight, "the bottom line is that he abandons his family. It is Nel who ends up as sole parent; she cleans houses to support the three children who for many years became her life."

Because *Sula* is the story of a community, the lives of its inhabitants are inextricably interwoven. After the death of Sula—the pariah, the devil, the outcast—the community's role of defining itself through acceptance and disapproval of one of its members shifts. No longer is the she-devil the focus of their collective energies. The misery of the awful winter that follows Sula's death deepens their discontent and stirs up the rage that has lain dormant and without a focus. Shadrack's parade comes on such a bright sunny morning that the townspeople are drawn in a spirit of badly needed camaraderie and fun. Somehow the dancing, laughing parade finds its way to the New River tunnel. The years of frustration, of pent-up anger, become an uncontrollable wave of rage as the marchers hack and hurl at the monument to the White world's refusal to let them in. The violence and tragedy at the tunnel are fitting and ironic because the rage represents a final act of defiance for promises unkept, committed on National Suicide Day, a holiday intended to allay fears of death so that people could get on with their lives.

Early in this article, I noted Wayman's observation that work shapes our lives, and I asked what happens when a person has no work or when a person is forced to engage in work that is demeaning or unsuitable. I also noted Morrison's comment that "Aggression is not as new to black women as it is to white women." In *Sula*, Morrison offers the deadly consequences when the natural feelings of aggression lack a suitable outlet because it is through our work that we define ourselves. Work need not be confined to the concept of earning a living: Work can also be understood as that outlet that allows our creative energies to surface. For Sula, her defiance in refusing to accept demeaning employment or to accept a life prescribed by others may not have been such a tragedy had she had access to an art form with which to express herself. Sula was stubbornly unwilling to define herself as part of the Medallion community and to conform to its standards, and by deliberately placing herself outside of the accepted boundaries, she stood alone. In her quest to "make herself," Sula was following a path that had never been trod before, a path for which she had no tools and no directions. Sula may have succeeded in making herself, but the making process involved pain not only for herself but for all those whose lives she touched.

It is hard to feel sympathy for Jude, the betrayer. We grant him the frustration he must have endured in his job as a waiter, but in seeking a respite from his frustration, he ruins the life of Nel, the wife who was willing to merge her own self into his to allow him to feel like a man.

And finally, we just consider the collective rage unleashed at the tunnel that fateful January 3 on National Suicide Day. Morrison first notes the anger when she describes Jude's humiliation at being turned away from the hiring shack for six days running. It was his need to assuage the rage; it was his determination to take on a man's role that pressed him into settling down with Nel.

And what of the other strong and willing young Black men who were also frustrated by a system that would not allow them to define their manhood through work? The outburst at the tunnel was led by young and enraged men whose audacious acts emboldened the others as they were joined by women and children, smashing the tunnel they could never build.

Morrison points out that there are "several levels of the pariah figure" in her writing. She sees the Black community itself as a pariah community. "Black people are pariahs," she continues. The civilization of Black people that lives apart from but in juxtaposition to other civilizations is a pariah relationship. Morrison explains that although the Black community of Medallion recognized Sula as a pariah, they "thought evil had a natural place in the universe; they did not wish to eradicate it. They just wished to protect themselves from it." The Black community of Medallion allowed Sula to exist as part of the natural order of things. They neither encouraged nor discouraged her as she lived her life; they simply watched and waited.

In *Sula*, Toni Morrison has created an unforgettable story of the friendship of two African American women and has graciously allowed us to enter the community of the Bottom in Medallion, Ohio. More specifically, Morrison has created individual characters and a community of characters whose concept of self has been thwarted by the absence of opportunities for respectable, gainful employment. Sula's lack of an occupation or the absence of clay through which she might express her creative energies denies her the means of defining herself. As desperately as Sula desires to make herself, a racist society will not allow her that opportunity. Similarly, the destruction of the tunnel by the community illustrates the frustration inherent in the consistent refusal of meaningful employment to those who are capable and willing workers but are denied because of their color. Jude's feeling that he is undervalued leads him to a superficial sexual episode with Sula, whose own idleness leads her to engage in meaningless sexual encounters as a means of filling up space in her empty life. Nel's sense of worth is made possible by her acceptance of menial work and her choice to live within the community rather than outside its boundaries as Sula has chosen to do.

By introducing us to the souls who lived and died in the Bottom, Morrison has given us an understanding of social, psychological, and sociological issues that might have been evident only to African Americans. She has lovingly portrayed a mythical community of unforgettable characters now gone forever but not forgotten.

BARBARA CHRISTIAN

The Contemporary Fables of Toni Morrison

Toni Morrison's works are fantastic earthy realism. Deeply rooted in history and mythology, her work resonates with mixtures of pleasure and pain, wonder and horror. Primal in their essence, her characters come at you with the force and beauty of gushing water, seemingly fantastic but as basic as the earth they stand on. They erupt, out of the world, sometimes gently, often with force and terror. Her work is sensuality combined with an intrigue that only a piercing intellect could create.

Two of her three novels: *The Bluest Eye* (1970) and *Sula* (1974) reveal a consistency of vision, for they illustrate the growth of a theme as it goes through many transformations in much the same way as a good jazz musician finds the hidden melodies within a musical phrase. Both novels chronicle the search for beauty amidst the restrictions of life, both from within and without. In both novels, the black woman, as girl and grown woman, is the turning character, and the friendship between two women or girls serves as the yardstick by which the overwhelming contradictions of life are measured. Double-faced, her focal characters look outward and search inward, trying to find some continuity between the seasons, the earth, other people, the cycles of life, and their own particular lives. Often they find that there is conflict between their own nature and the society that man has made, to the extent that one seems to be an inversion of the other. Her novels are rich then, not only in human characterizations but also in the signs, symbols, omens, sent by nature. Wind and fire, robins as a plague in the spring, marigolds that won't sprout, are as much characterizations in her novels as the human beings who people them. [. . .]

> Sula was a heavy brown with large quiet eyes, one of which featured a birthmark that spread from the middle of the lid toward the eyebrow, shaped something like a stemmed rose. It gave her otherwise plain face a broken excitement and blue-blade threat like the keloid scar of the razored man who sometimes played checkers with her grandmother. The birthmark was to grow darker, as the years passed, but now it was the same shade as her gold-flecked eyes, which to the end were as steady and clean as rain.

Toni Morrison's first novel, *The Bluest Eye*, reveals the inversions of an order that result in a black girl's belief that she possesses the greatest treasure, the bluest eyes imaginable. As such, it is a patterned fabric in which the warp is the myth of beauty and desirability in our society itself, while the weft, the part that shows, is the personal history of Pecola Breedlove. In *Sula*, her second novel, Morrison again takes on an apparently simple theme, the friendship of two black girls. One, Nel Wright, follows the pattern of life society has laid out for her, and the other, Sula Peace, tries to create her own pattern, to achieve her own self. Again, as in *The Bluest Eye*, the theme is but a sign of all that the novel explores, for the search for self is continually thwarted by the society from which Sula Peace comes. So the novel is not only about Nel Wright and Sula Peace, it is most emphatically about the culture that spawns them. In *The Bluest Eye*, Pecola's destiny is ultimately determined by the myth of beauty and goodness one culture has foisted on another. In Sula, the patterns of both cultures are distinct, yet share common factors. Sula's destiny is charted by the mythology of Evil and Nature her hometown ascribes to and by the view the Bottom as well as the larger society hold of woman, her span and space. In exploring this community's system of beliefs, Morrison weaves a fable about the relationship between conformity and experiment, survival and creativity. This mythological system is continually discerned in the novel's fabric through death, so ordinary in its eternal presence that it might otherwise be missed, through the drama of time as a significant event, and through the pervasive use of nature as both a creative and destructive force. As in *The Bluest Eye*, the novel's patterns help to transform a seemingly obvious theme.

Overtly, the novel is divided into an introduction, two parts—one devoted to years in the twenties, to Sula and Nel's growing up, and the other to years in the late thirties and early forties, to these women, now grown—and finally, as if an epilogue, there is 1965, a year of remembrance and understanding for Nel Greene. But Morrison immediately signals her reader that this tale about the friendship between Nel Wright and Sula Peace is integrally related to the survival of their community. The novel begins not with the presentation of these characters but with the death of their hometown. In Sula, as in *The Bluest Eye*, Morrison uses the motif of inversion, of derangement, as the natural order is turned upside down as a result of human society.

The introduction announces the pervasive presence of Death, as the Bottom is being torn down to make room for a golf course. We begin with the end, the death of a community of black folk, which is being deleted by the onward march of "progress," a community in which pain was so much a part of the pleasure of living that the Bottom's mores might be misleading. Then we leap from end to beginning, a beginning that was a joke, a nigger joke, because the laughter is so much a way of dealing with the pain. The Bottom, the Negro neighborhood of the town Medallion, was a white man's gift of land to a slave who had performed some heavy duties for him. Although the Bottom was really hill land where planting was backbreaking and the weather harsh, the master had persuaded the slave that this land was more desirable than valley land, that it was called the Bottom because it was the bottom of Heaven—"best land there is." Inverted, the truth is inverted, and so the Bottom on the top came to be.

This little nigger joke of how the Bottom came to be is juxtaposed in the novel to the origins of National Suicide Day, the Bottom's unique holiday. The beginning is the end, so to speak. National Suicide Day had been initiated by Shadrack, a shell-shocked soldier "who was not so much afraid of death or dying as the unexpectedness of both. It was a way of controlling the fear of death." In the essence of ritual, he initiated a day devoted to that fear, "so that everyone could get it out of the way."

What does National Suicide Day have to do with what follows—the story of Nel and her family, the story of Sula and her family, the story of their friendship? Their story, the story of the Bottom, is punctuated by death. Death occurs in each chapter and is the beginning of, or climax of, the experience in that particular section of the novel. Death becomes a way of focusing experience. As each year gives way to another, so each death gives way to a new view of life, a new discovery, a new feeling for truth.

Death is the haunt, personified by Shadrack, that moves the story; the tale of the Wright and Peace families and particularly of Nel and Sula, is the matter with which we are preoccupied. So the chapters proceed as if we are being shown the history of these families and finally the intertwining of two lives, Sula and Nel's, as they affect the Bottom, that nigger joke. The distinctive characteristics of these families from the Bottom, then, alert us to the specific belief system of their community, and the introduction of the novel, the juxtaposition of its end and its beginning, and the origins of National Suicide Day are indications that this story is a lesson in the nature of survival and continuity.

As the beginning is in the end, the end is in the beginning. Time becomes important only as it marks an event, for the people of the Bottom do not see its reckoning as an autonomous terminology. So each chapter in *Sula* is headed by a year, a time that allows us to focus on the climax of that section. The delineation of a particular year is a focus, not a limitation, as Morrison uses with great craftsmanship, this cultural characteristic of the Bottom. In adapting this quality to the novel, she heightens the magic of the written word—the flexibility to move from time to time, from one setting to another, without the need for changing props or signaling a new drift of images. So each chapter is not about the particular year for which it is named—rather some crucial event happens in that year which demands background, its whys and hows, the reasons for the event's significance. As the author, she is beyond time, collapsing the past, present, and future into the now so we might understand and feel the significance. The structure, then, so apparently neatly defined by the march of time, by a chronological pattern, is always transforming itself, for in fact we do not move forward in a straight line. Rather a particular point in time is but the focus of inter-twining circles of other times and events. It is as if we were hearing an old African folktale—mythological in tone—in which content revitalizes an empty terminological system. The then is in the now; the now in the then; and the teller spins ever-intricate webs of connectiveness, until the web is completed or broken.

The mythological tone of this tale is heightened further by Morrison's pervasive use of nature images. Throughout *Sula*, images of fire, water, wind and earth are closely linked to the eternal presence of death and the Bottom's concept of time. As a result, the novel projects an integral world view, for the qualities of creativity and destructiveness are continually transforming the images of nature.

Morrison's use of nature images is not arbitrary. As in *The Bluest Eye*, the way in which the characters perceive nature is crucial to an understanding of their universe:

> In spite of their fear, they reacted to an oppressive oddity, or what they called evil days, with an acceptance that bordered on welcome. Such evil must be avoided, they felt, and precautions must naturally be taken to protect themselves from it. But they

let it run its course, fulfill itself, and never invented ways either to alter it, to annihilate it or to prevent its happening again. So also were they with people.

What was taken by outsiders to be slackness, slovenliness or even generosity was in fact a full recognition of the legitimacy of forces other than good ones. They did not believe death was accidental—life might be, but death was deliberate. They did not believe that Nature was ever askew—only inconvenient. Plague and drought were as "natural" as springtime. If milk could curdle, God knows robins could fall. The purpose of evil was to survive it and they determined (without ever knowing they had made up their minds to do it) to survive floods, white people, tuberculosis, famine and ignorance. They knew anger well but not despair, and they didn't stone sinners for the same reason that they didn't commit suicide—it was beneath them.

Because the author probes the philosophical system compressed in these few paragraphs, this novel becomes not only an intense tale of two women's friendship but also a forceful drama of contending mythic beliefs. Her characters' philosophy of life contains no idyllic view of nature, no sympathy with the natural as an ideal, except to survive it. Theirs is a philosophy grounded in a history of struggling continually to survive, a philosophy that exhibits a cynicism about the limits of living. Nature's signs, although they are seldom controlled by the actions of men, must, in this view, relate to the course of human events. Rain falls alike on good men and bad; all are subject to the plague of robins. But the plague must mean something. As Eva greets Sula when she unexpectedly shows up in the Bottom after ten years' absence: "I might have knowed them birds meant something." Nature *is* a sign that can be read, and usually its message relates to the lives of the folk.

While the structural elements of Death, Time, and Nature unify the novel, the story of the Wright women and the Peace women specify the community's perception of itself, for its view of women is inexorably connected to its concept of survival. Part I of this patterned tale emphasizes the myriad forms of woman's behavior that the community incorporates, even as it dramatizes the beginnings of Nel and Sula's friendship. In using these two very different families, the author dramatizes not only the levels of this community's tolerance in relation to women but also its spiritual richness and poverty.

Nel's mother had been born in the Sundown House in New Orleans. The rest of her life was about getting as far away from the wild blood that brothel represents as she could. A high-toned lady, she fashioned her own daughter to be obedient, to be bland: "she drove her daughter's imagination underground," for fear that it might revert. Our introduction to Helene Wright and to Nel in the chapter "1920" comes, as it often does in this novel, through death. Helene's grandmother, who had taken her away from the Sundown House and raised her under "the dolesome eyes of a multicolored Virgin Mary," has died. Her funeral means that Helene has to do what she most fears—come close, too close, to the Sundown House. She will have to acknowledge her own mother, the whore who smells like gardenias and darkens her eyebrows with burnt matches. The trip South is significant, hence the marking of the year, for it is the first and last time Nel will leave Medallion. It is an opportunity for her to see her own mother, so adored by her father and so held in awe by the Bottom, reduced to "custard" by a white conductor. It is during this trip that she learns she is herself: "I'm me," Nel whispers. Each time she said the word "me, there was a gathering in her like power, like joy, like fear." It was her new sense of me-ness that allowed her to cultivate a friend, Sula Peace, of whom her mother initially disapproves.

Sula's ancestry is counterpoint to Nel's. The tone of their respective houses emphasizes the contrast:

> Nel who regarded the oppressive neatness of her home with dread, felt comfortable in it with Sula, who loved it and would sit on the red velvet sofa for 10 to 20 minutes at a time—still as dawn. As for Nel, she preferred Sula's woolly house where a pot of something was always cooking on the stove; where the mother, Hannah, never scolded or gave directions; where all sorts of people dropped in; where newspapers were stacked in the hallway, and dirty dishes left for hours at a time in the sink, and where a one-legged grandmother named Eva handed you goobers from deep inside her pockets or read you a dream.

As Helene Wright, the light-skinned lady, has a most dubious background, so the Peace women are convoluted, marvelous folk. As portrayals of black women, they are as complex and nonstereotypical as any you will find in literature. Only such ancestral vitality and complexity could have produced Sula, as undefinable as she is black, as unique as she is a woman. When we are first introduced to Eva, her grandmother, and Hannah, her mother, we might at first mistake them for the banal stereotypes of black women in literature and film. Eva, as the mammy, is willing to save her children at all costs, even to the point of sticking her leg under a train to sell it. Hannah, as the loose, comely black woman, will "fuck practically anything."

But even as we meet them, any comparisons with the "mammy" or the "loose woman" image is immediately put to rest.

Far from being the big-breasted, kind, religious, forever coping, asexual, loving-white-folks mammy, Eva is arrogant, independent, decidedly a man lover who loves and hates intensely. She is strong by virtue of her will, wit, and idiosyncrasies rather than because of her physique. That strength is nurtured and sustained by her hatred for Big Boy, the unfaithful father of her three children, a hatred that she says keeps her alive and happy. Her utterances throughout the book fall on the mean side of sharpness, refined by a rich imagination and a colorful folk wit. She answers what she considers to be foolish questions with nippy answers. So when her daughter Hannah asks her mother if she ever coddled her children, Eva's answer is richly to the point:

> "Play? Wasn't nobody playing in 1895. . . . What would I look like leapin' round that room playin' with youngins with three beets to my name?. . . No time, there wasn't no time. Not none. Soon as I get one day done here comes a night. With you coughin' and me watchin' so TB wouldn't take you off and if you was sleepin' quiet I thought, O lord they dead and put my hand over your mouth to feel if the breath was comin'. What you talkin' 'bout did I love you girl. I stayed alive for you can't you get that through your thick head or what is that between your ears, heifer?"

She loved her children enough to stay alive and keep them alive; she needn't be physically endearing to them. Thus she retreats to her upstairs bedroom where she spends most of her time, but from which she directs the lives of her children, friends, strays, and a constant stream of boarders.

If Eva has got any of the traditional mammy qualities, it is that she is domineering, without any reason to feel that she should be otherwise. She does as she pleases. As a mother she had given life, and so when her son Plum returns from the war and attempts to "crawl back into her womb," she acts in her usual decisive manner; she burns him to death. Her explanation to Hannah for her actions reverberate with the hidden power inherent in the act of creativity, the power to destroy:

> "After all that carryin' on, just gettin' him out and keepin' him alive, he wanted to crawl back in my womb and well. . . . I ain't got the room no more even if he could do it. . . . He was a man, girl, a big old growed-up man. I didn't have that much room. I

kept on dreaming it. Dreaming it and I knowed it was true. One night it wouldn't be no dream. It'd be true and I would have done it, would have let him if I'd've had the room but a big man can't be a baby all wrapped up inside his mammy no more; he suffo-cate. I done everything I could to make him leave me and go on and live and be a man but he wouldn't and I had to keep him out so I just thought of a way he could die like a man not all scrunched up inside my womb, but like a man."

Like the primeval Earth Mother Goddess, feared and worshipped by man, like the goddesses of antiquity, older even than the biblical Eve, Eva both gives life and takes it away. She performs a ritual killing inspired by love—a ritual of sacrifice by fire.

In conjuring up this ritual, Morrison dramatically fuses her major structural elements, for she uses Time as the significant event and fire as a destructive element in describing an act that is the most unnatural death of all, a mother's killing of her own son. Eva's burning of Plum takes place in the year 1921 and is the climatic event ending that chapter. The motif of death is resounded here as it was in the chapter "1920," but this time it is not death as a result of old age, but a killing. Although Plum's death ends "1921," Eva's explanation of her actions does not occur until two years later, in 1923, the year she will witness Hannah's accidental death by fire. Between these two chapters, "1921" and "1923," the chapter "1922" focuses on an acci-dental death by water. Like water, fire has always been a sign of creativity and destructiveness in the human imagination. Morrison uses this forceful symbol in her brilliant treatment of a taboo subject, a mother's murder of her son. But she does not stop there. In weaving her fable, the author connects Eva's destruction of her creation, Plum, to Nature's accidental burning of the beautiful Hannah.

Hannah, Eva's second daughter, is a lovely character. Widowed young and left with her daughter Sula, she returns to her mother's house, evidently intent on never marrying again, perhaps because she has inherited from her mother the love of maleness for its own sake. "What she wanted, after Rekus [her husband] died and what she succeeded in having more often than not, was some touching everyday." But far from being the seductress traditionally dressed in red, who manipulates men to her own ends, Hannah is funky elegance, making no special effort to be alluring other than her natural sensuality, setting no demands on the men she knows. She remains indepen-dent in her self, for although she would make love to practically any man, she is extremely careful about whom she sleeps with, for "sleeping with someone implied for her a measure of trust and a definite commitment." So she becomes, as Morrison puts it, "a daylight lover," sex being a part of the ordinary and pleasant things she does every day, rather than a hidden activity at night. Hannah's personality, though, is not wound around sex; she emerges as the practical actor in the bustling house she lives in—the manager, so to speak. Now and then we get glimpses of her questionings, her wonderings, as in her fatal question to Eva about Plum's death. She is honest, as Eva is, but not in her mother's flamboyant fashion. Her succinct appraisal of her feelings for Sula, whom she says she loves but doesn't like, is spoken in anything but dramatic tones.

Just as Plum's murder is enmeshed in the recurring dream of incest that Eva cannot dispel, Hannah's terrible death is foreshadowed by dreams, strange human actions, and omens from nature. In her manner of writing around the point of focus, of playing variations on top of variations, Morrison tells us the second strange thing that happens first. Hannah asks her mother a pointed question, "Mamma, did you ever love us?" in her effort to understand why her mother killed her only son. In true Hannah fashion, it had taken her two years to broach the question, a question that must be answered before she dies, even if it means tangling with her ornery mother. The urgency with which Hannah approaches her mother is, of course, in the realm of human choice; the first strange omen, though, was beyond human control. There had been an unusual wind the night before Hannah's questionings, wind without rain that brought more heat rather than a cooling rain to the Bottom. Then there had been Sula's unusual craziness the day before as if she didn't know what hit her, coupled with Hannah's dream of a wedding in the red dress. Those familiar with dream books, as Eva was, know that a wedding signifies death. But the signs were flying so hot and heavy, Eva scarcely had time to notice any of them. Thoroughly thrown off by the weirdness of the day, Eva cannot find her comb, her favorite object, in her room where no one ever moved anything. As she is looking for it, she sees Hannah burning.

What Morrison does in creating this tragedy of Hannah's burning, reminiscent of the burning of witches, is to pile up sign upon sign, some caused by human being themselves, others beyond their control, that in hindsight can be read as indications of an imminent tragedy. What a concentration of images, as the earthly and the supernatural, the seemingly trivial and the substantial mesh, it would seem, in a "perfection of judgment" upon Eva, who burns her only son only to see her daughter steamed to death because of a shift in the wind. The author has, in the classic sense, distilled the folk's sense of time by compressing the unseen with the known, the seemingly indifferent and idiosyncratic forces of nature with the order of events willed by human beings. Whatever goes around comes around. As if continuing that never-ending spiral, Eva insists that she was sure she saw Sula watch her mother burning, not with terror but interest. Eva's presumptuous act of burning her own son has triggered a series of effects that will haunt her many years hence when Sula will do battle with her. Her entire family is scorched by her act. In breaking a taboo, Eva provokes not only human repercussions but nature's wrath as well.

By dramatizing significant events in the lives of diverse characters such as Helene Wright and Eva and Hannah Peace, the novel outlines the precise perimeters of the Bottom's tolerance in relation to a woman's behavior. This community absorbs many styles—Helene's ladylike and hypocritical demeanor, Hannah's elegant sensuality, even Eva's arrogant murder of her son—as long as they remain within its definition of woman as wife, mother, or man lover. The Bottom's apparent toleration of these many styles is as restrictive as it is generous. Morrison focuses on this cultural characteristic in her presentation of the development of Nel and Sula's friendship. In addition, by placing the beginnings of their friendship between chapter "1921," when Eva burns Plum to death, and chapter "1923," the time of the accidental burning of Hannah, Morrison reminds us of the impact their female relatives are having on these impressionable twelve-year-old girls.

Out of their awareness that their lives, as black females, are restricted by their community and by the outer society, Nel and Sula are drawn to each other. As only-girl children, each takes the other as sister, sharing each other's dreams of freedom and excitement:

> So when they met, first in those chocolate halls and next through the ropes of the swing, they felt the ease and comfort of old friends. Because each had discovered years before that they were neither white nor male, and that all freedom and triumph was forbidden to them, they had set about creating something else to be. Their meeting was fortunate, for it let them use each other to grow on. Daughters of distant mothers and incomprehensible fathers (Sula's because he was dead; Nel's because he wasn't), they found in each other's eyes the intimacy they were looking for.

Nel and Sula's friendship is sustained not only by their recognition of each other's restrictions but also by their anticipation of sexuality and by an ultimate bond, the responsibility for unintentionally causing the death of another. However, although the two girls share these strong bonds, they are different, for Sula, who is the adventurer, often allows "her emotions to dictate her behavior," and Nel is more cautious, more consistent. As a result, in this chapter, Sula appears to be the more focal actor of the two.

The chapter "1922" is deceptive in its flow, for it is so innocent in springtime visions, so bittersweet in its images of budding twelve-year-old girls, that the drama of Chicken Little's drowning catches us off guard. But a note of pain, ever so slightly touched on, begins a shift in tone when Sula overhears her mother's comment that she may love her, but she does not like her. The pain of her mother's assertion is mingled with the beginning of sexual stirrings that she and Nel feel as they play by the river. Overflowing with the energy of repressed pain and pleasure, the emotional Sula swings the little boy, Chicken Little, until he falls into the river, never to be seen again.

Because of the feelings that led to it, this accidental death by water is Sula's baptism into her search for some continuity between the natural world and the social world, between the precariousness of life and the inevitability of death. The author emphasizes the impact this death has on Sula by having Shadrack, as well as Nel, witness it. A veteran of the witnessing of horrific death, Shadrack attempts to give Sula some sense of its meaning. As the originator of National Suicide Day, he assures her of her own permanency, that she need not have fear of death. Because of his own singular concern with this fear, his one utterance in the book, the word *always*, takes on mythic proportions. Although Shadrack does not intend the meaning Sula attributes to this word, he is in a sense right, for Chicken Little's death and the emotions that surround it will always be with her, not the drowning itself so much as the feeling that she cannot rely either on herself or on others. Perhaps the old women at Chicken Little's funeral are right when

> they danced and screamed, not to protest God's will but to acknowledge it and confirm once more their conviction that the only way to avoid the Hand of God is to get in it.

Morrison concludes Part I by reiterating her major structural elements, for Part I ends not with the death of someone but with a wedding, the wedding of Nel and Jude in the year 1927. Their marriage becomes *the* event in the Bottom, bringing together the community in a moment of feasting, revelry, and renewal. But as Eva has already told us, and as Hannah's death clearly illustrates, the dream of a wedding means death. This wedding seems to mean death, not only for Nel and Sula's girl friendship but for Jude and Nel's previous sense of themselves.

The delineation of Nel and Sula's personalities and the particular roads they take are finely drawn in this chapter, particularly in relation to the mores of the Bottom. Just as Sula was more focal in the chapter about these young girls' personal explorations of life and death, so Nel is the major actor in this chapter about the community's initiation of young adults into its fold. Jude chooses Nel because she has no desire to make herself and delights in caring about someone else. Like so many young men in his community, he begins thinking of marriage because he needs desperately to accomplish something of significance, this something being a job at helping to build the new River Road:

> It was while he was full of such dreams his body already feeling the rough work clothes, his hands already curved to the pick handle, that he spoke to Nel about getting married. She seemed receptive but hardly anxious. It was after he stood in lines for six days running and saw the gang boss pick out thin-armed white boys from the Virginia hills and the bull-necked Greeks and Italians and heard over and over, "Nothing else today. Come back tomorrow," that he got the message. So it was rage and the determination to take on a man's role anyhow that made him press Nel about settling down. He needed some of his appetites filled, some posture of adulthood recognized, but mostly he wanted someone to care about his hurt, to care very deeply.

Jude's reasons for pressing Nel into marriage reinforce our sense of the Bottom's definition of woman. As his helpmate, Nel is a buffer between his desire for his own autonomy and the restrictions the outside world places on him. Her marriage to him will replace the need he so intensely feels to have some impact on the world and thus enable him to accept his state.

As the Bottom dances and eats, as Nel responds to Jude's kiss, Sula takes another road distinct and apart from the community. We are left to contemplate Nel and Sula's childhood as reflected in the structural lines of Morrison's tale. Nel Wright's sense of her own identity had begun with her trip to her great-grandmother's funeral and the beginning of her friendship with Sula Peace. Our first insight into Sula's ancestry begins with our hesitant comprehension of Eva's fire murder of her only son to save his manhood. Sula's personality is gravely affected by the events that surround the watery death of Chicken Little. Her mother, Hannah, as if a witch, is seared to death in so tragic and senseless a way that supernatural omens are needed to justify it. As their childhood ends, all of these events reach their logical conclusion. Nel, the daughter of the proper Helene Wright, marries Jude, losing the sense of her own identity she had gotten a glimpse of in her friendship with Sula, and Sula, daughter of the distinctive Peace women, leaves the Bottom. The patterned story of Nel and Sula's friendship, woven as it is with threads of their community's culture and their families' histories, is rhythmically embroidered with knots of death and stunningly colored by the elemental forces of Nature.

Part I explores the many styles of women's behavior that the Bottom is willing to absorb, while it traces the friendship of Nel and Sula as young girls. In contrast, Part II emphasizes the forms that this community will not tolerate, while it examines the friendship and estrangement of Nel and Sula as adult women. Foremost to Part II is the Bottom's concept of evil, for that is the way in which they characterize intolerable behavior. Although there is a progression in theme, however, the structural elements of this fable remain the same. The author immediately reiterates her framework by beginning Part II with an uncommon freak of nature, a plague of robins. Like the marigolds that would not sprout in *The Bluest Eye*, this oddity of nature holds sway in the imagination, conjuring images of dread or at least of the unknown.

In Part II, as in Part I, Nature's signs are intertwined with the persistent recurrence of death, and the time when a particular death is focused upon is the core around which each chapter is built. However, although the deaths in Part I are primarily physical, the deaths in Part II are emotional and spiritual as well. In the chapter "1937," Nel and Sula's friendship is presumably killed because Sula sleeps with Jude, Nel's husband. In the chapter "1939," Sula and Ajax's relationship is killed by Sula's attempt to possess Ajax. In 1940 Sula dies physically, but we feel to some extent that her death is due to spiritual malnutrition as much as any physical cause. In 1941 a significant number of folk in the Bottom are killed in their attempt to destroy the tunnel that they were not allowed to build. In effect they bring about their own deaths because they have been spiritually as well as physically drained by poverty, harsh weather, and starvation—a powerlessness. Death is not just a physical occurrence. Its presence is related to the folk's spiritual needs left unfulfilled by Nature and society.

Related to death, in Part II is the figure of Sula and the images of nature that accompany her. Interestingly, the elements of air and earth are as pervasive as the elements of fire and water in the previous section. So in the chapter "1937," Sula's return is heralded by a plague of robins and by "the peculiar quality of that May," a quality that Nel alone notices. More than anything, Sula's lover, Ajax, wants to fly a plane. Sula thinks of Ajax's body in images of gold, alabaster, and loam, which she waters, and of sex with him as "the high silence of orgasm." As Sula dies in chapter "1940," she remembers the word *always* that Shadrack had uttered on the day of Chicken Little's drowning and feels her death to be "a sleep of water always." In keeping with that image of water, her funeral is concluded by a shower of rain. The collapse of the tunnel in chapter "1941," is preceded not only by Sula's death but by the sudden change from extreme cold to intense heat, which causes the earth to shift and the river to overflow. On that climactic January, Shadrack watches his ritual, National Suicide Day, come to life before his very eyes as water, earth, wind, and fire combine to create a holocaust. Part II then begins with an oddity of nature and ends with a natural disaster, one seeming to announce the return of Sula to the Bottom, the other seeming to underscore her death.

In addition to the elements of Death and Nature, Time, in Part II, continues to be crucial to Morrison's patterning of her fable. The way in which the events are arranged is not so much chronology as it is the juxta-position of two views about the nature of living. By using Nel and Sula, two parts of an intense friendship, as the embodiment of these views, Morrison personalizes the philosophical content of her tale. But these points of view would not assume mythic proportions as they do in this novel if they were merely idiosyncratic, if they were not set within the context of a culture. This novel is a fable because it presents a culture's philosophy about life and death, good and evil.

The community sees Sula as the embodiment of evil. All of their ills and sufferings take visual form in her being. From the year 1937, when Sula returns to the Bottom, to the year 1940, when she dies, a presence charges the Bottom with an energy, the fuse of which is to defeat her by surviving her. What is it about Sula Peace that turns this community into a buttressed fort against her? The reasons are not so much explanation as intersecting circles of fear, the greatest one being the fear of difference.

Ironically, Sula is both the sum of her ancestors and greater than each part. Like Eva, she is tough, ornery, and nippy. Her first action upon her return to the Bottom, in fact, is to do battle with her grandmother and to banish her to an old folks home, contrary to the mores of the Bottom. But Sula's expulsion of Eva is not her mortal sin. She and her grandmother clash on the issue that will emphasize her difference in a community that believes it needs consistency to survive: Sula wants to make herself rather than others. In a scorching dialogue between Sula and her grandmother, the perfection of judgment upon Eva comes full circle. Eva assaults Sula with the question:

> ". . . When you gone to get married? You need to have some babies. It'll settle you."
>
> "I don't want to make somebody else. I want to make myself."
>
> "Selfish. Ain't no woman got no business floatin' around without no man."
>
> "You did."
>
> "Not by choice."

"Mama did."

"Not by choice, I said it ain't right for you to want to stay off by yourself. You need . . . I'm a tell you what you need."

Sula sat up. "I need you to shut your mouth."

When Eva replies that God will strike her down, Sula retorts:

"Which God? The one who watched you burn Plum. . . . Maybe one night when you dozing in that wagon flicking flies and swallowing spit, maybe I'll just tip on up here with some kerosene and—who knows—you may make the brightest flame of them all."

As if she had carefully studied her grandmother, Sula introduces the one threat that would drive fear into Eva's heart. In so doing she dethrones the haughty mistress of the house. What is most interesting, though, is Eva's resistance to Sula's need to make herself, a concept totally alien to one who loves maleness for its own sake. Yet Sula has inherited this need for independence, this arrogance, this orneriness, at least partially from the Eva who had the gall to destroy her only son to save his maleness.

Like Hannah, Sula sleeps with the husbands of her neighbors indiscriminately. But although Hannah made the men feel complete and seemed to compliment the women by wanting their husbands, Sula sleeps with them once and discards them. Unlike her mother, Sula does not experience sex as a pleasant pastime. Orgasm becomes the moment for her when she feels her full strength and power at the same time that she experiences complete aloneness. Orgasm, for Sula, "was not eternity but the death of time and a loneliness so profound the word itself had no meaning." In sex she knows not her partner but herself.

Because of her drive for self-knowledge, and because of the imagination she brings to the memories of her ancestors and to her own experiences, Sula emerges as a unique woman. In two beautifully terse analyses, Morrison illuminates her character:

Sula was distinctly different. Eva's arrogance and Hannah's self indulgence merged in her and, with a twist that was all her own imagination, she lived out her days exploring her own thoughts and emotions giving them full reign, feeling no obligation to please anybody unless their pleasure pleased her. As willing to feel pain as to give pain, to feel pleasure as to give pleasure, hers was an experimental life—ever since her mother's remarks sent her

flying up those stairs, ever since her one major feeling of responsibility had been exorcised on the bank of a river with a closed
place in the middle. The first experience taught her that there
was no other that you could count on; the second that there was
no self to count on either. She had no center, no speck around
which to grow.

She had been looking along for a friend, and it took her a while
to discover that a lover was not a comrade and could never be—
for a woman. And that no one would ever be that version of
herself which she sought to reach out to and touch with an
ungloved hand. There was only her own mood and whim, and if
that was all there was, she decided to turn the naked hand toward
it, discover it and let others become as intimate with their own
selves as she was.

In a way, her strangeness, her naiveté, her craving for the other
half of her equation was the consequence of an idle imagination.
Had she paints, or clay, or knew the discipline of the dance, or
strings; had she anything to engage her tremendous curiosity and
her gift for metaphor, she might have exchanged the restlessness
and preoccupation with whim for an activity that provided her
with all she yearned for. And like any artist with no art form, she
became dangerous.

Sula has the distinction of being herself in a community that believes that
self-hood can only be selfishness. Her view of life is different from others, as if
the birthmark above one of her eyes has either distorted or enlarged her vision.
It is with maddening recognition that we grasp Sula's tragedy—she is too full,
and yet too static, to grow. She has stared into that abyss where nothing in life
can be relied on—where nothing really matters. Like Cholly Breedlove in *The
Bluest Eye*, she has developed the freedom of narcissism allowed only to the
gods. Such freedom is not allowed to mere mortals as the oldest stories of all
cultures testify. Sula is unique, though, even in the company of mortals who try
to live life as if they are divine, for she is a woman. Her life, according to the
customs of all traditions, is not hers to experiment with, to create or destroy.
Her life is meant to result in other lives. So like Pauline Breedlove in *The Bluest
Eye*, she is an artist without an art form. When Sula stares into the abyss that
sex so clearly evokes for her, she is not looking for another entity but for
another version of herself, for a total union possible only when each perceives
the other as possibly being his or her self. Since woman is not usually

perceived by man in that total sense, Sula abandons any attempt at union and seeks only herself. Since she cannot have everything, she will at least, or at most, have herself. Marked at birth, she will pursue her own uniqueness.

But such total absorption leads to destructiveness, for the world, used to compromise, will not accept, cannot understand, such concentration—perhaps it must not, to maintain even a slim semblance of order. Using the inexplicable fact that Shadrack is civil to Sula while he shuns everyone else, convinced that she is committing the unforgettable sin—sleeping with white men—and buttressed by her disregard for their God-ordained ways, the town turns Sula into a witch, conjuring spells against her power and acting righteously to prove themselves better than the ignoble she-devil. This lone woman's effect on her community recalls the always perplexing mystery of humanity's need for an evil one, for a devil:

> Their conviction of Sula's evil changed them in accountable yet mysterious ways. Once the source of their personal misfortune was identified, they had leave to protect and love one another. They began to cherish their husbands and wives, protect their children, repair their homes and in general band together against the devil in their midst.

All things have their use and even Sula's evil nature is used by her community to validate and enrich its own existence. As pariah, she gives them a focus through which they achieve some unity, at least temporarily, just as Pecola's madness in *The Bluest Eye* is used by the townsfolk as evidence of their own sanity, their own strength, their own beauty. The need human beings continually exhibit for a scapegoat, so they can justify themselves, is one of the mysteries of human existence that Morrison consistently probes in her works. Why is it that human beings need an enemy, or a martyr, to come together, to feel their own worth, or merely to survive? Why is it that human beings are fascinated with "evil," creating images in its likeness, as children create monsters? It is significant, too, the emphasis the author places on women as accessible scapegoat figures for communities, for any obviously conscious disregard of cultural mores on their part seems to represent not only a threat to the community but to the whole species as well—hence the preponderance of witches, pariahs, and insane women in the history of humanity.

Most importantly, through Morrison's characterization of Eva, Hannah, and Sula, we see that it is not merely social deviance that makes one a pariah. That cursed label is given only to one whose behavior seems so different from, so *at odds with*, the prevailing norm that it cannot be absorbed into the unconscious of the community. In this case, from her birth, the community's unconscious had already been prepared to accept Sula as distinct. It is significant that Sula's birthmark is perceived in different ways, depending on the perspective of the beholder. When Morrison first describes it, "it is something like a stemmed rose" that adds excitement to an otherwise plain face. To Shadrack, who reveres fish, it is the mark of a tadpole, identifying Sula as a friend. To Jude, the mark resembles a rattlesnake, the sting of which is taken away by Sula's smile. To the folk, the mark is Evil, the mark of Hannah's ashes, identifying Sula from her very beginning as a devil. So Sula, not Eva or Hannah, is a pariah because she is distinctly different, because she is consciously seeking to make herself rather than others, and she is totally unconcerned about what others think; in other words, she does not care.

Although Sula does not care about what the community thinks, she does care about Nel, the friend to whom she returns in the Bottom, and she comes to care about Ajax, her lover, for a time. Morrison weaves in a specific pattern the strands of the community's belief system together with the estrangement of Nel and Sula and the love affair of Ajax and Sula so we might better understand the complexity of both points of view. First, the author tells us about the community's view of Nature and Evil, after which we experience the estrangement of Nel and Sula and the community's designation of Sula as a witch. Finally, the story of Sula's and Ajax's relationship is followed by Sula's death and the death of the folk in that tunnel. In carefully charting her pattern, Morrison asks us to contemplate the meaning of her design.

The story of the apparent dissolution of the strong friendship between Nel and Sula occurs within the context of the Bottom's need to band against Sula and as such is the embodied formulation of the gap between Sula and the community from which she comes. Unlike the other folk in the Bottom, Nel is elated when Sula returns. Her joy is expressed, as their fear is, in terms of nature. She

> . . . noticed the peculiar quality of the May that followed the leaving of the birds. It had a sheen, a glimmering as of green, rain-soaked Saturday nights (lit by the excitement of newly installed street lights; of lemon yellow afternoons bright with iced drinks and splashes of daffodils).

For Nel, the world again becomes magical and interesting because of Sula's presence. She emphasizes their unity, how talking to Sula was like talking to herself. Yet Sula's gift of magic becomes a spiritual death for Nel because these two women are no longer one. They have taken different roads in life and have formed the meaning-ness of their lives into different patterns. Nel's life, in essence, revolves around Jude, her husband, and their three children, while Sula's life revolves around her own exploratory imagination. When Sula sleeps with Jude, obviously not so much as an act of passion, but more as an exploratory act, or even, we suspect, as a means to more intimacy with Nel, she breaks the one taboo that could shatter their girlhood friendship. Their respective reactions to this act counterpoint one another, revealing their different value systems.

In her soliloquy, Nel stares into that abyss that Sula experienced so sharply when she overheard Hannah admit that she did not like her. That is, Nel learns that one can never wholly rely on anyone. She remembers Sula's words, "The real hell of Hell is that it is forever," and counters "Sula was wrong. Hell ain't things lasting forever, Hell is change." Unable to get away from her self, which is pain, and the pain, which is her self, she learns, too, as Sula had, that there is no self to rely on. Her pain and her fear of it become in her mind a dirty ball of fur and string signifying nothing. What Sula does for Nel, as she has always done in their friendship, is to share her experimental knowledge with her. By so doing Sula underscores the illusion on which Nel's life is based. From a practical point of view, Nel has been prepared solely for the role of being a handmaiden to Jude or to someone like him. By sleeping with Jude, Sula strips Nel of her illusion, leaving her with nothing she can rely on. In contrast to Sula, who turns this jarring knowledge into a reason for exploration, Nel *knows* that "her thighs are forever empty," that her life is finished, and that she nonetheless longs for those who had crushed her:

> That was too much. To lose Jude and not have Sula to talk to about it because it was Sula that he had left her for.

In one stroke, Nel loses the bases of her emotional life, her husband, Jude, and her only friend, Sula. What else is there for her to do but die—slowly.

Between Nel's soliloquy about her pain and Sula's reactions to their broken friendship, Morrison inserts the community's judgment of Sula as a witch and Sula's acceptance of that judgment. The folk's judgment of Sula is partly based on Sula's infidelity to her friend Nel; in part, Sula's acceptance of their judgment is her realization that her only true friend has become one of *them*. Sula had thought of Nel as being one with her and finds out, at least from her point of view, that Nel is just like all the women she has known who hold onto their men "because they were only afraid of losing their jobs." Nel becomes like the others, the people she visualizes as spiders, afraid of experiment, afraid of living. So their friendship freezes to death, Sula surmises, because Nel becomes dead like the rest of the town.

These are Nel and Sula's perceptions about what has happened, perceptions on opposite sides of the spectrum. But Morrison's unrelenting probing assails us with a complicated truth that lies somewhere between the pain and emptiness of Nel, husbandless with three children, left to live without any hope of really living, and Sula's pure view of people who are afraid to live because they are possessive, because they do not want to experience pain and therefore never experience pleasure. As Sula explores her feelings about her estrangement from Nel, she characterizes the women of the Bottom in this way:

> The narrower their lives, the wider their hips. Those with husbands had folded themselves into starched coffins, their sides bursting with other people's skinned dreams and bony regrets. Those without men were like sour-tipped needles featuring one constant empty eye. Those with men had had the sweetness sucked from their breath by ovens and steam kettles. Their children were like distant but exposed wounds whose aches were not less intimate because separate from their flesh. They had looked at the world and back at their children, back at the world and back again at their children, and Sula knew that one clear young eye was all that kept the knife away from the throat's curve.

But Sula, too, is not immune from the need for permanence and consistency. Morrison juxtaposes Sula's caustic analysis of the women in the Bottom with her relationship with Ajax, a relationship in which Sula discovers the desire to be possessive.

Sula and Ajax's love relationship emerges as the fullest communication between a man and woman in Morrison's works. As persons, they are well suited to each other. Ajax, beautifully male and heroic (as his name implies) had been the object of Nel and Sula's adolescent dreams of anticipated sexuality. His two loves, his conjure woman mother and airplanes, tell us that he expects women to be mentally as well as physically interesting, and that he wants more than anything to fly, far above the limits set for him. Like Sula, he resists limitations and ties. But unlike her, he has found an object other than himself on which to focus his imagination, although it is interesting that he, too, will never be able to fulfill his dream, will never be able to fly a plane. They love each other; in that they find another version of themselves in each other, at least for a while. He is attracted to Sula, suspecting that "this was perhaps the only other woman other than his mother he knew whose life was her own, who could deal with life efficiently and who was not interested in nailing him." Their relationship solidifies because they have genuine conversations, the real pleasure that Sula is seeking. But having discovered this pleasure, Sula wants to keep it, possess it, always have it when she wants it. So in the manner of age-old seduction, she adorns herself, cleans the house, and whispers to him, "Lean on me," words that epitomize the relationship between Nel and Jude, words that thrust the concept of dependence and therefore of possessiveness into their relationship. Knowing the signs, Ajax rushes off to watch the planes that he will never be allowed to fly.

Now, Sula experiences the pain of absence she had unwittingly inflicted on her friend Nel. Perhaps women feel wronged when men leave them, not only, or sometimes not at all, because they will lose their jobs, but because of the pain of absence. Sula experiences:

> An absence so decorative, so ornate, it was difficult for her to understand how she had ever endured, without falling dead or being consumed, his magnificent presence.

Yet she knows that the relationship would have ended eventually, for had he not left, her insatiable curiosity would have compelled her to dig deeper and deeper into his psyche until she hurt him. Realizing the essential loneliness of her stance in life, she sings, "There aren't any more new songs, and I have sung all the ones there are." What else is there left for her to do but die?

Although Nel and Sula have taken opposite paths, they are both dying. But Nel is dying, as Sula says, "like a stump," while Sula feels that she is "going down like one of those redwoods." Death brings them together again when Nel comes to see Sula on her deathbed. Both thirty, the evil Sula is dying physically, the Bottom feels, as retribution for her sins, while the virtuous Nel's "hot brown eyes had turned to agate, and her skin had taken on the sheen of maple struck down, split and sanded at the height of its green." Sula had lived gloriously before she was struck down; Nel, on the other hand, endures physically, but only at the price of never having fulfilled herself. Their conversation, an echo of Eva's conversation with Sula, concerns how much one is allowed to live:

> "You can't have it all, Sula."
> "Why? I can do it all, why can't I have it all?"
> "You *can't* do it all. You a woman and a colored woman at that. You can't act like a man. You can't be walking around all

independent-like, doing whatever you like, taking what you want, leaving what you don't."

Their exchange illuminates the difference between their philosophies. Sula exclaims:

> "You think I don't know what your life is like just because I ain't living it? I know what every colored woman in this country is doing."
> "What's that?"
> "Dying. Just like me. But the difference is they dying like a stump. Me, I going down like one of those redwoods. I sure did live in this world."
> "Really? What have you got to show for it?"
> "Show? To who? Girl, I got my mind. And what goes on in it. Which is to say, I got me."
> "Lonely, ain't it?"
> "Yes. But my lonely is *mine*. Now your lonely is somebody else's. Made by somebody else and handed to you. Ain't that something? A second-hand lonely."

As Nel leaves her, Sula crystallizes the difference.

> "How you know?" Sula asked.
> "Know what?" Nel wouldn't look at her.
> "About who was *good*. How you know it was you?"
> "What you mean?"
> "I mean maybe it wasn't you. Maybe it was me."

In her final speech in this novel, Sula questions the community's insistence on its own goodness and its designation of anything that falls outside its ken as evil. She does this most specifically in relation to their view of woman, which she proclaims is entirely to the community's use without any concern for the women who must live it. In spite of the community's judgments, however, and despite their estrangement, Nel and Sula still relate to each other as they had in childhood. Although the Bottom has labeled the behavior of one of them as evil and the other as good, they continue to complement one another. As the exploratory half in their relationship, Sula had always been the one to share with Nel what it was to experience this or that. So Sula had been Nel's source of liberation from stern parents or from a rigid community that sought to destroy any imagination she had. Nel had been Sula's source of stability when crises occurred, as in the death of Chicken Little. When Nel experiences the pain of Jude's absence, it is to Sula that she wants to talk, an impossibility since Sula is the reason for his leaving. When Sula is dying, her last thought is to share with Nel this most personal of experiences. "Well, I'll be damned," she thought, "it didn't even hurt. Wait'll I tell Nel." We later learn that when Sula is dead, Nel is the one in the Bottom who makes the arrangements for her funeral and is the only one who formally attends it. The practical element in their relationship, Nel always performs well in a crisis.

In the pursuit of complex truth, Morrison has juxtaposed the world of Nel next to the world of Sula, the world in which practicality and survival are foremost to the world in which exploration and imagination make life worth living. Which world view holds the answer to life? Does either? Nel does as she is told; any sparkle she has is rubbed down to a dull glow so she can become a sensible, comforting wife, so she can do those things, however tedious, necessary for survival. But her world is dependent on another, the world of her husband or her children. Since these worlds collapse, she is left without a context. Sula pursues herself, exploring her emotions and imagination. Her world is hers, but left without a focus for her imagination, she becomes destructive, and because her stance seems contrary to the survival of her community, she is left alone, estranged from others. Finally, she turns in on herself, but the self, as her experience with Chicken Little or as her relationship with Ajax proves, cannot be totally relied on either.

Although Sula dies, Morrison does not want us to conclude that the philosophy of the Bottom is superior. The folk's major premise is that the way to conquer evil is to survive it, to outlast it. So when Sula dies, the folk feel they have won, that a brighter day is dawning, that there will be work for black men in building the tunnel, which has been planned, abandoned, and replanned. The chapter "1941" makes it plain that the evil they need to conquer cannot merely be outlasted, and that Sula's presence in the Bottom has little to do with brighter days. If anything, her absence makes things worse, for without a pariah, the folk revert to not caring about each other. What becomes clear is that Nature will always inflict disasters on them, that the evil of racism will result in jobless men and women, and that death will be always with them. With or without a pariah, evil days continue, and although the philosophy of survival may be useful in combatting them, it is a limited method. As if reminding the Bottom that it is still vulnerable to catastrophe, regardless of Sula's death, the natural fall of the year is replaced by an early frost, destroying the crops, resulting in sickness of the body and in a spiritless, stingy Thanksgiving. Then the frost is followed by the false hope of a summery January, a heat that will cause the earth to shift in the tunnel they all yearn to build. In fact, if anything, Sula's death, coupled with the natural and social ills that affect them, bring mass death to the Bottom.

Consistent in the novel, Shadrack appears as the figure who stands for the fear of death. Ironically, this shell-shocked soldier realizes through the death of Sula that his National Suicide Day ritual does not ward off death. He had reassured Sula, his only visitor in all those years, that she would *always* be. Yet she, too, had died and would never come again. On January third, on National Suicide Day, he pays no attention to the details of his ritual for he no longer believes in its efficacy, and, ironically, on this particular day, national suicide happens not in ritual but in fact. Looking at death in the sunshine and being unafraid, laughing folk follow Shadrack:

> As the initial group of about twenty people passed more houses, they called to the people standing in doors and leaning out of windows to join them; to help them open further this slit in the veil, this respite from an anxiety from dignity, from gravity, from the weight of that very adult pain that had undergirded them all those years before. Called to them to come out and play in the sunshine—as though the sunshine would last, as though there really was hope. The same hope that kept them picking beans for other farmers, kept them from finally leaving as they talked of doing; kept them knee-deep in other people's dirt; kept them excited about other people's wars; kept them solicitous of white people's children; kept them convinced that some magic "government" was going to lift them up, out and away from the dirt, those beans, those wars.

Revitalized by false hope, they dance to the site of promise—the tunnel—and in an act of defiance try to kill the tunnel they were forbidden to build. The heat, the false hope, causes the earth to shift and the water to break. Many are suffocated, drowned, or crushed to death as Shadrack rings his bell, proclaiming the unexpectedness of death. Too long insistent on outlasting evil, worn down by natural and social forces, the folk's one defiant gesture is built on a false hope that keeps them in shackles.

Morrison's fable emphasizes the paradox inherent in the philosophy of survival. True, when one is not able to destroy evil, one must try to outlast it. But human beings have to demand more from life than mere survival, or they may not survive at all. To really live life, there must be some imagination, some exploration, so there can be some creative action.

The last chapter of the novel, "1965," hammers this point home, for although some of the folk have survived and there has been some progress, the Bottom and its distinctiveness have disappeared. Ironically, black folk had moved from the Bottom only to realize too late that hill land had become valuable. In terms of monetary value, it had become, in fact, what the white farmer had told his slave a hundred years before, "the bottom of Heaven."

Structurally, this chapter acts as the Bottom's eulogy, weaving all the novel's threads together into a completed fabric. Nel is, as she must be, our point of view character, for through Sula, she has participated in another world view, distinct from her own. She alone can recognize the pattern that was being woven all those years. In talking with Eva, the mother who has outlasted her progeny, Nel is confronted with the waste and arrogance inherent in living solely to make others. Confronted by Eva's meanness, Nel recognizes the Bottom's narrowness, finally its undoing, even as she can still appreciate its marvelous distinctiveness. Nel's conversation with Eva also reminds us of the futile deaths that pervade this book: the deaths of Plum, Chicken Little, Hannah, and finally Sula. In confusing Nel with Sula, Eva reminds Nel of the unity of feeling she once had with this cursed woman. As if to heighten our awareness of the death of the Bottom, Nel goes to the cemetery, the only remaining monument of this community. On her way she passes Shadrack, the symbol of the fear of death throughout this novel. It is fitting that these two should be our final witnesses to the fable for they represent throughout the novel the personal embodiment of the community's concept of survival that is rooted not in the wish to live but in the fear of dying.

As a result of her confrontation with the pattern of her life, Nel realizes the emptiness she had felt all of these years was not the pain of Jude's absence but that of Sula's. It is with Sula that she had experienced the excitement of being human and had had the opportunity to go beyond the Bottom's narrow principle of survival. Through Sula, she could have transformed her own life just as the Bottom might have. If she and it had sought to understand what Sula meant, if she and it had explored the possibilities of life, perhaps Sula might have survived, Nel might have lived, and the Bottom might still be. As it is, the tale of Sula, the marked woman, and her community, the Bottom, remains the stuff out of which legends are made.

HORTENSE J. SPILLERS

A Hateful Passion, a Lost Love

> When I think of how essentially alone black women have been—alone
> because of our bodies, over which we have had so little control; alone because
> the damage done to our men has prevented their closeness and protection;
> and alone because we have had no one to tell us stories about ourselves; I
> realize that black women writers are an important and comforting presence
> in my life. Only they know my story. It is absolutely necessary that they be
> permitted to discover and interpret the entire range and spectrum of the
> experience of black women and not be stymied by preconceived conclusions.
> Because of these writers, there are more models of how it is possible for us to
> live, there are more choices for black women to make, and there is a larger
> space in the universe for us.

Toni Morrison's *Sula* is a rebel idea, both for her creator and for Morrison's audience. To read *Sula* is to encounter a sentimental education so sharply discontinuous from the dominant traditions of Afro-American literature in the way that it compels and/or deadlocks the responses that the novel, for all its brevity and quiet intrusion on the landscape of American fiction, is, to my mind, the single most important irruption of black women's writing in our era. I am not claiming for this novel any more than its due; *Sula* (1973) is not a stylistic innovation. But in bringing to light dark impulses no longer contraband in the black American female's cultural

This article is a revised version of an article originally published in *Feminist Studies* 9, no. 2 (Summer 1983): pp. 293–323, by permission of the publisher, *Feminist Studies*, Inc.

address, the novel inscribes a new dimension of being, moving at last in contradistinction to the tide of virtue and pathos which tends to overwhelm black female characterization in a monolith of terms and possibilities. I regard Sula the character as a literal and figurative breakthrough toward the assertion of what we may call, in relation to her literary "relatives," new female being.

Without predecessors in the recent past of Afro-American literature, Sula is anticipated by a figure four decades removed from Morrison's symbol smasher: Janie Starks in Zora Neale Hurston's *Their Eyes Were Watching God* (1937). By intruding still a third figure—Vyry Ware of Margaret Walker's *Jubilee* (1966)—we lay hold of a pattern of contrast among three African-American female writers, who pose not only differences of character in their perception of female possibilities, but also a widely divergent vocabulary of feeling. This article traces the changes in black female characterization from *Sula* back toward the literary past, beginning with Margaret Walker's Vyry and Zora Neale Hurston's Janie, forward again to *Sula* and Morrison. It argues that the agents which these novels project are strikingly different, and that the differences take shape primarily around questions of moral and social value. And it explores the mediations through which all three writers translate sociomoral constructs into literary modes of discourse.

Margaret Walker's Vyry Ware belongs to, embodies, a corporate ideal. The black woman in her characterization exists for the race, in its behalf, and in maternal relationship to its profoundest needs and wishes. Sula, on the other hand, lives for Sula and has no wish to "mother" anyone, let alone the black race in some symbolic concession to a collective need. If Vyry is woman-for-the-other, then Sula is woman-for-self. Janie Starks represents a dialectical point between the antitheses, and the primary puzzle of *Their Eyes Were Watching God* is the contradiction of motives through which Janie Starks has her being; in other words, Janie might have been Sula, but the latter only through a resolution of negative impulses. These three characters, then, describe peak points in a cultural and historical configuration of literary issues. In Sula's case, the old love of the collective, for the collective, is lost, and passions are turned antagonistic, since, as the myth of the black woman goes, the latter is loving only insofar as she protects her children and forgives her man. The title of this article is a kind of shorthand for these longhanded notations.

The scheme of these observations, as I have already implied, is not strictly chronological. Hurston's affinities are much closer to Morrison's than Walker's, even though Hurston's *Their Eyes Were Watching God* was written nearly fifty years ago. The critical scheme I offer here is not precisely linear, because the literary movement I perceive, which theoretically might take in more women writers than my representative selections, does not progress neatly from year to year in an orderly advance of literary issues and strategies. My method aims at a dialectics of process, with these affinities and emphases tending to move in cycles rather than straight lines. I see no myth of descent operating here as in Harold Bloom's "anxiety of influence," exerted, in an oedipal-like formation, by great writers on their successors. The idea-form which I trace here, articulated in three individual writers' metaphors and patterns of theme and structure, does not emerge within this community of writers in strict sequential order. Ironically, it is exactly the right *not* to accede to the simplifications and mystifications of a strictly historiographical time line that now promises the greatest freedom of discourse to black people, to black women, as critics, teachers, writers, and thinkers.

As the opening exercise in the cultural and literary perspective that this article wishes to consider, then, we turn immediately to Morrison's Sula, the "youngest" of three heroines. Few of the time-honored motifs of female behavioral description will suit her: not "seduction and betrayal," applied to a network of English and American fictions; not the category of "holy fool," as exemplified in various Baldwinian configurations of female character; not the patient long-suffering female, nor the female authenticated by male imagination. Compared with past heroines of black American fiction, Sula exists foremost in her own consciousness. To that extent, *Sula* and *Their Eyes Were Watching God* are studies in contrast to Walker and share the same fabric of values. The problem that Morrison poses in Sula is the degree to which her heroine (or antiheroine, depending on one's reading of the character) is self-betrayed. The audience does not have an easy time in responding to the agent, because the usual sentiments about black women have been excised, and what we confront instead is the entanglement of our own conflicting desires, our own contradictory motivations concerning issues of individual woman-freedom. Sula is both loved and hated by the reader, embraced and rejected simultaneously because her audience is forced to accept the corruption of absolutes and what has been left in their place— the complex, alienated, transitory gestures of a personality who has no framework of moral reference beyond or other than herself.

Insofar as Sula is not a loving human being, extending few of the traditional loyalties to those around her, she reverses the customary trend of "moral growth" and embodies, contrarily, a figure of genuine moral ambiguity about whom few comforting conclusions may be drawn. Through Sula's unalterable "badness," black and female are now made to appear as a *single* subject in its own right, fully aware of a plenitude of predicative possibilities, for good and ill.

In Sula's case, virtue is not the sole alternative to powerlessness, or even the primary one, or perhaps even an alternative at all. In the interest of complexity, Sula is Morrison's deliberate hypothesis. A conditional subjunctive replaces an indicative certainty: "In a way her strangeness, her naiveté, her craving for the other half of her equation was the consequence of an idle imagination. Had she paints, or clay, or knew the discipline of the dance or strings; had she anything to engage her tremendous curiosity and her gift for metaphor, she might have exchanged the restlessness and preoccupation with whim for an activity that provided her with all she yearned for. And like any *artist with no art form* she became dangerous."

In careful, exquisite terms Sula has been endowed with dimensions of other possibility. How they are frustrated occupies us for most of the novel, but what strikes me keenly about the passage is that Morrison imagines a character whose destiny is not coterminous with naturalistic or mystical boundaries. Indeed the possibility of art, of intellectual vocation for black female character, has been offered as style of defense against the naked brutality of conditions. The efficacy of art cannot be isolated from its social and political means, but Sula is specifically circumscribed by the lack of an explicit tradition of imagination or aesthetic work, and not by the evil force of "white" society, or the absence of a man, or even the presence of a mean one.

Morrison, then, imagines a character whose failings are directly traceable to the absence of a discursive/imaginative project—some *thing* to do, some object-subject relationship which establishes the identity in time and space. We do not see Sula in relationship to an "oppressor," a "whitey," a male, a dominant and dominating being outside the self. No Manichean analysis demanding a polarity of interest—black/white, male/female, good/bad—will work here. Instead, Sula emerges as an embodiment of a metaphysical chaos in pursuit of an activity both proper and sufficient to herself. Whatever Sula has become, whatever she is, is a matter of her own choices, often ill-formed and ill-informed. Even her loneliness, she says to her best friend Nel is her own—"My own lonely," she claims in typical Sulabravado, as she lies dying. Despite our misgivings at Sula's insistence and at the very degree of alienation Morrison accords her, we are prepared to accept her negative, naysaying freedom as a necessary declaration of independence by the black female writer in her pursuit of a vocabulary of gesture—both verbal and motor—that leads us as well as the author away from the limited repertoire of powerless virtue and sentimental pathos. Sula is neither tragic nor pathetic; she does not amuse or accommodate. For black audiences, she is not consciousness of the black race personified, nor "tragic mulatto," nor, for white ones, is she "mammie," "Negress," "coon," or "maid." She is herself, and Morrison, quite rightly, seems little concerned if any of us, at this late date of Sula's appearance in the "house of fiction," minds her heroine or not.

We view Morrison's decision with interest because it departs dramatically from both the iconography of virtue and endurance and from the ideology of the infamous Ogre/Bitch complex, alternately poised as the dominant traits of black female personality when the black female personality exists at all in the vocabulary of public symbols. Sula demands, I believe, that we not only see anew, but also *speak* anew in laying to rest the several manifestations of apartheid in its actual practice and in the formulation of the critical postulates that govern our various epistemologies.

That writers like Morrison, Toni Cade Bambara, and Paule Marshall among them, participate in a tradition of black women writing in their own behalf, close to its moment of inception, lends their work thorough complexity. With the exception of a handful of autobiographical narratives from the nineteenth century, the black woman's realities are virtually suppressed until the period of the Harlem Renaissance and later. Essentially, the black woman as artist, as intellectual spokesperson for her own cultural apprenticeship, has not existed before, for anyone. At the source of her own symbol-making task, this community of writers confronts, therefore, a tradition of work that is quite recent, its continuities broken and sporadic.

It is not at all an exaggeration to say that the black woman's presence as character and movement in the American world has been *ascribed* a status of impoverishment or pathology, or, at best, an essence that droops down in the midst of things, as de Beauvoir describes female mystery in *The Second Sex*. Against this social knowledge, black women writers likely agree on a single point: whatever the portrayal of female character yields, it will be rendered from the point of view of one whose eyes are not alien to the humanity in front of them. What we can safely assume, then, is that black women write as partisans to a particular historical order—their own, the black and female one, with its hideous strictures against literacy and its subtle activities of censorship even now against words and deeds that would deny or defy the black woman myth. What we can assume with less confidence is that their partisanship, as in the rebellion of Sula, will yield a synonymity of conclusions.

The contrast between Sula and Margaret Walker's Vyry Ware is the difference between captive woman and free woman, but the distinction between them has as much to do with aspects of agency and characterization as it does with the kind of sensibility or sympathy that a writer requires in building one kind of character and not another. In other words, *what* we think of Sula and Vyry, for instance, has something to do with *how* we are taught to *see* and *value* them. In the terms of fiction which they each propose, *Jubilee, Their Eyes Were Watching God*, and *Sula* all represent varying degrees of plausibility, but the critical question is not whether the events they portray are plausible, or whether they confirm what we already believe, or think we do, but, rather, how each writer deploys a concept of character. Of the three, Toni Morrison looks forward to an era of dissensions: Sula's passions are hateful, as we have observed, and though we are not certain that the loss of conventional love brings her down, we are sure that she overthrows received moralities in a heedless quest for her own irreducible self. This radical intrusion of waywardness lends a different thematic emphasis to the woman's tale of generation, receding in Sula's awareness, and the result is a novel whose formal strategies are ambiguous and even discomforting in their uncertainties. Once we have examined an analogy of the archetype from which Sula deviates by turning to Margaret Walker's *Jubilee* and have explored Hurston's novel as a structural advance of the literary issues, we will return to *Sula* in a consideration of myth/countermyth as a discourse ordained by history.

In radical opposition to notions of discontinuity, confronting us as a fictional world of consecrated time and space, *Jubilee* worries one of the traditional notions of realism—the stirring to life of the common people—to a modified definition. Walker completed her big novel in the mid sixties at the University of Iowa Creative Writers' Workshop. She tells the story of the novel, twenty years in the making, in *How I Wrote* Jubilee. This novel of historical content has no immediate precedent in Afro-American literary tradition. To that extent, it bears little structural resemblance to Hurston's work before it, although both Hurston and Walker implement a search for roots, or to Morrison's work after it. *Jubilee*, therefore, assumes a special place in the canon.

From Walker's own point of view, the novel is historical, taking its models from the Russian writers of historical fiction, particularly Tolstoy. In its panoramic display, its massive configurations of characters and implied presences, its movement from a dense point of American history—the era of the Civil War—toward an inevitable, irreversible outcome—the emancipation of 10 million African Americans—*Jubilee* is certainly historical. Even though it is a tale whose end is written on the brain, in the heart, so that there is not even a chance that we will be mistaken about closure, the novel unfolds as if the issues were new. We are sufficiently excited to keep turning the page of a twice-told tale accurately reiterating what we have come to believe is the truth about the "Peculiar Institution." But the high credibility of the text in this case leads us to wonder, eventually, what else is embedded in it that compels us to read our fate by its lights. My own interpretation of the novel is that it is not only historical, but also, and primarily, Historical. In other words, "Historical," in this sense, is a metaphor for the unfolding of the Divine Will. This angle on reality is defined by Paul Tillich as a theonomy. Human history is shot through with Divine Presence so that its being and time are consistent with a plan that elaborates and completes the will of God. In this view of things, human doings are only illusions of a counterfeit autonomy; in Walker's novel agents (or characters) are moving and are moved under the aegis of a Higher and Hidden Authority.

For Vyry Ware, the heroine of *Jubilee* and her family, honor, courage, endurance—in short, the heroic as transparent prophetic utterance—become the privileged center of human response. If Walker's characters are ultimately seen as one-dimensional, either good or bad, speaking in a public rhetoric that assumes the heroic or its opposite, then such portrayal is apt to a fiction whose value is subsumed in a theonomous frame of moral reference. From this angle of advocacy and preservation the writer does not penetrate the core of experience, but encircles it. The heroic intention has no interest in fluctuations or transformations or palpitations of conscience—these will pass away—but monumentality, or fixedness, becomes its striving. Destiny is disclosed to the hero or the heroine as an already-fixed and named event, and this steady reference point is the secret of permanence.

Set on a Georgia plantation before the Civil War, the novel is divided into three parts. The first recalls the infancy and youth of Vyry Ware, the central figure of the novel, and rehearses various modes of the domestic South in slavery. The second part recapitulates the war and its impact on the intimate life of families and individuals. One of the significant threads of the Peculiar Institution in objective time is closely imitated here—how the exigencies of war lead to the destruction of plantation hierarchy. In this vacuum of order a landscape of deracinated women and men dominates the countryside, and Walker's intensity of detail involves the reader in a scene of universal mobility—everything is moving, animate and inanimate, away from the centers of war toward peace, always imminent, in the shadows of Sherman's torch. Vyry and her first love Randall Ware are numbered among the casualties. They are separated as the years of war unhinge all former reality.

The third and final segment of the novel marks Vyry's maturity and the rebirth of a semblance of order in the South. The future is promising for the emancipated, and Vyry takes a new lover, Innis Brown, before the return of Randall Ware. This typing up the various threads of the narrative is undercut by a bitterly ironical perspective. The former enslaved will struggle as she or he has before now, with this difference: free by law, each remains a victim of arbitrary force, but such recognition is the reader's alone. This edge of perception reads into the novel an element of pathos so keenly defined that Vyry's fate verges on the tragic.

Variously encoded by signs associated with a magical/superstitious world order, echoes of maxims and common speech, *Jubilee* is immersed in the material. We are made to feel, in other words, the brutal pull of necessity—the captive's harsh relationship to this earth and its unrelenting requirements of labor—as they impel the captive consciousness toward a terrible knowledge of the tenuousness between life and death. The novel conjoins natural setting and social necessity in a dance of temporal unfolding; in fact, the institution of slavery described here is an elaboration of immanence so decisive in its hold on the human scene imposed upon it that Walker's humanity is actually "ventriloquized" through the medium of a third-person narrator. The narrative technique (with its overlay of mystical piety) is negotiated between omniscient and concealed narrators. Whatever the characters think, however they move and feel about their being, all is rendered through the eyes of another consciousness, not their own. We might say that the characters embody, then, historical symbols—a captive class and their captors—which have been encoded or transliterated as actors in a fiction. Walker's agents are types or valences, and the masks through which they speak might be assumed as well by any other name.

In attributing to Walker a theonomous view of human reality, I am also saying that her characters are larger than life; that they are overdrawn, that, in fact, their compelling agency and motivation are ahistorical, despite the novel's solid historical grounding. Walker's *lexis* operates under quite complicated laws, complicated because such vocabulary is no longer accessible, or even acceptable, to various mythoi of contemporary fiction. Walker is posing a subterranean structure of God terms, articulated in the novel through what we can identify as the *peripeteia*—that point of radical change in the direction that the forces of the novel are moving; in historical and secular terms this change is called emancipation. Historiographic method in accounting for the "long-range" and "immediate" causes of the Civil War and its aftermath does not name "God" as a factor in the liberation of black Americans, and neither does Walker in any explicit way. But it seems clear to me that "God" is precisely what she means in all the grandeur and challenge of the Nominative, clear that the agency of Omnipresence—even more reverberative in its imprecise and ubiquitous *thereness*—is for Walker the source of one of the most decisive abruptions in our history.

Walker adopts a syntax and semantics whose meanings are recognizable in an explanation of affairs in human time. But these delegated efficacies register at a deeper level of import so that "nature," for instance, is nature and something more, and character itself acts in accordance with the same kind of mystical or "unrealistic" tendencies.

Walker's backdrop of natural representation has such forcefulness in the work that dialogue itself is undercut by its dominance, but her still life is counterposed by human doings which elaborate the malignancies of nature, that is, torture, beatings, mental cruelty, the ugly effects of nature embodied in the formal and institutional. The slaveholder and his class, in the abrogation of sympathy, lose their human form. The captors' descent into nature is seen as pernicious self-indulgence, ratified by institutional sanction, but it also violates a deeper structural motive which Walker manipulates in the development of character. Though natural and social events run parallel, they are conjoined by special arrangement, and then there is a name for it—the act of magic or invocation that the enslaved opposes to the arbitrary willfulness of authority.

The evocation of a magical program defines the preeminent formalistic features of the opening segments of the novel. Prayers for the sick and dying and the special atmosphere that surrounds the deathwatch are treated from the outset with particular thematic prominence. In several instances mood is conveyed more by conventional notation—the number thirteen, boiling black pot, full moon, squinch owl, black crone—than any decisive nuance of thought or detail; or more precisely, fear is disembodied from internal agitations of feeling and becomes an attribute of things. "Midnight came and thirteen people waited for death. The black pot boiled, and the full moon rode the clouds high in the heavens and straight up over their heads. . . . It was not a night for people to sleep easy. Every now and then the squinch owl hollered and the crackling fire would glare and the black pot boil. . . ."

The suspense that gathers about this scene is brought on by the active interaction of forces that move beyond and above the characters. An outburst would surprise. Sis. Hetta's death is expected here, and nothing more. The odd and insistent contiguity that Walker establishes among a variety of natural and cultural-material signs—"black pot boiled"; "full moon rode"—identifies the kind of magical/mystical grammar of terms to which I have referred.

"Black pot" and "full moon" may be recognized as elements that properly belong to the terrain of witchcraft, but we must understand that magic and witchcraft—two semiological "stops" usually associated with African-American rebellion and revolutionary fervor throughout the New World under the whip of slavery—are ritual terms of a shorthand which authors adopt to describe a system of beliefs and practices not entirely accessible to us now. In other worlds, Walker is pointing toward a larger spiritual and religious context through these notations, so that ordinary diurnal events in the novel are invested with extraordinary meaning. My own terms—theonomous meaning—would relate this extraordinary attribution to the Unseen, for which Protestant theology offers other clusters of anomalous phenomena, including "enthusiasm," "ecstasy," or the equivalent of Emile Durkheim's demon of oratorical power. In specific instances of the novel, we see only pointers toward, or markers of, an entirely compelling structure of feelings and beliefs, of which "black pot," for instance, is a single sign. The risk I am taking here is to urge a synonymity between "God" and, for want of a better term, "magic." At least I am suggesting that Walker's vocabulary of God terms includes magic and the magical and the enslaved person's special relationship to natural forces.

Walker achieves this "extra" reading by creating a parallelism between natural and social/domestic issues that dominates the form of the novel. In its reinforcements, there is an absence of differentiation, or of the interplay between dominant and subdominant motifs. A nocturnal order pervades *Jubilee*—life under the confines of the slave community, where movement is constantly under surveillance; secret meetings; flights from the overseer's awful authority; illegal and informal pacts and alliances between slaves; and above all, the slave's terrible vulnerability to fluctuations of fate.

The scene of Vyry's capture after an attempted escape on the eve of the Civil War will provide a final example. After their union Vyry and Randall Ware, the free black man, have two children, Jim and Minna, and Ware makes plans for their liberation. His idea is that he or Vyry will return for the children later, but Vyry refuses to desert them. Her negotiation of a painful passage across the countryside toward the point of rendezvous groans with material burden. It has rained the day of their attempted escape, and mud is dense around the slave quarters by nightfall. Vyry travels with the two children—Jim toddling and the younger child Minna in her arms. The notion of struggle, both against the elements and the powerful other, is so forceful an aspect of tone that the passage itself painfully anticipates the fatefulness of Vyry's move; here are the nodal points:

> Every step Vyry and Jim took, they could feel the mud sucking their feet down and fighting them as they withdrew their feet from its elastic hold. . . . The baby still slept fitfully while Vyry pressed her way doggedly to the swamps. . . . At last they were in sight of the swamps. Feeling sorry for little Jim she decided to rest a few minutes before trying to wade the creek. . . . She sat down on an old log, meaning to rest only a few minutes. . . . A bad spasm clutched her stomach instinctively. She tensed her

body with the sure intuition that she was not only being watched but that the watchful figures would soon surround her. Impassively she saw the patteroller and guards, together with Grimes [the overseer] emerge from the shadows and walk toward her. . . .

This grim detail concludes with Vyry's capture and brutal punishment—"seventy-five lashes on her naked back." That Vyry has been robbed of selfhood on its most fundamental level is clear enough, but the passage further suggests that her movements replicate the paralysis of nightmare. One would move, but cannot, and awakens in spasms of terror. This direct articulation of nightmare content—puzzles and haltings, impediments and frights—dictates the crucial psychological boundaries of *Jubilee* and decides, accordingly, the aesthetic rule.

The idea that emerges here is that Vyry's condition is the equivalent of nightmare, a nocturnal order of things that works its way into the resonances of the novel's structure. Her paralysis is symptomatic of a complex of fear and repression in the service of death. We could argue that the culture of slavery projected in the novel—its modalities of work and celebration, its civic functions and legal codes, its elaborate orders of brutality and mutilation—presents a spectacle of a *culture* in the service of death. Given this reality, the slave subject has no life, but only the stirrings of it. Vyry, trapped in a bad dream, cannot shake loose, and this terrible imposed impotence foreshadows the theme of liberation and a higher liberation as well in which case the stalled movement is overcome in a gesture of revolutionary consciousness. For Vyry the freeing act is sparked by war whose intricate, formal causes are remote to her, though its mandates will require the reorganization of her human resources along new lines of stress. Above all, Vyry must move now without hesitation as the old order collapses around her.

For Vyry's class, the postwar years stand as the revelation of the emotional stirrings they have felt all along. "Mine Eyes Have Seen the Glory of the Coming of the Lord" (the title of one of Walker's chapters) is as much a promise as it is an exercise in common meter, but the terms of the promise that Walker imitates are neither modern nor secular. They are eternal and self-generating, authored elsewhere, beyond the reach of human inquiry. Along this axis of time, with its accent on the eternal order of things, women and men in destiny move consistent with the stars of heaven.

This blending of a material culture located in the nineteenth century with a theme which appears timeless and is decisively embedded in a Christian metaphysic reveals the biographical inspiration behind Walker's work. *Jubilee* is, in effect, the tale translated of the author's female ancestors. This is a story of the foremothers, a celebration of their stunning faith and intractable powers of endurance. In that sense, it is not so much a study of characters as it is an interrogation into the African-American character in its poignant national destiny and through its female line of spiritual descent. A long and protracted praise piece, a transformed and elaborated prayer, *Jubilee* is Walker's invocation to the guiding spirit and genius of her people. Such a novel is not "experimental." In short, it does not introduce ambiguity or irony or uncertainty or perhaps even "individualism" as potentially thematic material because it is a detailed sketch of a *collective* survival. The waywardness of a Sula Peace, or even a Janie Stark's movement toward an individualistic liberation—a separate peace—is a trait of character development engendered by a radically different Weltanschauung.

Their Eyes Were Watching God enforces a similar notion of eternal order in the organic metaphorical structure through which Hurston manipulates her characters, but the complexities of motivation in the novel move the reader some distance from the limited range of responses evoked by *Jubilee*. Janie Starks, the heroine of the novel, defines a conglomerate of human and social interests so contradictory in its emphasis that a study of structural ambiguity in fiction might well include Janie Starks *and* her author. Perhaps "uncertainty" is a more useful word in this case than "ambiguity," since Hurston avoids the full elaboration or display of tensions that Janie herself appears to anticipate. In short, Janie Starks is a bundle of contradictions: raised by women, chiefly her grandmother, to seek security in a male in his properties, Janie quite early in her career rejects Nanny's wisdom. In love with adventure, in love with the very idea of adventure, Janie is determined to know exactly what independence for the female means for her. This includes the critical quest of sexual self-determination. Janie's quite moving sense of integrity, however, is undercut in puzzling and peculiar ways.

Janie marries her first husband Logan Killicks because her grandmother wants her to do so, but Janie has little interest in a man who is not only not "glamorous" (as Joe Starks and Virgible "Teacake" Woods will be), but also not enlightened in his outlook on the world and the specifically amorous requirements of female/male relationship. Killicks gets the brunt of a kind of social criticism in *Their Eyes Were Watching God* which mocks the rural person—hardworking, unsophisticated, "straight-arrow," earnest—and Hurston makes her point by having Killicks violate essentially Janie's "dream of the horizon." Janie will shortly desert Killicks for a man far more in keeping with her ideas concerning the romantic, concerning male gracefulness. Jody Starks, up from Georgia and headed for an adventure in real estate and town government, takes the place of Logan Killicks with an immediacy, which in "real" life would be somewhat disturbing, a bit indecent; but here the "interruption" is altogether lyrical, appropriate, and unmourned. Starks's appearance and intention are even "cinematic" in their decidedly cryptic and romantic tenor—Janie literally goes off "down the road" with the man.

Their destination is Eatonville, Florida, a town which Joe Starks will bring to life with his own lovely ego, shortly to turn arrogant and insulting as he attempts to impose on Janie his old-fashioned ideas about woman's place and possibilities. The closure on this marriage is not a happy one either, troubled by Starks's chauvinistic recriminations and Janie's own disenchantment. Starks dies of a kidney ailment, leaving Janie "Mrs. Mayor" of Eatonville and not particularly concerned, we are led to believe, to be attached again.

Janie's new love affair with Teacake is untrammeled by incompatibility between the pair, though her friends express great concern that Teacake's social and financial status is not what it ought to be, let alone comparable to Jody Starks's. Janie is, however, at once traditionally romantic in her apparently male-centered yearnings and independent in her own imagination and the readiness to make her own choices. The convergence of these two emotional components is, in fact, not the diametrical opposition which contemporary feminists sometimes suppose; heterosexual love is neither inherently perverse nor necessarily dependence-engendering, except that the power equation between female and male tends to corrupt intimacies. The trouble, then, with the relationship between Janie and Teacake is not its heterosexual ambience, but a curiously exaggerated submissiveness on Janie's part that certain other elements of the heroine's character contradict.

When, for instance, Janie follows Teacake to the Florida Everglades to become a migrant farm worker for several seasons, their love is solid and reliable, but the male in this instance is also perfectly capable, under Hurston's gaze, of exhibiting qualities of jealousy and possession so decisive that his occasional physical abuse of the female and his not-so-subtle manipulation of other females' sexual attraction to him seem condoned in the name of love. Hurston's pursuit of an alleged folk philosophy in this case—as in, all women enjoy an occasional violent outburst from their men because they know then that they are loved—is a concession to an obscene idea. One example will suffice. "Before the week was over he had whipped Janie. Not because her behavior justified his jealousy, but it relieved that awful fear inside him. Being able to whip her reassured him in possession. No brutal beating at all. He just slapped her around a bit to show he was boss. . . . It aroused a sort of envy in both men and women. The way he petted and pampered her as if those two or three slaps had nearly killed her made the women see visions and the helpless way she hung on him made men dream dreams. . . ."

One might well wonder, and with a great deal of moral, if not poetic, justification if the scene above describes a *working posture* that Hurston herself might have adopted with various lovers. This scene is paradigmatic of the very quality of ambiguity/ambivalence that I earlier identified for this novel. The piece threatens to abandon primitive modes of consciousness and response from the beginning, but Hurston seems thwarted in bringing this incipience to fruition for reasons which might have to do with the way that the author understood certain popular demands brought to bear on her art. Hurston has detailed some of her notions of what Anglo-American audiences expected of the black writer and the black female writer of her time, but it is not clear to me what African-American audiences expected of their chroniclers. The more difficult question, however, is what Hurston demanded of herself in imagining what was possible for the female, and it appears that beyond a certain point she could not, or would not plunge. *Their Eyes Were Watching God,* for all its quite impressive feminist possibilities, is an instance of "double consciousness," to employ W. E. B. Du Bois's conceptualization in quite another sense and intention. Looking two ways at once, it captivates Janie Starks in an entanglement of conflicting desires.

More concentrated in dramatic focus than *Jubilee*, Hurston's novel was written during the mid thirties; finished in seven weeks during the author's visit to Haiti, the novel is not simply compact. It is hurried, intense, and above all, haunted by an uneasy measure of control. One suspects that Hurston has not said everything she means, but means everything she says. Within a persistent scheme of metaphor, she seems held back from the awful scream that she has forced Janie to repress through unrelieved tides of change. We mistrust Janie's serenity, spoken to her friend Phoeby Watson in the close of the novel; complementarily, the reconciliation is barely acceptable in either structural or dramatic terms. Janie Starks, not unlike her creator, is gifted with a dimension of worldliness and ambition that puts her in touch with broader experience. This daughter of sharecroppers is not content to be heroic under submissive conditions (except with Teacake?); for her, then, nothing in the manners of small town Florida bears repeating. Its hateful, antisocial inclinations are symbolized by Janie's grandmother, whom she hates "and [has] hidden from herself all these years under the cloak of pity." "Here Nanny had taken the biggest thing God ever made, the horizon . . . and pinched it into such a little bit of a thing that she could tie it about her granddaughter's neck tight enough to choke her. She hated the old woman who had twisted her so in the name of love . . ."

The grandmother not only represents a personal trauma for Janie (as the grandmother does in the author's autobiography), but also terror and repression, intruding a vision of impoverishment within the race. Clustered around the symbolic and living grandmother are the anonymous detractors of experience who assume no discriminating feature or motivation beyond the level of the mass. Hurston's rage is directed against this faceless brood with a moral ferociousness that verges on misogyny. This profound undercurrent is relieved, however, by a drift toward caricature. Exaggerating the fat of misshapen men and calling attention to their sexual impotence in public, gaining dimensions of comic monologue, and leaving no genuine clue for those who gaze at her, Janie has elements of a secret life which sustains her through the adventures of three husbands, a flood, justifiable homicide, trial, and vindication.

The psychological bent informing Janie's character is deflected by an anthropological strategy that all but ruins this study of a female soul. The pseudodialect of Southern patois gives Janie back to the folk ultimately, but this "return" contradicts other syntactical choices which Hurston superimposes on the structure through visions of Janie's interior life and Hurston's own narrative style. Janie implies new moral persuasions, while Hurston has her looking back, even returning, to the small town she desperately wishes to be free of. This dilemma of choices haunts the book from the very beginning and may, indeed, shed light on the "ancestral imperative." That Janie does not break from her Southern past, symbolized in the "old talk," but grasps how she might do so is the central problematic feature of the novel, previously alluded to as an undercurrent of doubt running through Hurston's strategies.

Written long before *Jubilee, Their Eyes Were Watching God* anticipates the thematic emphases prominent in *Sula* to the extent that in both the latter novels only the adventurous, deracinated personality is heroic, and that in both, the roots of experience are poisonous. One would do well to avoid the plunge down to the roots, seeking, rather, to lose oneself in a larger world of chance and danger. That woman must break loose from the hold of biography as older generations impose it, even the broader movements of tribe, constitutes a controlling theme of Hurston's work.

Images of space and time, inaugurated in the opening pages of the novel, are sounded across it with oracular intensity, defining the dream of Janie Starks as a cosmic disembodiment that renders her experience unitary with the great fantastic ages. "Ships at a distance have every man's wish on board. For some they come in with the tide." Consonant with this history of fantasy life, Janie is something of a solitary reaper, disillusioned, stoical, in her perception of fate and death. "So the beginning of this was a woman and she had come back from burying the dead. . . . The people all saw her because it was sundown. The sun was gone, but he had left his footprints in the sky. It was time to hear things and talk . . .".

The novel is essentially informed by these ahistorical, specifically rustic, image clusters, giving the whole a topological consistency. Hurston, however, attempts to counterpoise this timeless current with elements of psychic specificity—Janie's growth toward an understanding of mutability and change and other aspects of internal movement. The novel's power of revelation, nonetheless, is rather persistently sabotaged at those times when Hurston intrudes metaphorical symbolism as a substitute for the hard precision of thought. Janie actually promises more than the author delivers. As a result, the novel is facile at times when it ought to be moving, captivated in stereotype when it should be dynamic.

The flood that devastates the Florida Everglades and the homes of the migrant farm workers of which Janie and Teacake are a part provides an example. The storm sequence is the novel's high point, its chief dramatic fulcrum, on which rests the motivation that will spur both Janie's self-defense against a rabid Teacake and her return to Eatonville and the Starks house. Waiting in their cabins for the storm to recede, Janie, Teacake, and their fellow laborers are senseless with wonder at its power, "They seemed to be staring at the dark, but their eyes were watching God." What one wants in this sequence is a crack in the mental surface of character so acute that the flood cleaves the narrative precisely in half, pre- and post-diluvial responses so distinctly contrasting that the opening lines—"their souls asking if He meant to measure their puny might against His"—mature into the ineluctable event. The reader expects convergence of outer scene and its inner correspondence, but Hurston appears to forego the fruition of this parallel rhythm, content on delineating the external behavior of the agents.

Nothing specific to the inner life of Janie appears again for several pages; the awe that greets the display of natural phenomena is replayed through the imagination of a third-person observer, dry feet and all, well above the action of furious winds. We miss the concentration on Janie's internal life which saves the entire first half of the narrative from the pathos of character buffeted by external circumstances. Janie never quite regains her former brilliance, and when we meet her considered judgments again, she has fled the 'Glades, after having had to shoot Teacake in self-defense [as a result of his violence, rabies-induced] and is seeking peace in the town where she has been "first lady." "Here was peace. She pulled in her horizon like a great fish-net. Pulled it from around the waist of the world and draped it over her shoulder. So much of life in its meshes! She called in her soul to come and see . . ."

One is not certain how these images of loss and labor should be read, nor why they strike with such finality, except that the lines make a good ending, this rolling in of fish nets and cleaning of meshes, but if we take Janie as a kind of adventurer, as a woman well familiar with the rites of burial and grief, then we read this closure as a eulogy for the living; Janie has been "buried" along with Teacake.

The fault with this scene is not that Janie has loved Teacake, but, rather, that the author has broken the potential pattern of revolt by having her resigned, as if she were ready for a geriatric retirement, to the town of frustrated love. We know that all novels do end, even if they end with "the," and so it is probably fitting for Janie to have a rest after the tragic events unleashed by the flood. But her decision to go back to Eatonville after the trial strikes me as a naive fictional pose. Or, more precisely, what she thinks about her life at that point seems inappropriate to the courageous defiance that she has often embodied all along. The logic of the novel tends to abrogate neat conclusions, and their indulgence in the end essentially mitigates the complex painful knowledge that Janie has gained about herself and the other.

The promise to seize upon the central dramatic moment of a woman's self-realization fizzles out in a litany of poetic platitudes about as opposite to Janie's dream of the horizon as the grandmother's obsessive fear of experience has been. We miss the knowledge or wisdom of revelation in the perfectly resolved ending—what is it that Janie knows now that she has come back from burying the dead of the sodden and bloated? Are the words merely decorative, or do they mobilize us toward a deeper mysterious sense? In a mode of fictive assumptions similar to Margaret Walker's, Zora Neale Hurston inherits a fabric of mystery without rethreading it. That is one kind of strategic decision. There are others.

Sula, by contrast, closes with less assurance. "'All that time, all that time, I thought I was missing Jude.' And the loss pressed down on her chest and came up into her throat. 'We was girls together,' she said as though explaining something. 'O Lord, Sula,' she cried, 'girl, girl, girlgirlgirl.'"

Nel's lament not only closes *Sula*, but also reinforces the crucial dramatic questions which the novel has introduced—the very mystery of a Sula Peace and the extent to which the town of Medallion, Ohio, has been compelled by her, how they yearn for her, even to the point, oddly enough, of a collective rejection. Nel and Sula are more than girls together. They sustain the loss of innocence and its subsequent responsibilities with a degree of tormented passion seldom allowed even to lovers. More than anyone else in Medallion, they have been intimate witnesses of their mutual coming of age in a sequence of gestures that anticipates an ultimate disaffection between them, but the rhythm of its disclosure, determined early on by the reader as inexorable, is sporadic and intermittent enough in the sight of the two women that its fulfillment comes to both as a trauma of recognition. Nel

Wright's "girl," repeated five times and run together in an explosion not only of the syntactical integrity of the line, but also of Nel's very heartbeat, is piercing and sudden remorse—remorse so long suspended, so elaborate in its deceptions and evasions that it could very well intimate the onset of a sickness-unto-death.

When Sula comes of age, she leaves Medallion for a decade in the wake, significantly, of Nel's marriage to Jude and her resignation to staid domestic life. Sula's return to Medallion, in a plague of robins, no less, would mark the restoration of an old friendship; Sula, instead, becomes Jude's lover for a brief time before abandoning him as she does other husbands of the town. Nel and Sula's "confrontation," on the deathbed of the latter, tells the reader and the best friend very little about what it is that makes Sula run. All that she admits is that she has "lived" and that if she and Nel had been such good friends, in fact, then her momentary "theft" of Jude might not have made any difference. Nel does not forgive Sula, but experiences, instead, a sense of emptiness and despair grounded, she later discovers after it doesn't matter anymore, in her own personal loss of Sula. She has not missed Jude, she finds out that afternoon, but her alter ego passionately embodied in the other woman. It turns out that the same degree of emotional ambivalence that haunts Nel plagues the female reader of this novel. What is it about this woman Sula that triggers such attraction and repulsion at once? We have no certain answers, just as Nel does not, but, rather, resign ourselves to a complex resonance of healing which suggests that Sula is both necessary and frightening as a character realization.

In the relationship between Nel and Sula, Morrison demonstrates the female's rites-of-passage in their peculiar richness and impoverishment; the fabric of paradoxes—betrayals and sympathies, silences and aggressions, advances and sudden retreats—transmitted from mother to daughter, female to female, by mimetic gesture. That women learn primarily from other women strategies of survival and "homicide" is not news to anyone; indeed, this vocabulary of reference constitutes the chief revisionist, albeit implicit, feature of the women's liberation effort. Because Morrison has no political axe to grind in this novel—in other words, she is not writing according to a formula which demands that her female agents demonstrate a simple, transparent love between women—she is free, therefore, to pursue the delicate tissue of intimate patterns of response between women. In doing so, she identifies those meanings of womanhood which statements of public policy are rhetorically bound to suppress.

One of the structural marvels of *Sula* is its capacity to telescope the process of generation and its consequent network of convoluted relationships. *Sula* is a woman's text par excellence, even subscribing in its behavior to Woolf's intimations that the woman's book, given the severe demands on her time, is spare. The novel is less than two hundred pages of prose, but within its imaginative economy various equations of domestic power are explored. For instance, Sula's relationships to her mother Hannah and grandmother Eva Peace are portrayed in selective moments. In other words, Sula's destiny is located only in part by Nel, while the older Peace women in their indifference to decorous social behavior provide the soil in which her moral isolation is seeded and nurtured. Hannah and Eva have quite another story to tell apart from Sula's, much of it induced by Eva's abandonment by her husband BoyBoy and her awful defiance in response. The reader is not privy to various tales of transmission between Eva and Hannah, but we decide by inference that their collective wisdom leads Hannah herself to an authenticity of person not alterable by the iron-clad duties of motherhood, nor the sweet, submissive obligations of female love. In short, Hannah Peace is self-indulgent, full of disregard for the traditional repertoire of women's vanity-related gestures, and the reader tends to love her for it— the "sweet, low and guileless" flirting, no patting of the hair, or rushing to change clothes, or quickly applying makeup, but barefoot in summer, "in the winter her feet in a man's leather slippers with the backs flattened under her heels. . . . Her voice trailed, dipped and bowed; she gave a chord to the simplest words. Nobody, but nobody, could say 'hey sugar' like Hannah . . . ."

Just as Hannah's temperament is "light and playful," Morrison's prose glides over the surface of events with a careful allegiance to the riffs of folk utterance—deliberate, inclusive, very often on the verge of laughter—but the profound deception of this kind of plain talk, allegedly "unsophisticated," is the vigil it keeps in killing silence about what it suspects, even knows, but never expresses. This hidden agenda has a malicious side which Sula inherits without moral revision and correction. Morrison's stylistic choice in this passage is a significant clue to a reading of Hannah's character, a freedom of movement, a liberty of responses, worked out in a local school of realism. Hannah Peace is certainly not a philosopher, not even in secret, but that she rationalizes her address to the other in an unfailing economy of nuances implies a potential for philosophical grace. Among the women of *Sula*, the light rhythms usually conceal a deeper problem.

One of the more perplexing characters of recent American fiction, Eva Peace embodies a figure of both insatiable generosity and insatiable demanding. Like Hannah, Eva is seldom frustrated by the trammels of self-criticism, the terrible indecisiveness and scrupulosity released by doubt. Because Eva goes ahead without halting, ever, we could call her fault nothing less than innocence, and its imponderable cruelty informs her character with a kind of Old Testament logic. Eva behaves as though she were herself the sole instrument of divine inscrutable will. We are not exactly certain what oracular fever decides that she must immolate her son Plum. Perhaps even his heroin addiction does not entirely explain it, but she literally rises to the task in moments of decisiveness, orchestrated in pity and judgment. Like an avenging deity who must sacrifice its creation in order to purify it, Eva swings and swoops on her terrible crutches from her son's room, about to prepare his fire. She holds him in her arms, recalling moments from his childhood before dousing him with kerosene:

> He opened his eyes and saw what he imagined was the great wing of an eagle pouring a wet lightness over him. Some kind of baptism, some kind of blessing, he thought. Everything is going to be all right, it said. Knowing that it was so he closed his eyes and sank back into the bright hole of sleep.
>
> Eva stepped back from the bed and let the crutches rest under her arms. She rolled a bit of newspaper into a tight stick about six inches long, lit it and threw it onto the bed where the kerosene-soaked Plum lay in smug delight. Quickly, as the *whoosh* of flames engulfed him, she shut the door and made her slow and painful journey back to the top of the house. . . .

Not on any level is the reader offered easy access to this scene. Its enumerated, overworked pathos, weighed against the victim's painful ignorance not only of his imminent death, but also of the requirements of his manhood generates contradictory feelings between shock and relief. The reader resents the authorial manipulation that engenders such feelings. The act itself, so violently divergent from the normal course of maternal actions and expectations, marks a subclimax. Further, it foreshadows the network of destruction, both willful and fortuitous, that ensnares Sula and Nel in an entanglement of predecided motivations. Eva, in effect, determines her own judgment, which Sula will seal without a hint or recourse to the deceptions or allegiances of kinship. Sula, who puts Eva in old age in an asylum, does not mistake her decision as a stroke of love or duty, nor does it echo any of the ambiguities of mercy.

Like Eva's, Sula's program of action as an adult woman is spontaneous and direct, but the reader in Sula's case does not temper her or his angle on Sula's behavior with compassion or second thought, as she or he tends to do in Eva's case. It could be argued, for instance, that Eva sacrifices Plum in order to save him, and however grotesque we probably adjudge her act, inspired by a moral order excluding contingency and doubt, no such excuse can be offered in Sula's behalf. We must also remember that Sula's nubile *singleness* and refusal of the acts and rites of maternity have implicitly corrupted her in our unconscious judgment and at a level of duplicity which our present "sexual arrangements" protect and mandate. We encounter the raw details of her individualism, not engaged by naturalistic piety or existential rage, as a paradigm of wanton vanity. Her moral shape, however, does not come unprecedented or autonomously derived. Merging Eva's arrogance on the one hand and Hannah's self-indulgence on the other, "with a twist that was all her own imagination, she lived out her days exploring her own thoughts and emotions, giving them full reign, feeling no obligation to please anybody unless their pleasure pleased her."

Just as Hannah and Eva have been Sula's principal models, they have also determined certain issues which she will live out in her own career. It is probably not accidental that the question that haunts Hannah—have I been loved?—devolves on Sula with redoubtable fury. If it is true that love does not exist until it is named, then the answer to the enigma of Sula Peace is not any more forthcoming than if it were not so. Yet, certainly the enormous consequences of being loved or not are relevant by implication to the agents of the novel. Morrison does not elaborate, but the instances of the question's appearance—halting, uncertain, embarrassed, or inappropriate words on a character's tongue—conceal the single most important missing element in the women's encounter with each other. A revealing conversation between Eva and Hannah suggests that even for the adult female the intricacies and entanglements of mother love (or perhaps woman love without distinction) is a dangerous inquiry to engage. Hannah cannot even formulate the sentences that would say the magic words, but angles in on the problem with a childlike timidity which she can neither fake nor conceal. "I know you fed us and all. I was talking 'bout something else. Like. Like. Playin' with us. Did you ever, you know, play with us?"

This conversation may be compared with one that Sula overhears the summer of her twelfth year, between Hannah and a couple of friends. The three women confirm for each other the agonies of childrearing, but can never quite bring themselves around to admitting that love is contingent and human and all too often connected with notions of duty. Hannah tells one of the friends that her quality of love is sufficient. "You love [your child], like I love Sula. I just don't like her. That's the difference." And that's the "difference" that sends Sula "flying up the stairs," blankly "aware of a sting in her eye," until recalled by Nel's voice.

To pin the entire revelation of the source of Sula's later character development on this single episode would be a fallacy of overdetermination, but its strategic location in the text suggests that its function is crucial to the unfolding of events to come, to the way that Sula responds to them, and to the manner in which we interpret her responses. At least two other events unmistakably hark back to it. Chicken Little joins Sula and Nel later on the same afternoon in their play by the river. In the course of things Sula picked him up and "swung" him outward and then around and around. His knickers ballooned and his shrieks of frightened joy startled the birds and the fat grasshoppers. When he slipped from her hands and sailed out over the water they could still hear his bubbly laughter . . . ."

Frozen in a moment of terror, neither girl can do more than stare at the "closed place in the water." Morrison aptly recreates the stark helplessness of two trapped people, gaining a dimension of horror because the people are children, drawn up short in a world of chance and danger. That they do nothing in particular, except recognize that Shadrack, the town's crack-brained veteran of World War I, has seen them and will not tell, consigns them both to a territory of their own most terrible judgment and isolation. In this case the adult conscience of each springs forth in the eyes of the other, leaving childhood abruptly in its wake. The killing edge is that the act itself must remain a secret. Unlike other acts of rites-of-passage, this one must not be communicated. At Chicken Little's funeral, Sula "simply cried," and from his grave site she and Nel, fingers laced, trot up the road "on a summer day wondering what happened to butterflies in the winter."

The interweave of lyricism and dramatic event is consistent with Morrison's strategies. Their juxtaposition does not appear to function ironically, but to present dual motifs in a progressive revelation that allows the reader to "swallow" dramatic occurrences whose rhetoric, on the face of it, is unacceptable. At the same time we get in right perspective Sula's *lack* of tension—a tension that distinguishes the character stunned by her own ignorance, or by malice in the order of things. Sula, by contrast, just goes along, "completely free of ambition, with no affection for money, property, or things, no greed, no desire to command attention or compliments—no ego. For that reason she felt no compulsion to verify herself—be consistent with herself." That Sula apparently wants nothing, is curiously free of mimetic desire and its consequent pull toward willfulness, keep pity in check and release unease in its absence.

Sula's lack of egoism—which appears an incorrect assessment on the narrator's part—renders her an antipassionate spectator of the human scene, even beholding her mother's death by fire in calculated coolness. Weeks after Chicken's burial Hannah is in the backyard of the Peace household, lighting a fire in which she accidentally catches herself and burns to death. Eva recalls afterward that "she had seen Sula standing on the back porch just looking." When her friends insist that she is more than likely mistaken since Sula was "probably struck dumb" by the awful spectacle, Eva remains quietly convinced "that Sula had watched Hannah burn not because she was para-lyzed, but because she was interested. . . ."

This moment of Sula's interestedness, and we tend to give Eva the benefit of the doubt in this case, must be contrasted to her response to Chicken's drowning, precluding us from remaining impartial judges of her behavior, even as we understand its sources in the earlier event. Drawn into a cycle of negation, Sula at twelve is Sula at twenty, and the instruments of perception which the reader uses to decipher her character do not alter over the whole terrain of the work. From this point on, any course of action that she takes is already presumed by negating choices. Whether she steals Nel's husband or a million dollars matters less to the reader than to the other char-acters, since we clearly grasp the structure of her function as that of a radical amorality and consequently of a radical freedom. We would like to love Sula, or damn her, inasmuch as the myth of the black American woman allows only Manichean responses, but it is impossible to do either. We can only behold in an absolute suspension of final judgment.

Morrison induces this ambiguous reading through an economy of means, none of which relate to the classic *bête noire* of black experience—the powerful predominance of white and the endless litany of hateful responses associated with it. That Sula is not bound by the customary alliances to natu-ralism or historical determinism at least tells us what imperatives she does not pursue. Still, deciding what traditions do inspire her character is not made easier.

I would suggest that Hurston's Janie Starks presents a clear prece-dent. Though not conforming at every point, I think the two characters lend themselves to a comparative formula. In both cases, the writer wishes to examine the particular details and propositions of liberty under constricted conditions in a low mimetic mode of realism, that is, an instance of realism in which the characters are not decisively superior in moral or social condition to the reader. Both Janie and Sula are provided an arena of action within certain limits. In the former case, the character's dreams are usually too encompassing to be accommodated within the space that circumscribes her. The stuff of her dreams, then, remains disem-bodied, ethereal, out of time, nor are her dreams fully differentiated, inas-much as all we know about them is their metaphorical conformity to certain natural or romantic configurations. It is probably accurate to say that the crucial absence for Janie has been an intellectual chance, or the absence of a syntax distinctive enough in its analytical requirements to realign a particular order of events to its own demands. In other words, Janie is stuck in the limitations of dialect, while her creator is free to make use of a range of linguistic resources to achieve her vision.

The principle of absence that remains inchoate for Janie is articulate for Sula in terms whose intellectual implications are unmistakable—Sula lacks the shaping vision of art, and the absence is as telling in the formation of her character as the lack of money or an appropriately ordered space might be for the heroines, for example, of Henry James's *Portrait of a Lady* or *Wings of the Dove*; in both of James's works the heroines are provided with money, a term that James's narrator assigns great weight in deciding what strategies enable women to do battle with the world, though the equation between gold and freedom is ironically burdened here. In Woolf's conception of personal and creative freedom for the woman, *money*, *space*, and *time* figure prominently.

It is notable that Janie and Sula, within the social modalities that determine them, are actually quite well off. Their suffering, therefore, transcends the visceral and concrete, moving progressively toward the domain of symbols. In sharp contrast to Walker's Vyry, the latter-day heroines approach the threshold of speaking and acting *for self*, or the organization of one's resources with preeminent reference to the highest form of self-regard, the urge to speak one's own words urgently. Hurston and Morrison after her are both in the process of abandoning the vision of the corporate good as a mode of heroic suffering. Precisely what will take its place defines the dilemma of *Sula* and its protagonist. The dilemma itself highlights problems of figuration for black female characters whose future, whose terms of existence, are not entirely known at the moment.

The character of Sula impresses the reader as a problem in interpretation because, for one thing, the objective myth of the black American woman, at least from the black woman's point of view, is drawn in valorized images that intrude against the text, or compete with it like a jealous goddess. That this privileged other narrative is counterbalanced by its opposite, equally exaggerated and distorted, simply reinforces the heroics to the extent that the black woman herself imagines only one heroine—and that is herself. *Sula* attempts a correction of this uninterrupted superiority on the one hand and unrelieved pathology on the other; the reader's dilemma arises in having to choose. The duplicitous reader embraces the heroics with no intent of disproof or unbelief, while the brave one recognizes that the negating countermyth would try to establish a dialectical movement between the subperspectives, gaining a totally altered perspective in the process. In other words, Sula, Vyry, and Janie need not be seen as the terms of an either/or proposition. The three characters here may be identified as subperspectives, or *angles onto* a larger seeing. The struggle that we bring with us to *Sula*, indeed, the implicit proposition upon which the text is based, is the imperative that requires our coming to terms with the very complexities that a juggling of perspectives demands.

Sula is not the "other" as one kind of reading would suggest, or perhaps as we might wish, but a figure of the rejected and vain part of the self—ourselves—who in its thorough corruption and selfishness cannot utter, believe in, nor prepare for, love. I am not entirely sure that Sula speaks for us on the lower frequencies—though she could very well. The importance of this text is that she speaks at all.

In a conversation with Robert Stepto, Toni Morrison confirms certain critical conjectures that are made here concerning the character of Sula. "[She] was hard for me; very difficult to make up that kind of character. Not difficult to think it up, but difficult to describe a woman who could be used as classic type of evil force. Other people could use her that way. And at the same time, I didn't want to make her freakish or repulsive or unattractive. I was interested at that time in doing a very old, worn-out idea, which was to do something with good and evil, but putting it in different terms. . . ."

As Morrison goes on to discuss the idea, Sula and Nel are to her mind an alterity of agents—"two sides of the same person, or two sides of one extraordinary character." Morrison does not attribute the birth of her idea to any particular cultural or historical event and certainly not to the most recent wave of American feminism, but it does seem fairly clear that a Sula Peace is *for black American literature*, if not for the incredibly rich potential of black American female personality, a radical alternative to Vyry Ware and less so, to placid Janie Crawford Starks. "This was really part of the difficulty—I didn't know anyone like her. I never knew a woman like that at any rate. But I knew women who looked like that, who looked like they *could* be like that. And then you remember women who were a little bit different in [one's] town, you know."

If we identify Sula as a kind of countermythology, we are saying that she is no longer bound by a rigid pattern of predictions, predilections, and anticipations. Even though she is a character in a novel, her strategic place as *potential being* might argue that *subversion* itself—law breaking—is an aspect of liberation that women must confront from its various angles, in its different guises. Sula's outlawry may not be the best kind, but that she has the will toward rebellion itself *is* the stunning idea. This project in liberation, paradoxically, has no particular dimension in time, yet it is for all time.

STEPHANIE A. DEMETRAKOPOULOS

Sula *and the Primacy of Woman-to-Woman Bonds*

S*ula* is for me the most powerful of Toni Morrison's works. I think this is not a judgment unique to me. I spoke on Morrison at the National Association of Women's Studies convention several years ago, and I took it for granted that the audience (about 100 women, around one-third of whom were Black) shared the aesthetics of whatever committee selected *Song of Solomon* as her best work and so awarded her the National Book Critics Circle Award for Fiction. Several members of the audience objected when I mentioned my assumption in my introduction, so I decided to poll the audience. Not one woman there preferred *Song of Solomon* over *Sula*. I wonder if masculine aesthetics were not, at least unconsciously, standards for measuring *Song of Solomon* as better than *Sula*.

At the end of *Sula*, Nel cries out for, longs for, her friend and soul sister Sula; I was overcome when I first read the book, and I still have to choke back tears when I teach the novel and reread these last pages. I have had one deep and yet severed relationship with a woman that made me suffer more acute loss and grief than either of my divorces. The relationship was of a different nature than Sula's and Nel's, but it was just as primal and as much a ground of being in my life as theirs. I think one of the reasons that I so deeply respond to the novel is that it is the first time I have read a written work that reflects my own experience of the depth and profound meaning of women's

From *New Dimensions of Spirituality: A Biracial and Bicultural Reading of the Novels of Toni Morrison*. © 1987 by Karla F. C. Holloway and Stephanie A. Demetrakopoulos. Reproduced with permission of Greenwood Publishing Group, Inc., Westport, CT.

bonds. It is to other women that we go for the deepest understanding, for the most uncontingent love. Women without female bonds are, in my opinion, the most lost and alienated of human beings. And one friend can never replace another. So when Maya Angelou says that *Sula* is "the book I've been waiting to read all my life," I have to agree; and this in spite of the fact that my life has been books—they are the lifeblood of English teachers. But no other book has ever moved me in the same way—as deeply, yes, but not in the same way as *Sula*. It touches chords no other novel has.

In this chapter I will outline the archetypes and significance of the novel, why it so stirs the feminine soul, and reminds us of the deeper meanings of Everywoman's sojourn through the world.

I chiefly analyze *Sula* through a framework of both Christian and Greek goddess figures. I think of *Sula* in these terms for more than one reason. Partly it is because as a Jungian and a feminist I have studied and thought in these images for years. But also, the ancient Greeks created gods and goddesses so much in the image of humanity, so essentially anthropomorphic, that they represent and even make sacred many aspects of humanity since repressed by the heavy hand of Christianity. Sometimes the Greek goddesses are truly representative of women, but, of course, sometimes they are emblematic of patriarchal fear and loathing of the feminine. Thus even these ancient images must be used with care. When certain of these ancient images and Morrison's images parallel so closely as they often do, they validate one another.

Part of my methodology involves gender essences as defined in alchemy, an ancient symbolic system for describing the human psyche. This methodology works well with Morrison's novels, which are in essence primordial and elemental, as I shall show. I here remind the reader that the masculine elements are fire, air, and sulphur; the feminine are water, earth, and salt. In the latter stages of life, the masculine sulphur and the feminine salt are connected by mercury, embodied in Olympian godhead as Hermes, the messenger God. This latter pattern, the psychic, internal connection of the masculine and feminine in later life, is especially significant to *Sula*.

The novel is structured around the bonds of the two main characters, Nel and Sula, who come from opposite types of matrilineal lines. We meet three generations of these families; in addition, all of Sula's and most of Nel's life patterns are lived out in the novel. The tension between these opposite female typologies is the dynamic of the whole work. The novel is thus rich in knowledge and wisdom about both change and stability in women's bonds in various life stages. Because each women's identity is at least partially forged vis-à-vis the masculine principle, both within herself and as embodied in men, the male/female relationships will also receive some attention as I work through the complex patterns of the major female characters as feminine typologies.

This chapter falls into four interrelated sections that I draw together in my conclusion. The first two sections analyze and contrast the matrilineal lines of Nel and Sula; the third section treats the quest of Sula and her demise in the face of the masculine; the fourth section analyzes the aged Eva as a sibyl, an aggrieved Demeter-Sophia who is Nel's mentor into old age.

Nel's Matrilineal Line: Eve/Mary Duality

Because the novel is finally Nel's, I will begin by discussing how her background is typical of most women. She is Everywoman. The repression of parts of self is, however, even more intense in Nel's case since she carries the additional burden of shadow that white culture projects onto Black people. But she is still typical of most women in Western culture. Nel's matrilineal line suffers from an Eve/Mary bedrock of feminine duality, the whore/Madonna polarity. Nel's mother, Helene, has been carefully taught to hate her own mother, Rochelle, an Eve figure, a "Creole whore." Helene was raised by her grandmother "under the dolesome eyes of a multicolored Virgin Mary, counseling her to be constantly on guard for any sign of her mother's wild blood." When ten-year-old Nel goes with Helene to bury Helene's pious grandmother, Nel meets her own still beautiful prostitute grandmother. Helene lets her mother Rochelle know that she does not want to have anything to do with her. Rochelle accepts this and leaves, but not without a tight, hard, anguished final embrace of her granddaughter Nel. That first and last embrace is an emblem of great loss. It reflects the separatism among women caused by polarized and largely Christian, male-created images of the feminine; the women lose their roots and connections, their continuity. (As I shall show, Nel's family structure is nevertheless matrifocal, even perhaps matriarchal although it defines itself through patriarchal and church-generated stereotypes.)

These images of a demonically sexual ancestor, whose blood may resurge in Nel and destroy her, are what makes Helene drive Nel's young feminine imagination underground, causing the young woman to repress many parts of herself that struggle to emerge as adolescence impinges. In fact, it is her friend Sula's freedom simply to imagine that makes her so necessary to Nel. The feminine principle in Nel's own background is so orderly, contained, and stultifying that even Sula's disorderly house holds a fascination of the underworld for Nel. Helene projects and channels fear of her own mother's "outlaw" sexuality into a controlling repression of Nel's sexuality.

It is important to see that the women in Nel's family contain and connect with adult males although some of the men are mere accouterments. All three of the generations we meet are clearly matrifocal. Helene's husband Wiley Wright (*wiley, right*—the correct but escapist husband) is scarcely ever home because he is a seaman; he is peripheral both in the actual home and psychologically. Jude's name reveals his much more central role in Nel's life as an archetypal "Intimate Betrayer." Morrison makes us understand that Jude has his own reasons for bitterness and hatred that make him betray Nel—the pressures of being a Black man kept from promotion because of white men. But no matter how sympathetic one feels towards Jude's plight, the bottom line is that he abandons his family. It is Nel who ends up as sole parent; she cleans houses to support the three children who for many years become her life.

But unlike the women of Sula's line, Nel has had at least some years in her life with a man who did love her and to whom she revealed herself as an adult woman. In the myth of Amor and Psyche, Psyche's quest for womanhood, for adulthood, can only begin when she finally allows Amor to have a face, an identity, a separate and individual masculine consciousness. This identity is symbolized by her lighting a torch to see him after many nights of lovemaking in which he comes and goes after dark. When Psyche sees his face at last, she releases him from his purely divine masculine role and allows him to become a vulnerable, individual person. Having gazed daily at one another's individuality, pain, and vulnerability, Nel and Jude have a deep sense of the other. It is his betrayal in the face of this bond that so wounds Nel when Jude is unfaithful with Sula. Marriage can remove many masks and so rejection by the spouse can become one of the most painfully personal betrayals; as Nel says:

> But Jude . . . you *knew* me. All those days and years, Jude, you *knew* me. My ways and my hands and how my stomach folded and how we tried to get Mickey to nurse and how about the time when the landlord said . . . but you said . . . and I cried, Jude. You knew me and had listened to the things I said at night, and heard me in the bathroom and laughed at my raggedy girdle and I laughed too because I knew you too, Jude. So how could you leave me when you knew me?

Ironically, Nel has lived out the traditional "good woman" of the Mary tradition, yet she loses her man to a woman that she for many years thereafter labels as an Eve figure. Thus Morrison makes it clear that following the American (perhaps white) ways of marriage and monogamy is risky fulfillment for women; the separatism that the Peace matriarchy symbolizes is at least a less vulnerable way of life.

The Peace Women as the Ancient Goddesses
Demeter, Persephone, and Hestia

The images of the feminine that the Peace women embody are much more ancient, natural, and universal than Nel's line. The Greek goddesses (and perhaps others such as Kali, the destroyer) emerge as powerful twentieth-century feminine archetypes in these women. Eva is the founding matriarch and queen of the line; she establishes the values of this line. When we meet her, she is already in late middle age and the reigning deity in her household of daughter, granddaughter and various adopted, interchangeable, and peripheral male figures. Eva has earned her regal authority; in one of the most poignant and harrowing passages in all literature by women (and it could only be written by a woman), we see in a flashback what Eva has overcome in order to survive and give her children life. She was deserted in 1895, by a man who, unlike Jude, was abusive and childish, could never be known—so his abandoning her with three children is not a special loss to her personally as the loss of Jude was to Nel. But she and her three children face starvation. In order to feed her children, she has mysteriously sacrificed a leg and regularly thereafter receives money to live on. She loses her left leg which reflects the loss of the symbol making, intuitive side of the feminine, the softer gentler values of the feminine. She is strongly, fiercely, rationally and roughly protective until the end of her life, which I shall treat later. But as long as her children and grandchildren are in her care, her house is organized and carefully run, a haven for her women who do not have to submit their lives to the caprices of husbands or lovers.

Eva develops an antipathy for the co-equal masculine, which in her case is healthy. She understands as did the Renaissance Queen Elizabeth that to marry would simply empower a man to take from her the home and territory over which she must reign so that the young may grow up. Perhaps an ironic parody of the insane wife of Charlotte Brontë's *Jane Eyre*, she lives on the top floor of the house—but rather than a walled off insane part of the self, she is a deeply sane and cautiously protective Hestia, an overseeing Demeter. These are the two goddesses that I see as most operative, most strongly emerging in Eva. Recall that Hestia is in charge of the most crucial life support processes such as meals and household heating. She is also traditionally uncoupled, her virginity symbolic of the devotion and single-minded purity with which she tends and sustains the home. Eva returns to her virgin state after BoyBoy leaves; men remain amusing toys to her, but all her life energy is spent in establishing a home that reminds us perhaps of the guarded sanctity of a convent. Eva's house becomes a fortress for the women of her line. Her immobility is like that of a Hestian queen bee; she scarcely ever descends to the lower floors, but sits on a throne-like wagon device to receive her faceless, nameless, and interchangeable suitors. They surround and worship her, but are like the castrated priests of Isis, weak and wispy forces of the masculine.

Except for Jude and Ajax (more on him later), all the men in the novel are mere forces, their individuality never acknowledged by the Peace women:

> Those Peace women loved all men. It was man love that Eva bequeathed to her daughters. Probably, people said, because there were no men in the house, no men to run it. But actually that was not true. The Peace women loved maleness, for its own sake.

But their love is a strange *disengagé*—Hannah, Sula's mother, refuses to sleep with a man, instead has sex standing or lying in the pantry or parlor with whomever she chooses. Like the young Germaine Greer, Hannah never gives a man access to her sleeping quarters, her personal territory. Eva adopts Tar Baby, a drunken white man, but never sees him as a person. She adopts the three Deweys, whose name reminds us of Donald Duck's identical nephews. These three boys are white, black, and Chicano, a surreal trinity of races who become absolutely interchangeable to their teachers and entire household. Eva's adoption of these boys reflects her Demeter maternal urge. She would like to contain and mother forth all the lost sons she sees, but she is not able finally to permit each to move away towards his own unique individuation. This is partly because an individuated adult male would threaten her feminine stronghold. But it is even more because of Eva's loss of the more "sensitive water" (her leftness) aspect of femininity that allows others to individuate. She cannot afford this feminine virtue anymore; she must be hard to protect the perimeters of the small stronghold she has seized for her progeny. The culture around her has stripped her of the softer feminine and nurturing attitudes. This loss is early symbolized in the book when her quiet, more introverted daughter Pearl "shits worms" as a baby, then on reaching adolescence flees the mother home in order to establish a family of her own far away; this daughter symbolizes the loss of the Pearl of Great Price, these gentler feminine values that Eva cannot afford to give into.

Eva kills her other two children. These acts of euthanasia are perhaps the most brilliant, incisive passages of the novel in terms of feminine depth psychology. Her son Plum is the one male figure, the only *animus* image that Eva gives autonomy, a face, a future and that she allows herself to love with her full heart. She has literally sacrificed her own mobility for her children; her psychic future—movement, completion, and wholeness—rides on Plum.

She retains her female progeny in her well-stocked and managed fortress, but assigns her one son the role of the moving dynamic hero prince who will sally into the world and conquer it. Plum carries the Hermetic aspect of Eva's repressed animus. Hermes is the adventurous messenger, the man forever on the road, an emblem of imaginative roving. But like the other proto-genius black males in Morrison's novels, he is castrated on multiple levels in his sojourn in the white man's world. Like the town's mad prophet, Shadrack, Plum loses his masculine impetus, his initiative, in the white man's army. Shadrack returns mad; Plum comes home a drug addict.

Plum wants to be contained again by his mother and sleeps his life away in a bedroom directly beneath hers; Eva tells Hannah:

> He wanted to crawl back in my womb and well . . . I ain't got the room no more even if he could do it. There wasn't space for him in my womb. And he was crawlin' back. Being helpless and thinking baby thoughts and dreaming baby dreams and messing up his pants again and smiling all the time. I had room enough in my heart, but not in my womb, got no more. I birthed him once. I couldn't do it again. He was growed, a big, old thing. Godhave-mercy, I couldn't birth him twice.

Erich Neumann defines suicide as a regressive urge towards *uroboric* incest, a desire to merge with the Mother Earth and annihilate the consciousness causing such pain. But the perverse and horrible twist here is that in returning home the son appears to want his real mother to become the earth, the vegetative Demeter to whom he can return. She feels that he wants to implicate her in his waking death. But Eva has fought too hard to give her children a good and fruitful life. So the year he comes of age, Eva kills her beloved son. The protective ferocity, the tigress instinct, the ruthless love of Demeter transmutes into Kali, the mother destroyer who forces an end of the life cycle. The ease of her savage severing of these two grown children's life threads suggests to me how women often view euthanasia as pragmatic, expedient, overwhelmingly necessary in the scheme of things. There is not even remorse for Eva, just commitment—passionate and self-sacrificial—for life that has quality.

Whether a character dies by fire or by water is crucial thematically; for in this novel, the apocalypse seems to come from within. All of Eva's progeny die by fire. Eva burns Plum's bedroom with him in it; when Sula is a teenager, Hannah catches fire and Eva leaps from an upstairs bedroom trying to save her. Morrison implies that Eva smothers Hannah in the ambulance because Hannah is so horribly disfigured. Later, as the adult now in charge, Sula threatens Eva with fire to get her out of the house and into an old people's home. Sula dies of a terrible fever that comes on her after she falls in love for the first time in her life. The Peace females thus die of a double dose of the masculine element of fire; the Peace males, of the feminine element of water. It is important to see that Plum has already sunk into the depths of the unconscious, has been drowned by drugs, before Eva burns him. The adopted males die of literal water; the Deweys and Tar Baby are drowned on National Suicide Day. Early on, Sula drowns Chicken Little. It is as if the sexes are so polarized that each dies of the other's basic element. The contra-sexual, the opposite gender, is so unknown, so undifferentiated that it becomes demonic and killing. The whole Peace line dies of it. Thus Morrison images the apocalypse that results from sexual separatism. The problem this separation creates for Sula vis-à-vis the masculine is the subject of the next section.

Sula's Quest For Self

Emma Jung has written at length on how the animus can become the creative principle, the muse that carries woman's artistic desires into the world. Couple this theory with Morrison's statement that Sula is an *artiste manqué* because she never found a medium, a form; and her burning up with a fever over Ajax becomes strangely logical. Sula to this time had been acting out only masculine archetypes herself; like Hermes, she travels from town to town, never taking root and acting without *eros*, with self-interest only, as when she takes Jude from Nel or puts Eva in a rest home. Except for Nel, she has no identification with other women or with her own feminine self. She needs to ground herself in the earth and water (home and relationships) to ready herself for the salty wisdom that comes in the second stage of life for the older woman.

Sula's nesting instincts are finally awakened by Ajax and she suffers a terrible double dose of love. She asks him to satisfy all her long repressed needs for continuity and for family, plus she assigns all the divinity of the masculine principle to him. He becomes numinous as she projects all this onto a mere other human being; he unwittingly becomes life and death dealing, Cupid before Psyche lights the torch. Sula needs him to carry the masculine so that she can recover the feminine through their relationship. But like most of Morrison's male characters, Ajax wants to fly, to transcend; he is not the stable, but rather, the airy masculine. Like Icarus and Hermes, Ajax cannot be bound to one spot. The planes he so loves embody both his artistic medium and his picaresque masculinity. He will not, cannot, stay and carry the projection of Sula's animus so that she can find her own feminine principle. He can only accept her as a short-term mistress, the fickle and promiscuous face of Venus. Too late Sula finds out her desire for a home and her own man. Now she suffers as Nel did, but without the bonds of mothering, of responsibility to others, that hold Nel among the living until she finds a way to reformulate her life. Nel also has a mother and a community for contextual support. Sula is deeply alienated from both family and community; Sula is an artist who takes only herself as her medium. The novel proves the pain produced by such solipsism, such willful self-creation. She is left burning up with her animus values, a real double dose.

Comparison with Nel throws Sula's dilemma into greater relief. While devastated by Jude's betrayal, Nel has on the other hand gained some valuable access to her own feminine roots during her years and sojourn as his wife. She has established her home, found her earthy side that establishes roots. She has developed the feminine element of water, the harmonizing *eros* of woman that bonds together a family. She has her children, her Demeter roots. And she has some at least mildly satisfying love affairs after Jude leaves.

Sula has lived out the masculine elements, the fire and air that come and go whither they list; and she has corroded others' lives through the burning sulphur, an element that leaves brooding depressions in *materia* it touches, psychically imaged in Nel's long grief. Thus each woman in the novel is quite one-sided. Mercurial like fire and air, Sula needs grounding in the feminine principle, while Nel and Eva have no room for the play of fire and air in their natures. Nel is tied to her home and to an exhausting, tedious work in order to support it; when Eva tries to fly out the window to smother the flames devouring Hannah, she misses her mark, hitting the ground like the pinioned eagle she has become. Nel and Eva are too stable, weighty, full of *gravitas*, to let their creative instincts take flight.

Ajax's mother is an important foil both to Eva's stultified immobility and to Sula's freewheeling lack of connections. An "evil" conjure woman who supports seven sons with her medicine, Ajax's mother practices voodoo and herbal therapy as an art form for the intuitive and natural (organic) feminine she needs to express. Her religious singlemindedness comes, as Ajax rightly perceives, from a deeper spiritual passion than any of the Christian women in the community. He sees his mother as brilliant, strong, and free, and Sula is the first woman he has ever met like her. But Sula only seems like his mother. Sula's brand of freedom is sexual, like Hannah's; and this freedom has been maintained by her usually callous denial of needs other than her own. Sula also has strength in terms of autonomy, but it is not an enduring strength. Sula has never, like Ajax's mother, served others or cared for dependents. So Sula presents a confusing and inconsistent anima face or hook onto which Ajax can project a different feminine than he has previously experienced in his other lovers. He quickly abandons Sula when she cleans the house and puts a ribbon in her hair, becoming the elemental nesting woman.

While Ajax's mother has balanced the feminine sides that Sula and Nel stand for, Sula demonstrates the principle of *enantiodromia*, the "regulative function of opposites," the automatic recoil to the opposite pole when only one side of an archetype is lived out. Before her affair with Ajax, she lives out only the side of woman that embraces extremist or pathological masculine values, denial of roots and connections in preference for flying and drifting. She had lived out a culturally repressed side of the feminine so monomaniacally that when the other side of her is touched, she suddenly metamorphosizes into a caricature of Nel. Sula becomes a dependent, yearning woman who can be killed by the same deserting behavior that she herself has lived out.

We can further understand why Sula dies after Ajax's desertion by examining the cosmic bliss she experiences when they make love. Ajax transforms her very being, and they merge into a mystical, primoridal, and elemental oneness with the universe. Morrison's imagery becomes splendidly lyrical and biblical. Sula becomes the coupled Feminine, the perfect half of a "Royal Couple." His gold, alabaster, and loam (earthy fertility) balances and merges with her newly awakened feminine elements of silver (moon to his sun) and water. The alabaster image is probably not a common image of the masculine for women and reflects the artist's perspective in Sula that appreciates the pure, sculpturesque, and elemental masculine in Ajax. But Sula is inexperienced, becomes too watery, clinging, cloying, and frightens Ajax away; then the fire within her takes over as the watery feminine disappears without Ajax to inspire and contain it.

To sum up, Sula dies of becoming mature, which always means going through the Fall. She has tried to hang onto her prelapsarian, preoedipal, feminine oneness through her friendship with Nel and through never connecting permanently with a man. Sula dies of her undifferentiated animus, her undeveloped conscience. She has lived out a polarity that dies of separatism, of loneliness, of its own alienness. Her feminine roots connect only to her girlhood friend, not to the larger matriarchal system of her community. She has refused to move toward becoming part of that matrix of responsible "umbrella women" that Morrison has identified as the central stabilizing force in the Black community.

Her death does finally become peaceful, a sleep of water imagistically; and her last thoughts are of Nel. Nel is, of course, as much Sula's shadow as Sula is everyone's shadow. But Sula also loves Nel for herself and what they have shared, not just as a symbol of a polarity that might have helped Sula soften and move towards a life style she could survive. Though she initially dies of fire (a fever), she sinks into a comfort of water, of final psychic and spiritual oneness with Nel, the only human being she ever knew or loved. Sula's death is evoked through images of water and fetal positions; women writers often image death as another beginning.

The above patterns are like ripples that spread cosmically and infinitely. The whole novel's framework emphasizes the power of the elemental feminine; even the weather echoes the transformation of the watery feminine in the community and in the women themselves. As Eva calls desolately for her dead son Plum, a drying air sweeps through the town, suggesting her desolate yet repressed (dried up) grief and aloneness. A silver thaw comes when Sula dies; the positive feminine of the whole community ceases to flow as it loses the scapegoat that carried its deadly shadow. The silver thaw presages the sickness, the psychic hardening, that carries the community into the "phlegm of December," and precipitates National Suicide Day when Shadrack, also missing Sula, leads the town into a drowning tunnel in which the Deweys, Tar Baby, and many others die. As Morrison herself says, the town is a character. Thus many in the community die in Shadrack's apocalyptic double dose of the undifferentiated feminine element of water. As feminist theologians point out, when a woman fails to develop an integrated self, everyone who touches her suffers—it is not just her personal problem when a culture keeps a woman from growing into all that she could be. The town's resultant disasters are an important comment on the significance of community to lovers' relationships, and vice verse.

Sula's fall into a love relationship, into a coupled world, took place in a vacuum; Ajax and Sula live on the fringes of their community. Their relationship is not contextual and so the community is untouched by Sula's final capitulation to its values of connection and stability. James Hillman has said that you can only go as far with yourself as you have gone with another. Morrison's novels show that individual transformations need the ceremonial presence of the community to reify and support ritual passages. Sula and the community both suffer catastrophe from their alienation.

Eva as Sibyl, Aggrieved Demeter, and Sophia; Nel's Entrance To Old Age

All of this discussion brings us to the last scene that features Eva, who outlives all her children although she sacrificed so much for their lives. When Nel visits Eva in the old folks' home, Eva is constantly making the motions of ironing pleats. She is still making Hestian order, but the image of ironing is also probably an allusion to Tillie Olsen's story, "I Stand Here Ironing," in which a poverty-stricken mother stands and irons while pondering her lost child, her eldest daughter who has such artistic potential. The passion for physical and household order that contains and mutes the tragedies of life is still there in Eva but now in a mad form. She had been the principle of household management, an unrecognized *logos* in itself. Her rationality that managed, administered for others for so long is partially stilled by senility; the long-held-under visionary and irrational feminine erupt. She is feminine madness as Marguerite Duras defines it, a voice out of the silence and darkness, neurotic yet knowing what she wants. This madness set against the "norm" of masculine sanity is actually the truest and deepest kind of feminine sanity. Eva becomes the Sibyl that gives Nel the spiritual and psychological truth that Sula and Nel were and are one. Just as Pilate's dead father speaks to her in *Song of Solomon*, so does Plum now tell Eva the truths that are passed on to Nel. Women bereft of real men in this life connect with fantasy or "spirit" men. In spite of everything, Eva seems fully individuated, an admirable old woman even at this point. She is Hecate, the Medium, the Sibyl, the Truthsayer that still mothers forth the daughters but now in a psychological and metaphysical sense. She is an unfrocked priest, the aggrieved Demeter whose whole line is lost to her, but nevertheless gives the gift of completion to other women. I am unable to fault Eva for her life decisions or acts. Morrison thinks that Eva and Hannah have committed wrong or bad acts, but I think Eva is a portrait of archetypal feminine strengths that goes beyond the author's intentions. Eva has built a life and home as best she could when the only act of free will open to her was self-mutilation or letting her babies die. And she does not really *cause* any of her adult children's deaths; she merely hastens death to save them from misery. Her life has been economically, socially and historically determined in the most narrow way; but in spite of it all, her character is one of fierce protectiveness, gracious regality, magnanimity, deep intelligence, and great courage. And her sharp tongue is salt with wisdom. Eva becomes the Demeter/Sophia, the last phase of feminine wisdom which never stops mothering, informing younger persons of the deepest truths; for Eva mothers Nel into old age. Nel is fifty-five years old in the last pages of this novel, the year of entry into wisdom according to numerologists; it is the year that closes middle age according to many gerontologists. Personally I prefer the numerologists' beautiful image of fifty-five as the year that begins the rectangle of consolidation, of metaphysical wisdom.

Nel realizes Eva is right. Sula is Nel's image of individual, freely imagined feminine selfhood. Nel's deepest bond with another human being was with Sula—not with Jude or any man. I think it is this realization that

Angelou also celebrates; this is certainly the best and perhaps only portrait in all of literature of the true significance for women of feminine bonding.

The Nels of the world survive and their line survives. But it has been at the cost of repressing knowledge of the free and imaginative Sula buried and smoldering deep within. To know that she is there is the first step of feminine completion, a founding self-knowledge that gives spiritual breadth. Nel has always done what her culture said she should; Sula has not only done exactly what she wants but has also told Nel truths that go against all the conventions of their community. Sula stands for feminine freedom of thought even for a woman like Nel who has lived out the cultural norms. The Hermetic or mercurial connection between feminine salt and masculine sulphur in later life seems to underlie Nels epiphany. This is a corroding, painful connection for the traditionally feminine Nel; pain and exultation mingle in her cry for Sula. But it will also put Nel in touch with the masculine principles of flight and freedom, air and fire that Sula always brought into Nel's life. Paradoxically it is through the feminine other that Nel truly touches and releases the masculine within. So we see that the aged Eva starts Nel on her last stage of life with an internal grounding in the fusion of polarities that is perhaps more important than any kind of external reality.

It seems to me that *Sula* itself is in fact an image of feminine psychology and metaphysics that will help carry the human psyche further into the light of conscious articulation and self-knowledge. *Sula* embodies a connection between feminine archetypes that has been held down, repressed even within the feminine collective unconscious. The novel teaches us that women too need to be in touch with their lawless side, the roving woman, the Artemis in her hunting phase. Thus the novel leaps into unknown space, beyond the boundaries of self that male-authored literature has set for us. Where the knowledge will take us, no one can be sure of, and Morrison's last image in the novel reflects this; Nel cries for Sula, cries her loss out into the world, cries out her knowledge of Sula and her own Sula-self:

"All that time, all that time, I thought I was missing Jude."
And the loss pressed down on her chest and came up into her throat.
"We was girls together," she said as though explaining something.
"O Lord, Sula," she cried, "girl, girl, girlgirlgirl." It was a fine cry—loud and long—but it had no bottom and it had no top, just circles and circles of sorrow.

Nel's cry is like the stone in the water, radiating its impact to infinity or like the winding staircase in Melville's *Pierre*—one cannot see the infinite bottom or top of it. The novel thus suggests the cosmic value in women realizing how much they do love each other, of how much joy and pain they share. But still, at the end Nel is alone; Sula, dead; and we see how much of the pain is solitary. Even the realization of loss is often too late for the relationship itself.

Finally, while Morrison portrays all the life stages of her women, the final phases of completing the self in old age are crucial to her patterning. Eva grows more twisted, but more complete nevertheless. In fact, I tire of the word "wholeness" as the aim for human personality. The term implies that certain ingredients must be present. Eva is never able to make a deep or lasting connection with the masculine principle through a man, yet she must certainly be seen as a full, individuated, complex old woman. *Completion* may take different paths and different patterns; not each personality in one lifetime can assimilate the same ingredients. Eva has moved into an unmanned space in society, in the world, and become a woman, a person, of her own making. The novel implicitly asks some hard questions. Can feminine imagination only soar by copying male individuation (often so irresponsible and unnurturing) and cutting oneself off from alliances or partnerships with men? What would happen to the family, to children, if younger women were as free as Sula? Must a woman wait until her last stage of life to embrace her fullness of self? Can human culture afford otherwise? How important are men to the older woman?

The internal union of parts of the feminine (rather than the feminine with the masculine) seems to be what Morrison insists on for the last stage of woman's personality development. Nel considers the men she knew after Jude left: "But now she was fifty-five and hard put to remember what all that had been about." Re-membering her feminine soul, Nel's last stages of individuation begin as an epiphany of Sula. This epiphany of Sula is the trigger, catalyst, and foundation for Nel's last stages of feminine individuation and self-knowledge. And Eva is the mother body out of which this truth and the enlightened Nel issue. As Sula turned to Nel during death, so Nel merges with Sula as she looks to her own final stage of life.

Sula then is prophetic in its invitation to women readers to examine more consciously and sharply their alliance with other women. Many modern women will outlive the important male partners and friends in their lives; the meaning of the predominantly female community they will find themselves in needs consideration. As many social gerontologists have pointed out recently, we can only begin to know the meaning of old age, as many people, not the strongest, live longer. This is especially true for women, who until the last thirty years usually died much younger than men.

The aged Eva bodies forth the knowledge to Nel (Everywoman) that all parts of the feminine must be embraced for old age to be squarely faced from an ego centered in the fullest sense of self. Thus in Nel the two matrilineal lines coalesce and merge. Nel's feminine imagination has assimilated fire and air, can rove the inner universe. Perhaps intro-psychic connections with the masculine are the safest for women. Nel is after all the survivor of her world, but she finally contains her dead sisters, feminine alter egos, through bonds that go even beyond death. Eva, Sula, and Nel interconnect in the last pages of this novel, embodying a matriarchal consciousness that looms large as Eros ripened, full, and rooted, a feminine ground of being for us, their progeny.

I think it is important that no biological relationship symbolizes the psychic significance of female bondedness that Sula's and Nel's does. While I have found a love and belonging through female family members, I have found my deepest spiritual connections with women outside of my family, often women from very different backgrounds. These are the women that have made me grow, individuate beyond my own biology and history. I began this essay speaking of how the betrayal and loss in this novel made me understand the grief and pain of a similar situation in my life. That relationship is semi-estranged still, yet also resolved. For the undeniable love and bond I have with that woman in my life is even in our alienation "until death do us part"—I believe that Morrison's *Sula* helped me see that that particular woman would be part of me always, reconciled with or not. We must submit to the deep symbology and spiritual connection of the love of friends as surely as with biological relatives. I believe that we are in the beginning of a time when our spiritual bonds with self-made communities will be as important, as anchoring, as the family has been in the past. We will need lessons and theory and images of how to bond into a larger collective rather than just the biological matrix we will always have. In this way, *Sula* is futuristic.

This novel makes me realize anew the sacrifices that our foremothers made for us, their progeny. It also makes me realize that we with so much more opportunity must bear their often incomplete individuation into the future. To do so, we must make larger connections than they could afford; our Sula-selves must be more than internal realization.

MELVIN DIXON

Like an Eagle in the Air: Toni Morrison

In recent interviews Toni Morrison has talked about her midwestern, Ohio background and the possibilities it presents for new settings in Afro-American fiction. "It's an interesting state from the point of view of black people because it is right there by the Ohio River, in the south, and at its northern tip is Canada. And there were these fantastic abolitionists there, and also the Ku Klux Klan lived there . . . So I loved writing about that because it was so wide open." On another occasion she remarked, "Ohio offers an escape from stereotyped black settings. It is neither plantation nor ghetto." From a home that is neither typically North nor South, Morrison, like Ellison, who comes from Oklahoma, freely explores new physical and metaphorical landscapes in her fiction. She envisions space with fewer historically or politically fixed boundaries and endows her characters with considerable mobility. Her play of language upon and from within the land creates areas of symbolic activity for both author and protagonists: house and yard become scenes of psychological dislocation in *The Bluest Eye* (1970); land gradations and moral codes have inverted meaning in *Sula* (1973); mountain, farm, and island emerge as stages for enacting dramas of self-creation, racial visibility, and cultural performance in *Song of Solomon* (1977) and in *Tar Baby* (1981). Starting with her birthplace in Lorain, Ohio, and subsequent transformations of that place into

From *Ride Out the Wilderness: Geography and Identity in Afro-American Literature.* © 1987 by the Board of Trustees of the University of Illinois. Used with the permission of the University of Illinois Press.

several charged fields in fiction, Toni Morrison has imagined a complex and multitextured world.

The symbolic geography in Morrison's fiction emerges from the precise physical details that give her black neighborhoods so much startling character and presence. Medallion, Ohio, or Shalimar, Virginia, fixes firmly in the imagination and shapes either terrestrial or celestial images through which Morrison initiates a dialogue with earlier texts [. . .] most notably with Ralph Ellison's *Invisible Man*. In the three novels that have earned Morrison an indisputable prominence in contemporary American letters, the author enlarges and completes many previous attempts to show the importance of both place and person in the development of Afro-American culture. From the songs her characters sing to transform otherwise dreary households into spiritual havens, and from the journeys they undertake through history and myth as in the early slave narratives (as the author revealed, "You know, I go sometimes and, just for sustenance, I read those slave narratives—there are sometimes three or four sentences of half a page, each one of which could be developed in an art form, marvelous") comes the achievement of form and art in Morrison's fiction.

Attentive to the physical and cultural geography of the small black towns that have shaped her and her characters, Morrison constructs familiar yet new dialectical oppositions between enclosed and open spaces, between the fluid horizontality of neighborhoods (shifting, migrating populations, a profusion of character types and changing morals) and the fixed verticality, hence presumed stability, of the house. Morrison calls for an end to Ellisonian inertia and a delight in the free fall. These oppositions produce various exciting results that propel characters and readers toward the principal movement in Morrison's fiction: the leap from land into sky. Pecola Breedlove, for one, ventures to the "cave" of Elihue's mind (the cerebral force, readers will recall, that pushed Ellison's protagonist to consider ending his underground hibernation, "Because, damn it, there's the mind, the *mind*. It wouldn't let me rest") and its reservoir of conjure and magic. Pecola comes away with the cherished blue eyes that she alone can see (a blindness that completes the invisibility she had suffered from others). She wears a vision of the sky but never gains its reward of flight (is the name Pecola a variant of peacock?). For Pecola's aesthetic choice sinks her evermore into the mire of self-hatred that had initially created her desire. Sula, on the other hand, longs for flight and song but gets no farther than the upper rooms of Eva's house of death. The house opposes the space of Ellison's cellar, but it is filled with the same inertia (the stunted growth of the eternally juvenile Deweys is one example). The one character who eventually learns to resist the gravitational pull of social conformity and to grasp what his newly stretched imagination can reach is Milkman Dead. He earns the authority to sing his real name, for he not only has discovered the long-sought-for ancestor Solomon, he becomes him when he tries the air. That test of the air—the risk, the ultimate surrender to it, and the strengthening *ride*—culminates Morrison's metaphorical triumph over conventional terrestrial frontiers or boundaries to identity, moving up into the celestial infinity of its achievement. Milkman's journey from No Mercy Hospital to the cave in Danville, Pennsylvania, and from a wilderness hunt to a mountaintop discovery in Shalimar, Virginia, offers a more satisfying solution to black homelessness than the reflective yet artificial hibernation Ellison had proposed.

The Bluest Eye. "When the Land Kills of Its Own Volition"

Claudie MacTeer, the occasional and maturing narrator in Morrison's first novel, discovers one of the earth's peculiar traits that may mitigate the guilt that she feels for the failure of her marigold seeds to grow: "*For years I thought my sister was right: it was my fault. I had planned* [our seeds] *too far down in the earth. It never occurred to either of us that the earth itself might have been unyielding.*" This revelation brings only partial relief. It offers one explanation of the novel's theme: the loss of innocence. The underlying question concerns the earth's role in bringing on misfortune, in creating a climate for Pecola's suffering and insanity as well as confusing the parameters of moral responsibility. The actual telling of the story, the sharing of narration among several voices, including Pauline's interior monologues, leads Claudia to confess too late the community's and her own complicity in acquiescing to hostility by taking life's misery too much for granted. "We acquiesce and say the victim had no right to live. We are wrong, of course, but it doesn't matter. It's too late." The victim here is not only Pecola's premature and dead baby, sired by Pecola's own father, but also Pecola herself. The loss of Claudia's and Frieda's innocence, as they witness and report Pecola's decline, makes them victims as well.

The Bluest Eye is Morrison's study of a community out of touch with the land and the history that might have saved them. The displacement of blacks had begun long before Claudia's retrospective narration about the failed marigolds. The distance between their lives and the ideal American home or family, depicted in the passage from the grade-school reader that opens the novel, is also measured by the increasingly distorted passage, parts of which later introduce the subject of each subsequent chapter. This technique reveals the pervasive trauma of dislocation suffered by Pecola, Claudia, Soaphead Church, and the entire community. [. . .]

Sula. "It's the Bottom of Heaven—Best Land There Is"

A more complex figuration of land and identity emerges in *Sula*. Beyond the psychological boundaries that imprison Pecola and allow the MacTeer sisters to bear witness to the loss of sexual and mental place, *Sula* tells the story of two women who renegotiate the pressures of place and person through their long friendship, which is not without moments of rupture and discord. The growing bond between Nel Wright and Sula Mae Peace as well as their complementary personalities are first revealed to us by the contrasting features of the land.

Two key terrestrial images frame the novel: the hillside signifying the creation of the black community of Medallion, Ohio, known as the Bottom (through the chicanery of a white planter unwilling to fulfill his promise of valley land to an industrious and newly emancipated slave), and a tunnel under construction at New River Road that collapses upon participants in Shadrack's last march to commemorate National Suicide Day. At first glance, the hillside and the tunnel appear dichotomous. The hillside, or the Bottom, is named ironically, and it is viewed through a passing of time: "there was once a neighborhood." The phrase introduces a narrative about an entire community, but also prophesies its destruction, the hell of mutability alluded to by Nel: "Hell ain't things lasting forever. Hell is change."

One reading of these two regions suggests they have male and female characteristics: the phallic hillside and the vaginal tunnel, particularly when one recalls that the Bottom was established as a black community through a barter between two men. But Morrison gives the two regions feminine traits and infuses them with a preponderance of female properties, in the dual sense. One then suspects a different personification at work. Irene's Palace of Cosmetology, Reba's Grill, the dance of a "dark woman in a flowered dress doing a bit of cakewalk, a bit of black bottom, a bit of 'messing around' to the lively notes of a mouth organ," all depict a procreative, female environment. The hillside is nurturing; it is a veritable breast of the earth. Within a feminine figuration (accompanying the narrative of a nurturing friendship between Nel and Sula) the hillside complements rather than contrasts with the womblike tunnel, which upon "breaking water" becomes a haunting, unsuspecting grave when several Bottom luminaries drown. This "abortion" of life occurs right at the time Medallion is undergoing a kind of rebirth through urban renewal. Whites and blacks are changing geographical spaces:

the former moving to the cooler hills, the latter descending to the crowded valley floor. This change and death reverse the notion of economic upward mobility for Medallion blacks, who have only a promise of work on New River Road, and foreshadow the further decline, or bottoming *out*, of the community. The nurture-destruction tension in Morrison's figuration of the land this early in the novel more than prepares us for the complementary relationship, shifting moral dualism, and irony between Sula Mae Peace, who makes and unmakes peace in the community, and Nel Wright, who is never fully as right or as morally stalwart as she would like to appear.

The double figuration of the land as a framing device also foreshadows the novel's curiously double closure. One ending, effected by Shadrack's haunting, successful celebration of death, culminates his search for a "place for fear" as a way of "controlling it" and brings his social marginality to a shocking conclusion. A second ending, however, forces the reader to revise this reading of the novel. Nel's visit to the elderly Eva, now in a nursing home, picks up the unfinished business between Nel and Sula (here represented by Eva) with shattering results: Nel is forced to acknowledge the guilt she shares with Sula for the accidental drowning of Chicken Little who had slipped from Sula's swinging hands and had entered the "closed place of the water." The scene also foreshadows the tunnel's sudden collapse. Nel must also acknowledge the grief for Sula she had tried to suppress, only to discover in her solitary walk home that grief like guilt has no prescribed boundaries; it demands open public expression. When she realizes the extent of her accountability to Sula's friendship—"We was girls together"—Nel lets loose the emotion she had artificially held in check all these years: the cry without "bottom" or "top," but "circles and circles of sorrow." The ever-spiraling geometry of Nel's grief returns readers to the scene of Chicken Little's death and forces us to rethink and replace the event. Sula's "evil" now appears innocuous and Nel's guilt more calculating and malevolent. We must also reconsider Nel's [W]rightness, for her cry admits a moral responsibility for wrongdoing that was not Sula's alone. Riding the spiral of Nel's grief back through the novel, we encounter other geometrical and geographical images that clearly establish the theme of moral dualism and double meaning in society and in nature. *Sula* then becomes as much a novel about the shifting patterns of accountability in Sula and Nel's friendship as it concerns a community's acceptance of moral relativism.

The boomerang effect of the shifting moral and physical geography of Medallion, Ohio, can be seen, for example, in the medallion Sula wears, the birthmark above her eye, the meaning of which changes according to who reads it. Morrison's novel is as much about interpretation as it is about art. How members of the community *read* Sula tells us a great deal about their relation to the land, to themselves, and to the meaning they create. The first indication of this theme is the novel's epigraph, taken from *The Rose Tattoo*, which implicates an entire community, a "they," in the speaker's nonconformist assertion of self: *"Nobody knew my rose of the world but me. . . . I had too much glory. They don't want glory like that in nobody's heart."* No one really knows Sula or why she sets about—as she tells Eva—to "make herself." But nearly everyone has an opinion about Sula's medallion: a sign they believe of her "evil," her *"too much glory"* in flaunting her disregard of social conventions. At first Sula's birthmark is described as a "stemmed rose"; as she matures, it becomes a "stem and rose," suggesting the duality in nature as well as Sula's developing thorny yet attractive personality. With age, the mark becomes "the scary black thing over her eye." When Jude begins to see the mark as a "copperhead" and a "rattlesnake," he is seduced by Sula. And as Sula becomes the evil the community fears yet abides, her mark indicates either "Hannah's ashes" or, as Shadrack sees it, "a tadpole." No one, not even Nel, knows Sula's heart. Indeed, Sula's closest kin, in terms of the community's social and moral landscape, is none other than Shadrack whose madness makes him at once both an outsider and insider: "Once the people understood the boundaries and nature of his madness, they could fit him, so to speak, into the scheme of things." His shack in the woods or wilderness, halfway between the order of the town and the disorder of the lake where Chicken Little drowned, becomes Sula's refuge, a more useful shelter after the accident than Nel's calculated silence. When Shadrack answers "always" to the distraught Sula's unvoiced question, he seals the doubling of their characters in one word of recognition.

The shifting geometry of Sula's birthmark also shapes her actions throughout the novel and identifies the forces directing her. Readers will recall that we know nothing of Sula's life away from Medallion—her time spent in college, in New York, and in other parts of the country—because Sula's real character, however enigmatic, comes from this community, this Medallion. It is her home and, as suggested above, her landmark. When Sula returns home after an absence of ten years, she fully claims the territory as hers by dispossessing Eva of the house. Sula then occupies Eva's third floor bedroom. Her hibernation behind the boarded window seals her fate in the family and in the community. Sula's appropriation of height in the upper room does not, however, bring the desired refuge or elevation. Nor does it become the place of performance where the creation of character, the "making of oneself" can take place. Although she repossesses a space, Sula, like Cholly Breedlove, fails to find therein a voice for her identity. The self she finds in the house where she was born is still incomplete, as fragile and infantile as her uncle Plum. When Eva descended the stairs on her one leg—

the only time she actually went down those stairs—she found Plum in a stupor of drug addiction, trying to return to her womb. Childlike, he clearly needed a new identity, a new birth, but one that Eva could neither provide nor accommodate. She set fire to him. Plum's vision before he burned to death may offer a clue to Sula's fate: "He opened his eyes and saw what he imagined was the great wing of an eagle pouring a wet lightness over him. Some kind of baptism, some kind of blessing, he thought." Plum succumbs to the "bright hole of sleep" without achieving flight on the eagle's wing. Sula, who had returned to Medallion during a plague of robins, also yearns for flight as the fulfillment of the self-creation she thought she had achieved. In the upper room, now the setting for her ardent lovemaking with Ajax, Sula discovers her human frailty (sexual possessiveness and emotional vulnerability). It is also the place where she dies.

Flight appears in Morrison's oeuvre as early as *The Bluest Eye*. Pecola, enticed into Junior's house, encounters his black cat with fascinating blue eyes, suggesting the probability that a black person can also have blue eyes. Junior ruthlessly snatches the cat from Pecola and begins to "swing it around his head in a circle." Defying Pecola's cries for him to stop, Junior lets the cat go "in midmotion," throwing it against the window; it falls dead behind the radiator, its fur singeing. In a similar geometrical gesture, "Sula picked [Chicken Little] up by his hands and swung him outward then around and around," until he slips "from her hands and sailed away out over the water," still laughing in delight. When he lands in the "closed place in the water," his flight, like that of the blue-eyed cat, is aborted in death. But the height and sense of the free fall he achieves brings him to the cutting edge of the kind of freedom and transcendence Sula herself seeks.

Sula's own quest for height and power through performance occurs in Eva's third floor bedroom. Mounted *on top of* Ajax in their lovemaking, Sula "rocked there, swayed there, like a Georgia pine on its knees, high above the slipping, falling smile, high above the golden eyes and the velvet helmet of hair, rocking, swaying . . . She looked down, down from what seemed an awful height at the head of the man whose lemon-yellow gabardines had been the first sexual excitement she'd known. Letting her thoughts dwell on his face in order to confine, for just a while longer, the drift of her flesh toward the high silence of orgasm." Sula's discovery of height and freedom confirming her self-centered identity and place is only partially realized because the milk-bearing Ajax, in a gesture of sexual nurture, counters her contrived image of flight with a more realistic, attainable one of his own. When Sula experiences the human frailty of love and possessiveness that ultimately destroys her at the same time that it brings her closer to Nel, she becomes just domestic enough to make the adventuresome Ajax lose interest:

"when Ajax came that evening . . . the bathroom was gleaming, the bed was made, and the table was set for two." Ajax's compelling desire, however, is to attend an air show in Dayton. Sula has indeed met her match.

Moreover, Ajax shows how trivial, self-indulgent, and incomplete is Sula's notion of the "free fall," which she felt made her different from Nel, whose imagination had been driven "underground" by her repressive mother, and from the other women of Medallion. Ajax's presence heightens Sula's self-contradictions as he effectively matches her false, showy noncon-formity with his more authentic eccentricity: he is the son of a conjurer mother, and his knowledge of magic and lore surpasses Sula's allure. Here Morrison's prevailing metaphor of flight begins with a leap, or free fall, and offers a rectifying alternative to Ellison's idea of hibernation. As Sula hiber-nates on the upper floor at 7 Carpenter Road, not in an underground cellar, she longs for the kind of performance that would complete her discovery of self-mastery and complete control. This metaphor is hinted at in *The Bluest Eye*, sketched out and challenged by Ajax in *Sula*, and finds its fullest, if not most conclusive statement in *Song of Solomon*.

The relation between Sula and Nel ruptures when Sula interprets Nel's possessiveness of her husband, Jude, to mean that Nel is one of *them*, the conventional housewives of Medallion. Nel had earlier shared Sula's vision of "the slant of life that makes it possible to stretch [life] to its limits." Becoming the clichéd wronged wife, outraged at Jude and Sula's adultery, Nel is too quickly linked with other women in the community who had "interpreted" Sula as incarnating some kind of evil. They had measured themselves morally and socially by abiding "evil"—as Pauline Breedlove did with Cholly in *The Bluest Eye*—and garnering a false dignity, even heroism, by tolerating it: "The purpose of evil was to survive it." When Nel shows her natural jealousy and hurt, she begins to belong, in Sula's view, "to the town and all of its ways." Nel also begins to oppose Sula's notion of invention and free fall on which Sula had based her ascendant self-mastery and their complementary friendship: "But the free fall, oh no, that required—demanded—invention: a thing to do with the wings, a way of holding the legs and most of all a full surrender to the downward flight if they wished to taste their tongues or stay alive. But alive was what they, and now Nel, did not want to be. Too dangerous."

"Dangerous" more than evil is an accurate description of Sula. As an "artist with no art form" Sula is vulnerable to the shifting interpretations of the only form she carries in her very being: her birthmark. Like Hannah, Sula's art lay in lovemaking, in her enjoyment of the sheer abandon of sex. This clearly is how Sula makes the leap from sexual conventions that lead to marriage and braves the outer limits of promiscuity, the ultimate breach of which is to have sex with white men. It was through carefree sex, nonetheless, that Sula found the cutting edge and the leap of free fall, her performance:

> During the lovemaking she found and needed to find the cutting edge. When she left off cooperating with her body and began to assert herself in the act, particles of strength gathered in her like steel shavings drawn to a spacious magnetic center, forming a tight cluster that nothing, it seemed, could break. And there was utmost irony and outrage in lying *under* someone, in a position of surrender, feeling her own abiding strength and limitless power. But the cluster did break, fall apart, and in her panic to hold it together she *leaped* from the edge into soundlessness and went down howling, howling in a stinging awareness of the endings of things: an eye of sorrow in the midst of all that hurricane rage of joy. There, in the center of that silence was not eternity but the death of time and a loneliness so profound the word itself had no meaning. (emphasis mine)

In an interview published in *Nimrod*, Morrison once discussed the importance of venturing to the cutting edge and experiencing the leap. What is needed, she said, is complete self-control, divesting oneself of the vanities that weigh people down. This surrender is a triumph and results in a stark change of territory: from land to sky, from the confining boundaries of conventional morality and selfishness to the thrill of self-creation, a riding of the air. "Suppose it were literally so, what would it take to fly?" Morrison speculated. "But suppose you could just move one step up and fly? What would you have to be, and feel, and do, in order to do that?" *Sula* begins to answer Morrison's own question. The author, however, asks for more: "You would have to be able to surrender, give up all of the weights, all of the vanities, all of the ignorances. And you'd have to trust and have faith in the harmony of your body. You would also have to have perfect control." Sula indeed wishes for power, control, and the reward of flight. Ajax, the aviation-dreaming lover, brings her milk in blue, sky-colored glass bottles: "Ajax looked at her through the blue glass and held the milk aloft like a trophy." Perhaps it is Ajax who can lift Sula from the ground, or perhaps she will lift him up into the flight and transcendence he also seeks. The only uncertainty is Sula's ability to let herself go and to release Ajax from the confining domesticity of housebound sex.

Sula fails. Her wish for total freedom, for flight, becomes as much a delusion as Pecola's blue eyes. Even the unobstructed mobility or license granted by Sula's land/birthmark is illusory because Sula is both ostracized and nourished by the same community, the same land; her mobility is limited by the interpretive needs of the community, shown by Medallion's quick regression into antagonistic behavior once the "threat" of Sula passes with her death and just prior to the parade into the tunnel. The illusory nature of Sula's desire is revealed in the contrast between her and Ajax, who, like Bigger Thomas in *Native Son* or Buster and Riley in Ellison's story "That I Had the Wings," yearns for freedom through aviation. Although Ajax's dream is realized only in his frequent trips to airports, he establishes a degree of realism against Sula's illusion of control and flight through sex. (It is he who requests that she mount him.) He thinks equally about his conjurer mother and airplanes: "when he was not sitting enchanted listening to his mother's words, he thought of airplanes, and pilots, and the deep sky that held them both." The blue bottle of milk offered to Sula as a trophy connects her to the blue sky and the maternal milk. Flight and aviation as the exercise of creativity, the fulfillment of perfect control, hold both Sula and Ajax in its cobalt blue glow.

Yet the moment that Sula falls in love with Ajax and discovers possessiveness, both she and Ajax are more grounded than either desires. Ajax escapes this confinement by losing interest in Sula, but she remains trapped, totally overwhelmed by feeling human and vulnerable. When she takes Ajax through her newly cleaned house—"the spotless bathroom where dust had been swept from underneath the claw-foot tub"—she shows him her nest, a space for her hibernation, nurture, and fulfillment of sexual desire. Ajax makes love to her in the more conventional position, but he thinks less about Sula than "the date of the air show in Dayton." Sula is "under" him now, and he moves "with the steadiness and the intensity of a man about to leave for Dayton."

In his stunning absence, Sula tries to come to terms with her love for Ajax, for the flight of fancy he represented, for the adventuresome love, not the self-gratifying control that grounds her. Like Pecola, Sula is weighed down by the human, emotional vulnerability she succumbs to, particularly the self-willed grief she hibernates in, shut away in Eva's room. Like Cholly Breedlove, Sula reaches a momentary height of self-awareness in her admission of loneliness and possessiveness of Ajax (particularly when she realizes she never really possessed him, for she never knew his name), but she fails to give full voice to this spark of self-recognition. Hence, her freedom is never fully realized. Her flight is not only aborted, but Sula also dies. The song she wanted to sing might have saved her by providing a different kind of performance and presentation of self, as Milkman's song performance will. But the right lyrics elude her; she can only mouth repeated nonsense words. Sula, then, like Cholly, is a failed "person"-of-words, left dreaming, like Pecola, of "cobalt blue" without even an air show in Dayton to claim her: "When she awoke, there was a melody in her head she could not identify or recall ever hearing before. . . . Then it came to her—the name of the song and all its lyrics just as she had heard it many times before. . . . She lay down again on the bed and sang a little wandering tune made up of the words *I have sung all the songs all the songs I have sung all the songs there are* until, touched by her lullaby, she grew drowsy, and in the follow of near-sleep she tasted the acridness of gold, left the chill of alabaster and smelled the dark, sweet stench of loam." Sula succumbs to the "hollow," as Plum did at the "hole" of sleep because she could not give adequate voice and action to her vision. Instead of flying, she descends to the loam of the very land that had marked her from birth.

Sula's death offers no "invention," only descent; it is neither a free fall nor the redeeming flight she had longed for. One clue to her decline lies in Morrison's verbal design of Sula's place of hibernation, Eva's room with its blind window, boarded up indirectly by Sula herself. Sula's paralyzing interest in watching her mother Hannah burn necessitated Eva's leap of rescue out of that window. When Sula subsequently dispossesses Eva of that room, she puts herself in the physical, but not the emotional, space for the reconciliation Eva had attempted in her failed rescue of Hannah, and, para-doxically, in her mercy killing of Plum—to keep him from descending further into the stupor of drugs, or reducing his already fragile maturity to the helpless state of an infant wanting a return to the womb. Instead of a womb, Eva offered Plum the scent and vision of the eagle's wings. Instead of flight, Eva's upper room offers Sula the best setting for the only performance she is then capable of; her foetal plunge down an imaginary birth canal or tunnel (prefiguring the town's later disaster) is a perversion of the rebirth in death that Eva had granted Plum: "The sealed window soothed her with its sturdy termination, its unassailable finality. . . . It would be here, only here, held by this blind window high above the elm tree, that she might draw her legs up to her chest, close her eyes, put her thumb in her mouth and float over and down the tunnels, just missing the dark walls, down, down until she met a rain scent and would know the water was near, and she would curl into its heavy softness and it would envelope her, carry her, and wash her tired flesh always. Always."

Sula's plunge into the tunnel following a period of willful hibernation completes the solitude she had always wanted. This hibernation, however, had rendered her immobile, incapacitated (except in death), for Ajax's depar-ture and Sula's recognition of her human vulnerability stun her into physical and emotional paralysis. This backfire, or boomerang, reverses the moment of moral strength Eva felt in her husband BoyBoy's desertion, and now Eva, as a discerning, combative ancestor, cannot help Sula, for Eva has been safely locked away.

Neither Sula's solitude nor tunnel plunge is a fate left to her alone. Being a product of the land, a mark of the community, she reflects the fate of others. In the collapse of the half-finished tunnel at New River Road to the clanging tune of Sula's brother in marginality, Shadrack's pied-piper parade, the town, which had made Sula both person and pariah and a source of their negatively realized pride, meets its end. Both Sula and Shadrack have presided over figurations of the land that reveal underground refuge or hibernation to be the simple burial it is, which is what Wright's Fred Daniels discovered. Hibernation, despite the subversive bravura of Ellison's invisible man, does not lead to the effective overt activity or self-assertion he had promised. Morrison's more complex rendering of place and person in the collapse of the tunnel and the spirals of grief that bind Nel to repetitions of guilt, necessitates an end to hibernation, whether underground or three floors up. In *Song of Solomon*, Morrison offers the corrective reach of the mountaintop and a triumphant surrender to the air.

TRUDIER HARRIS

Sula: *Within and Beyond the African American Folk Tradition*

*T*he *Bluest Eye* (1970), with its grounding in Lorain, Ohio, provides at least geographical identification with events in the world as we know it. What the people do to each other there might be cruel and insensitive, but those characters approximate many we have seen. There is a verisimilitude in the cruelty of the children who reject Pecola, and we can easily visualize the likes of Pauline Breedlove in her adherence to a loyalty and love for the white family in preference for her own. With the creation of the Bottom in *Sula* (1974), Toni Morrison removes that grounding in a known place and locates her characters in a territory that invites the fantastic and the mythical as easily as the realistic. In the political-racial-economic confrontation surrounding its creation, the Bottom differs from other fictional communities; it was concocted out of hope, belief, and the power of dreams to transcend the harshness of the real world. It lends itself, therefore, much more readily to occurrences that are strange or fantastic and to characters who are at times more nether creatures than flesh and blood.

Toni Morrison has asserted that she writes the kind of books she wants to read. We might conclude, therefore, that in her use of folklore she is fascinated by the magic of fairy tales and intrigued with the horrors to be found in monsters, or at least in monstrous behavior. In *Sula*, Morrison continues her creation of literary folklore by drawing upon and expanding historical patterns.

From *Fiction and Folklore: The Novels of Toni Morrison*. © 1991 by Trudier Harris. Reprinted by permission of the University of Tennessee Press.

Morrison may begin with structural components of tales or peculiar traits of characters with which we may be superficially familiar, but she quickly embroiders upon these patterns. Her familiarity with African-American folk communities and with other oral traditions enables her to touch base with them in the outline of her materials, but to differ in the details. What Morrison does might be compared with what Charles Waddell Chesnutt did in *The Conjure Woman* (1899); beginning with the outlines of tales he had heard in North Carolina, he expanded details to shape political statements disguised as seemingly innocuous stories. Chesnutt's tales seem so true to black folk tradition that many students of his work have searched for exact parallels in published collections of folklore. Although Morrison surrounds her novel with an aura of unreality that discourages seeking exact parallels, her lore is further fictionalized beyond the mere germ of a traditional idea. Though we can see those basic inspirations in the ideas that shape the structure of the novel, delineate the characters, and develop the themes, it is also clear where Morrison has created something else.

Three oral sources are helpful in illuminating the structure of *Sula*. First of all, the structure evokes the formulaic opening of fairy tales from European cultures; secondly, it evokes a pattern of joking in African-American communities; and, thirdly, it evokes the form of the ballad, which, in its incremental development, in turn reminds us of jazz composition. In the first paragraph of the novel, Morrison establishes an almost mythical status for the Bottom, claiming kinship for it with the many places in which strange, almost supernatural, incidents have occurred. "In that place, where they tore the nightshade and blackberry patches from their roots to make room for the Medallion City Golf Course, there was once a neighborhood" deviates little from the "Once upon a time" formula for fairy tales; the fictional reality of the Bottom is thus juxtaposed with the lack of reality of some of those never-never lands. The formula establishes distance, a perspective from which to view the incidents about to be related. It is a signal that we can sit back and read of marvelous events, or at least that is what the formula usually conveys.

As we being our journey into that other world Morrison has created, we quickly discover a series of reversals: the fantastic events are disturbingly real, and the formula promising wondrous occurrences moves them from the realm of imagination to commonplaces such as war, poverty, and murder. The expected distance collapses, but it does not collapse thoroughly enough for us, without reservations, to accept Shadrack as the guy next door or Sula as the girl next door. Expected dragonslayers become frightened young soldiers afraid of their own hands, afraid that war has taught them not only to kill others but to kill themselves. Ogres are alcohol and drugs, and those strong enough to kill, such as Eva, cannot separate evil from the innocent victims it inhabits. Fires that save Hansel and Gretel or the three little pigs become scars upon the soul of a mother who kills her only son and upon a daughter who quietly watches her mother burn to death.

In another classic Morrison reversal, *Sula* is antithetical to the basic premise of the fairy tale—that the heroine is a helpless, passive creature who must depend upon some man, preferably a stranger, to save her from whatever "fate worse than death" she has innocently or stupidly managed to get herself into. There is little passivity in *Sula*, and innocence is not treasured; indeed, as is typical of Morrison's girl/women, Sula and Nel seem to blossom into adolescence with more knowledge than is comfortable for either of them. In fact, as the experimenter with life, the Ethan Brand type who explores the limits of sin, Sula is an active, destructive artist who, in the absence of "paints, or clay" or a knowledge of "dance, or strings" makes human beings her adventure in life. She is as active as Jack the giant killer and as amoral as Brer Rabbit the trickster.

In this literary folklore, therefore, there is a marked gap between expectation and outcome, between what the familiar leads us to anticipate and what Morrison's changing of the familiar actually provides. She undercuts any potential fairy tale outcomes by making Sula, her princess, a despicable user who needs rescue from no one; by making Eva, her fairy godmother, impotent at the most crucial moment of her life (Hannah's burning); and by making Shadrack, her potential prince, an outcast from the world where his services are most needed. None of these characters portends the "happily ever after" dimension of the formula. By novel's end, the princess is dead, the prince has unwittingly led many of her adversaries to their deaths, the twin sister is almost crazy with grief, and the kingdom is slowly being destroyed.

Its destruction has been foreshadowed in the second structural pattern underlying the novel, the "nigger joke" about the origin of the Bottom. The story fits a classic tale cycle of the black man being duped by the white man:

> A good white farmer promised freedom and a piece of bottom land to his slave if he would perform some very difficult chores. When the slave completed the work, he asked the farmer to keep his end of the bargain. Freedom was easy— the farmer had no objection to that. But he didn't want to give up any land. So he told the slave that he was very sorry that he had to give him valley land. He had hoped to give him a piece of the Bottom. The slave blinked and said he thought valley land was bottom land. The master said, "Oh, no! See those hills? That's bottom land, rich and fertile."

"But it's high up in the hills," said the slave.

"High up from us," said the master, "but when God looks down, it's the bottom. That's why we call it so. It's the bottom of heaven—best land there is."

So the slave pressed his master to try to get him some. He preferred it to the valley. And it was done. The nigger got the hilly land, where planting was backbreaking, where the soil slid down and washed away the seeds, and where the wind lingered all through the winter.

Which accounted for the fact that white people lived on the rich valley floor in that little river town in Ohio, and the blacks populated the hills above it, taking small consolation in the fact that every day they could literally look down on the white folks.

The tale presents two archetypes of African-American folklore: the white man of means and the "blinking," almost minstrel black man who learns too late the true nature of the bargain he has made. The basic discrepancy inherent in such interactions is also apparent: power (including the language skills to control or create reality) versus the absence of power. The twist in the tale is that the white farmer is the trickster, the figure who dupes instead of being duped.

The story is an etiological one, in that it serves to explain how the current state of affairs came to be. In a world in which the black man is destined to lose, because of or in spite of his labor, the slave here fares no better. The rules of the games will always be changed, as Daryl C. Dance astutely observes in her discussion of etiological tales in *Shuckin' and Jivin'* (1978) and elsewhere; the black man will always receive the reward of lesser value. But Morrison turns the joke around; it is difficult to grow things there, but it is "lovely up in the Bottom," and the trees are so "wonderful to see" that whites speculate on the Bottom indeed being "the bottom of heaven." In spite of their ancestors having been shortchanged, the black folks create reasonably happy lives for themselves in a place almost animate in its influence upon them.

Reminiscent of the storefront, communal, interactive culture that Zora Neale Hurston describes in *Mules and Men* (1935) and other works, the Bottom is a joke where the tables are turned, for a time, back on the joker. For that portion of the novel where the Bottom is vibrant—despite its occasional strangenesses—the last laugh is really on the whites, because they have not been able to destroy the will to survive of those blacks up in the Bottom. Indeed, the philosophy exemplified in the Bottom is one of survival at all costs, of making all mountains, built by whites or blacks, into mole hills. The black folks in the Bottom place white folks like the man in the tale in the large category of evil that will later contain Sula, and they resolve to withstand all of it. "The purpose of evil was to survive it and they determined (without ever knowing they had made up their minds to do it) to survive floods, white people, tuberculosis, famine and ignorance."

Morrison allows them to invert the stereotype of their existence (that they deserve and should be resigned to content themselves with less) for almost a hundred years. Ultimately, the structure imposed by the "nigger joke"—that outcomes will always fall short of expectations—reigns in the novel. Blacks who moved to the Bottom and expected to be left in peace are not. Eventually, the whites decide that the Bottom is ideal for suburbs and a golf course, so the blacks who have not voluntarily moved away are displaced once again. Although slight variations have occurred over the years, the basic structure is retained: whites get what they consider the best, and blacks must settle for what is left.

This structure also provides a backdrop against which to view the actions of the characters, especially those of Sula. In a world in which expectations are invariably short-circuited, it is not surprising to find Sula's actions a series of expectations that she measures against some invisible yardstick and finds wanting. Life is in many ways the "nigger joke" that has been played on her. From her twelve-year-old discovery that her mother "loved" rather than "liked" her, to her twenty-seven-year-old Weltschmerz, Sula learns that life holds few genuine adventures for her and even fewer pleasures. The cards dealt out to her are all marked with the notation that she is black and female; therefore, winning hands must be kept from her. Paralleling the structure that defines the fate of the Bottom, the fate of Sula's existence is similarly determined.

Sula's personality, along with the snake-like birthmark that so intrigues those who encounter her, makes her the closest thing to a witch that the Bottom will ever have. Yet, in its ability to contain contradictions, the community provides for her, as Morrison has noted on several occasions, the only place that will accept her and the only home she will ever know. Her wanderings away from the Bottom can only bring her full circle, like Eva, back to it, for it is able to absorb if not to condone her "otherness," and it gives her the identity that locks her both inside and outside the community's folk traditions. People in the community grant to her the power she has, and she accommodates them by living out their fantasies of otherness.

The third structural pattern in *Sula* evokes the ballad tradition, in which a "leaping and lingering" method of storytelling pauses on significant events in each character's life. In the ballad "Lord Rendal," for example, we are not told of Lord Rendal's birthplace or his growing up; we meet him as a young man who has gone into the woods and been poisoned by his "true love"—for some inexplicable reason. The murder, the encounter with his mother asking what has happened, and his request that his mother make his deathbed "soon" are the three significant points in his life. The whys and wherefores are less important than the consequences of the bloody confrontation. Thus Rendal's life is reduced to the three incidents that lead to his death; perhaps the ballad, over years of telling, has lost some of its detail, but probably not much. The form of the genre demands brevity and heightened scenes, the tableau scenes, as Axel Olrik calls them in reference to the major incidents recorded in folktales.

We can see a similar sparse depiction in the ballad of Barbara Allan, in which Sir John Graeme's failure to toast her is less central than the consequences of that action. As a result, he pines and dies; then Barbara, sensing that he has indeed cherished her, anticipates her own death. The deaths here, like the murder and anticipated death in "Lord Rendal," keep the listener's attention. The same is true of traditional African-American ballads, such as "Stagolee." The "central event" is the gun battle between Stagolee and the other man, who has various names, the most common of which is Billy Lyons. Background on the two men is not particularly important; indeed, Billy Lyons exists only to allow Stagolee to act out his fate as a bad man. Some versions of the ballad include Stagolee's early encounters with his father or law officers (individual will versus authority in any form), but the ballad is basically stripped to its essential details.

In an oral tradition, where memory could be subject to error, such standout scenes insured the singer a better chance of recalling what the audience was most interested in—the criminal activity surrounding rape, death, murder, hanging, and infanticide, and the pathos surrounding unrequited love. If there are valleys and peaks in an individual's life, then the peaks consistently receive attention ("peak" is used here to refer to emotional intensity, either good or bad, and not exclusively to pleasure or happiness). In relating her tale of passions, burnings, drownings, and witchery, Morrison, too, is interested in the highlights, the peaks, rather than the ordinariness represented by the valleys.

Morrison does not purport to be realistic to the minutiae of following characters on a day-to-day, year-by-year basis; her very labeling of the years she does dwell on (1919, 1920, 1921, 1922, 1923, 1927, 1937, 1939, 1940, 1941, 1965) indicates the leaping and lingering tradition. She selects the most impressive events and concentrates upon them for each of her most impressionable characters. The effects of the war upon Shadrack are finally more important than physically depicting him in battle, although the one scene he does recall is a striking one in which a soldier whose head has been blown off continues to run in spite of that catastrophe. The bloody images of the war lead to Shadrack's perennial celebration of National Suicide Day, and the visit from Sula, the other tableau scene in his life, serves as his last untainted tie to humanity.

Eva's life is crystallized in several scenes: pushing lard up Plum's rectum in the midst of unbearable poverty, knowing that hating BoyBoy after his return will give her peace, trying to save Hannah from a burning death, and being carted off to the old folks' home. The loss of her leg is certainly important, but we are left to speculate about the circumstances under which that occurred; what that loss enabled her to do is more significant. Nel and Sula's friendship solidifies on the day Sula hears Hannah's frank, but destructive, comment on her motherly feelings—which is also the day Sula accidentally kills Chicken Little. Nel's marriage collapses into the few minutes she finds Jude and Sula together, and her grief careens off the tombstones on the day, after her visit to Eva in the old folks' home, that she realizes the extent of her love for Sula. Perhaps the bits and pieces of these lives, as Morrison said about Cholly Breedlove, would make more sense in a musician's head, but they also make sense in the tradition that does not expect fairy tale completeness. Leaping and lingering, frequently with the bloody, or at least the violent, consequences of the ballad tradition, Morrison tells her story in sketches, in vignettes that encourage us to feel that we know her characters, but that really point out the facility with which their complexity is kept before us—and sometimes just beyond our reach.

The leaping and lingering of the ballad tradition suggests the jazz structuring of the novel, where the theme of death has many variations and improvisations upon it as Morrison manifests its meaning for various of the characters. Death is the stable point of this jazz composition, the center to which each year returns in spite of its individual departure. This allowance for individuality within an overall structure contrasts sharply with what is possible for Sula in the Bottom; the community would prefer that she play the straight refrain of the blues rather than the creative deviation allowable with the jazz comparison.

While these structural patterns are illuminating, they do not explain all that happens in the organization of the novel (we could also talk about the structure of a journey, in which Shadrack moves from innocence to experience to innocence, or where Nel moves from innocence to an almost unbearable knowledge); nor do they in any way confine Morrison to identification with these forms. Instead, they show how Morrison has used folk traditions to expand our expectations of what a novel should be and do. That expansion adds a richness and complexity to her work that is frequently absent in the works of other authors who draw upon oral traditions.

Within the structures Morrison devises for her novel, she creates many characters who echo either specific or general concepts from folk tradition. Local characters, such as Sula, and anecdotes about them, are particularly inspiring for Morrison. From Shadrack, who acts as a chorus to open and close this human drama, to the three deweys, Morrison's characters elicit comparison to those from other folk communities and various wonderlands. Communities that designate some of their inhabitants "weirdos," "crazies," and "loonies" have usually observed several traits in them. They are unusual in appearance and/or mannerisms, and frequently in terms of habitat. Youngsters are taught to fear boogie men and women, whose otherness may be defined by something as tangible as alcoholism or as intangible as an assumed ability to cast the evil eye. Some merely outsiders and others pariahs, these characters serve psychological as well as educational functions in their communities; they illustrate the dangers of talking with strangers (the possibility of disappearing into some peculiar abode), and their weirdness soothes the community as it measures its normalcy against their unusualness. That is certainly what the community does to Pecola Breedlove in *The Bluest Eye*; they can gauge how normal and beautiful they are by emphasizing Pecola's insanity and ugliness.

Omniscient narration gives readers an understanding of Shadrack's otherness, but the folks in the Bottom are never so privileged. They know that he went off to war normal and came back abnormal; the whys and wherefores of that transformation are mere abstractions and do not prevent them from defining Shadrack as one of the weirdos, however formed, who demands a special psychological and physical space in their worlds. A man who comes down the street ringing a cowbell and dangling a hanging rope every January third is not exactly an untainted representative of rationality, yet the community incorporates Shadrack's ceremony without diminishing itself or sanctioning him. They take note—from a distance when they can—of his cursing fits and drinking spells.

Still, like the local characters from oral tradition, he is able to make unspoken claims upon the community even as an outsider. The people in the Bottom evince a degree of responsibility for Shadrack (as one of the wounded whose injury is more intense than their own) by buying the fish he catches and by enduring his curses and morbid parades. He provides diversion from their normalcy; though they do not wish to emulate him, his antics make them secure in their own identities. Seeing Shadrack expose his private parts could only make the ladies more appreciative of their husbands' clothing and make the husbands appreciate the covering that prevents them from being evaluated so publicly. Shadrack's cabin by the river could hold out to them a possibility for freedom, but it is negated by their knowledge of his mental cages. Tolerated but not loved, a part of the community but not truly in it, Shadrack exemplifies the type of character around whom legends and anecdotes grow, who is a source of entertainment as well as a source of dread, who seems through his life-style to be imminently dispensable, but who is the epitome of the community penchant for survival.

It is appropriate that Shadrack is seen at the beginning and the ending of the novel, for the white man who made the Bottom a "nigger joke" and perpetuated white domination of black lives is representative of the system that has also overwhelmed Shadrack. His experiences in the army have been more costly than the slave's loss of land, and the effects have gone on longer. Not only has Shadrack been blasted mentally and suffered through more than forty years of that disorientation, but he must now watch with Nel as the remnants of the Bottom give way to a golf course and fancy houses.

In his strangeness, Shadrack is comparable to an overly sensitive poet/philosopher who has seen so much of the horror of life that he has been blasted beyond the reaches of mundane influences. He brings a knowledge to his people, but the ironic price of his experiences is that he has lost his ability to communicate in a language they understand. His bell and rope, initially more disturbing than enlightening, are more of a barrier to Shadrack's desire to impart truth than Tiresias's blindness or Diogenes's lamp. Rather than understanding that death can be put in perspective if it is given its recognizable place in human existence, the black folk of the Bottom are only reminded of its power to separate them from the living, of the mysteries it holds. To them, therefore, Shadrack is a loony who disturbs things that are best left alone; instead of reducing the fear of death, he evokes more.

Shadrack's mental blighting clearly sets him apart from the rest of the community. His insanity becomes one of the distinguishing physical characteristics that black folks have long used to recognize "otherness" in their midst. Such characteristics, like M'Dear's height and isolation from the community in *The Bluest Eye*, connect the possessor to powers beyond those of ordinary means. They hail such persons as conjurers, witches, or devil worshippers. Since the power identified with them can be used for evil as well a benign purposes, it ensures respect for them in the communities in which they dwell, respect that comes from fear or from belief. The inhabitants of the Bottom treat Sula's birthmark as such an indication of other-worldliness and use it to turn her into a witch. Who but a witch, the women probably rationalize, could use their husbands so thoroughly and discard them at whim? Who but a witch would progress to putting Eva in an old folks home?

The initial evidence against Sula is circumstantial, but it offers the beginning of the reinforcement of belief so central to the creation of outsiderness. From calling Sula a "roach" for putting Eva in the old folks home and a "bitch" for sleeping with Jude, the people in the Bottom come to recognize her true witchery when they discover she has slept with white men; that is the ultimate sign of deviation from their norm, and it puts Sula in league with all manner of strange beings. Knowing that strangeness does not mean weakness, they guard themselves accordingly: "So they laid broomsticks across their doors at night and sprinkled salt on porch steps." After a couple of attempts to "collect the dust from her footsteps," perhaps with the intention of using it in a potion against her, they content themselves with the power of gossip. They "know" she has power when Teapot trips and falls on her steps. The extent of her power gets verification in what happens to another neighbor: "Mr. Finely sat on his porch sucking chicken bones, as he had done for thirteen years, looked up, saw Sula, choked on a bone and died on the spot." They conclude that the birthmark over her eye "was Hannah's ashes marking her from the very beginning."

The birthmark explains why Sula is not content with the life the other women in the Bottom lead, why she must travel all over the country in search of something that they cannot begin to imagine. Indeed, her ten-year absence from the Bottom serves to highlight a mysterious, legendary quality about her in the same way that many figures in traditional narratives have some unexplained or missing part of their lives. Sula's difference, like Shadrack's, must be labeled so that the community can go on about its business. Since her neighbors have no words to explain Sula's personality and no previous encounters with anyone who could help them explain it, they label her difference as witchery and thereby justify shunning her. They can also soothe their ambivalent pride when she casts their husbands aside:

> Among the weighty evidence piling up was the fact that Sula did not look her age. She was near thirty and, unlike them, had lost no teeth, suffered no bruises, developed no ring of fat at the waist or pocket at the back of her neck. It was rumored that she had had no childhood diseases, was never known to have chicken pox, croup or even a runny nose. She had played rough as a child—where were the scars? Except for a funny-shaped finger and that evil birthmark, she was free of any normal signs of vulnerability. Some of the men, who as boys had dated her, remembered that on picnics neither gnats or mosquitoes would settle on her. Patsy, Hannah's one-time friend, agreed and said that not only that, but she had witnessed the fact that when Sula drank beer she never belched.

Imagination gives the community diversity from its own stupored monotony; it comes together to make a monster out of difference in the same way that various groups in *Song of Solomon* respond to Pilate's lack of a navel. Sula's "don't give a damn" attitude makes her an easy target for the tales, for she lacks an egotistical concern for reputation. Not interested in fighting back, her very silence gives truth to the rumors as far as the women are concerned. And indeed, they do not really need justification for the tales they tell; rumor exists for its own satisfaction. When Teapot falls down Sula's steps and fractures his skull, it is much more exciting to attribute the incident to witchery than to call it an accident. There is as much pleasure in telling the tales, perhaps more, than in looking into the truth of Sula's life.

The community also judges Sula to be in league with the devil because Shadrack is civil to her. When Dessie sees him tip his hat to Sula, she is convinced that she is witnessing a greeting between two of Satan's disciples. And woe to her that she does so, for a "big sty" is her reward for seeing what she should not have seen. Sula becomes the measure of evil for the community, their catch-all explanation for natural and unnatural occurrences, their chance to triumph, day after day, over the devil in their midst. Sula's place among them is as secure in its deviance as Shadrack's is in its insanity.

While the Bottom may work hard to prove that Sula is a witch, it already has one in its midst. Ajax's mother is reputed to be "an evil conjure woman" who, when Ajax is gone, sits "in her shack with six younger sons working roots." Her knowledge of good and evil is real, whereas the evidence of the knowledge assigned to Sula is "contrived." Perhaps because of her commitment to her sons, and theirs to her, this woman has found a place in the community; Sula is too antithetical to everything they believe in for them to accept her as readily. Ajax's mother would be beautiful, Morrison asserts, if she had any teeth or ever straightened her back, thereby emphasizing that her deviance is not the thing that sets her apart from her feminine self, which is a contrast to Sula. Stephanie A. Demetrakopoulos works through the implications of the masculine/feminine contrast of the two women in her discussion of the novel.

If Shadrack represents the outer realm of the community's obligation and focus, then the deweys represent its center. Shadowy though they may be at times, they are nevertheless firmly entrenched in Eva's house, which provides a center for the Bottom. From a folkloristic perspective, the deweys extend the concept of twins (exemplified in the novel by Sula and Nel) into triplets. As such, they have identical relationships to those around them and serve in identical capacities. It does not matter than Eva asks for *a* dewey to perform a chore, for they are all orphans, dependent, easily intimidated, and as strange as their personalities and Eva's house make them; they are "a trinity with a plural name . . . inseparable, loving nothing and no one but themselves." Made comical by their antics and diminutive size, they remain children into their adult years. In their youth, they provided the comic relief to the mystery surrounding Eva, to the brooding Sula, and to the sexually active Hannah. They are also a part of the joking cycle in the novel, for they illustrate the almost comic perversity with which good intentions are sometimes pervaded. They are wild things in the Bottom, who, as a part of that tables-turned phenomenon, debunk the myth of maternal concern surrounding adoptions. Though Eva provides shelter and food for the dewey's, she is about as much a mother to them as Teapot's Mamma is to him before his encounter with Sula.

The townspeople eventually notice that "the deweys would never grow. They had been forty-eight inches tall for years now." Their size, combined with their acquisition of only the basic, functional command of language, gives their mental otherness a physical dimension. Yet they nevertheless figure more frequently as a concept than as separate entities in the novel; the lower-case references to them reinforce this idea. The question to ask, then, is "What is a dewey?" A dewey is a shadowy presence at 7 Carpenter's Road, hard to visualize but always concretely creating problems or running errands. A dewey is an individual who exists on the borderline between tolerable behavior and trying out for reform school. A dewey is contained lawlessness, just as Shadrack is contained insanity. A dewey is rootless and uncommitted, existing from day to day with no knowledge of past or future. A dewey is an idea manifested in triplets whose very physical appearances defy that appellation. A dewey is the physical manifestation of Eva's power to control the environment around her.

Eva initiates the creation of the deweys as local characters, and Hannah and others perpetuate it when they force the teacher to admit all three youngsters—in spite of their differing ages—into the same grade. The denial of individual dewey reality gives way to one of Eva's pastimes: she creates the concept of the deweys for her own amusement. She names them and thereby determines their fate. Community sanctioning of her joke makes it all the more appealing; it gives Eva a goddess-like characteristic. In that folk-like community of the Bottom, where legends and superstitions abound, the path by which the deweys come to be local characters allows us to glimpse a clear-cut origin that has few counterparts in oral tradition.

In a less dramatic way, Eva also contributes to the community perception of Tar Baby, the white mountain drifter who finds his way into a small back room at 7 Carpenter's Road. As uprooted as Shadrack and the deweys, Tar Baby is another figure about whom tales can develop—Is he really white? Why does he drink? Why does he live in the Bottom rather than in Medallion? What drives him to sing "In the Sweet By-and-By" so pathetically? Eva directs the course of information about Tar Baby's ethnicity and makes a joke of it: "Most people said he was half white, but Eva said he was all white. That she knew blood when she saw it, and he didn't have none. When he first came to Medallion, the people called him Pretty Johnnie, but Eva looked at his milky skin and cornsilk hair and out of a mixture of fun and meanness called him Tar Baby." He provides Eva with another source of amusement. In her confinement to her sprawling house, she brings a world of diversions to fill the space when she does not wish to create her own. Tar Baby and the deweys are perhaps grateful for having the shelter of Eva's home; they desire about as much as she is willing to provide, thereby making her relationship to all of them as informal and as vaguely committed as their otherness and her temperament warrant. She can laugh at them or control them because she is ultimately disinterested in them; as a part of the landscape she has created in that huge house, they have as much or as little claim to belonging as any of the other inhabitants. Like a perverted artist out of a Hawthorne tale, Eva gives them a place in her home as well as a place in the lore of the Bottom; together, they increase Morrison's population of "grotesques," as Darwin T. Turner labels her characters.

However, to label them grotesques is perhaps to miss a fundamental component of the historical black communities that might have inspired the creation of the Bottom. Such communities have a large capacity for containing those unlike themselves, especially if the issue in question concerns sanity. Morrison writes of Shadrack: "Once the people understood the boundaries and nature of his madness, they could fit him, so to speak, into the scheme of things." Shadrack and other characters might be conspicuously different from the norm, but there is a space for them within the larger community. If they do no more than provide a yardstick for measuring acceptable group behavior, they nevertheless serve a function. When the Bottom no longer has Sula to establish its limits of morality, there is a noticeable hole, a palpable emptiness in the community. There was a place for her there, even if that place was not in line with the majority of the community's norms.

What Eva does with the deweys and Tar Baby, together with how the community responds to Sula, enhances the notion that the Bottom is a consciously contrived black folk community in which the folk create and venerate their own traditions, much as the people do in Paule Marshall's mythical Bournehills and in Zora Neale Hurston's Eatonville. Legends, superstitions (signs and beliefs), and rituals combine with the local characters to make *Sula* as akin to historic folk communities as any literary creation can be. In their observance of National Suicide Day, their most prominent ritual, the folks in the Bottom can be compared to contemporary communities observing rituals such as the Fourth of July or Groundhog Day, or to the Bournehillers' annual pageant to celebrate Cuffee Ned's rebellion. Cyclical, repetitive ceremonies provide these communities with a way of defining as well as explaining themselves.

The institutionalization of National Suicide Day is a measure of how thoroughly the community has absorbed Shadrack's strangeness as well as of how quietly that process of absorption takes place. The folks in the Bottom may not mark their wall calendars for the January third ritual, but they internalize the date and its events. Women mark labor and birth by that date as much as slaves in Alabama marked such occurrences by the years the stars fell. Even folks who choose to avoid doing things on National Suicide Day are nonetheless responding to its effect upon them. And the grandmother who maintains that "her hens always started a laying of double yolks right after Suicide Day" contributes her share to the ritual by building a superstitious lore around it. Familiarity and repetition enable the inhabitants of the Bottom to contain National Suicide Day. Initially unable and later unwilling to deny it a place, they soon discover that what seemed horrible was more sounding brass and tinkling cymbal than destructive. Unfortunately, their effort to see National Suicide Day more as symbol than substance backfires on that day in 1941 when Shadrack leads his jubilant followers to a muddy death in the tunnel at the end of the New River Road.

Again Morrison executes a reversal by giving true meaning to an initially farfetched and hollow idea. The respect for death that made Shadrack so crazy after participating in the white man's big war is now paralleled by the "murder" of black people by the whites who commissioned and worked on the tunnel. Over a period of fourteen years, the whites have killed black hopes for working on the new road as well as on the tunnel. Some men have died and others have grown up and gone away while waiting for those hopes to be fulfilled. Their hopes have been as inconsiderable as those of the slave who desired good bottom land. It is perversely fitting, therefore, that National Suicide Day be given the tangible reality that silence and neglect have conferred on it for all those years, and it is equally perversely fitting that the song they sing, "Shall We Gather at the River," is one that has traditionally brought comfort to black people and the expectation that life after this world would be much better than that lived here. When the deweys, Tar Baby, and others die in the tunnel, their deaths denote the end of a particular kind of hope, the end of an era of belief that justice would be done through an unprompted, natural cause. The tunnel catastrophe will provide tales for years to come about the "crazy" black folk of the Bottom who thought they could halt progress with their bodies. The story of their deaths will overshadow many of the tales that sustained these folk during their lifetime.

Just as it created local characters and instituted rituals, the Bottom also has its share of legends. Told for true, these stories take the shape of memorates, a first stage of legend formation in that the details of the narrative have not yet been fully fleshed out (and frequently the teller of the tale can claim to have been an eyewitness to the occurrence). For example, people surmise various causes for the disappearance of Eva's leg, but a prominent, single-stranded, developed story has not been accepted over others. Still, the one detail believed to be true is generally agreed upon: Eva sacrificed her leg for the money that would ensure her family's survival. How that essential fact was brought about is where the accounts differ: "Somebody said Eva stuck it under a train and made them pay off. Another said she sold it to a hospital for $10,000—at which Mr. Reed opened his eyes and asked, 'Nigger gal legs goin' for $10,000 a *piece*?' as though he could understand $10,000 a *pair*— but for *one*?" Sula absorbs the tale about Eva's leg, and, as an adult, uses it to try to equalize the distance between Eva and herself. When Eva claims that nobody can talk to her with disrespect, Sula maintains:

> "This body does. Just 'cause you was bad enough to cut off your own leg you think you got a right to kick everybody with the stump."
> "Who said I cut off my leg?"
> "Well, you stuck it under a train to collect insurance."

Sula turns perhaps the most significant occurrence in Eva's life against her by suggesting that the circumstances surrounding the loss of the leg place Eva in a category similar to Shadrack. The irony is that Eva has contributed to the growth of the lore about her missing leg. When she mentions it, usually "in some mood of fancy, she began some fearful story about it—generally to entertain children. How the leg got up by itself one day and walked on off. How she hobbled after it but it ran too fast. Or how she had a corn on her toe and it just grew and grew and grew until her whole foot was a corn and then it traveled on up her leg and wouldn't stop growing until she put a red rag at the top but by that time it was already at her knee." An active tradition bearer in much of the lore of the Bottom, Eva is no less stinting with tales about herself.

By contrast, Sula's derisive recounting of the tales about Eva's missing leg shows how she breaks with tradition and perhaps even alters the lore in an effort to undercut her biological relationship to Eva. By negatively reinforcing the stories, Sula shows a disrespect not only for Eva, but for the tradition itself. This small exchange illustrates well her severing of ties with the community. The lore is not entertaining for her; she uses it to control Eva's behavior and finally to threaten her. She redefines the function of folklore by telling her stories as a leveling device to gain power over Eva and to diminish her self-concept in the process. She therefore simultaneously devalues the vibrancy and purpose of the oral tradition while strengthening her reputation as a *ba-ad* woman.

Morrison's community has its superstitions and folk beliefs in addition to its folk characters. Traditionally, the natural world has been the logical place for people in folk communities to look for signs and meanings to be revealed to them. The unnatural and peculiar things that happen before Hannah's burning are a sign to Eva that some significant occurrence is about to take place. She cannot find her comb, which is out of its "natural" place; there is an unusually strong wind that does not bring the release of rain; and Hannah dreams of a wedding in which the bride wears a red dress, the color of which Eva will later interpret to mean that it portended Hannah's burning death. Her knowledge that dreams go by opposites strengthens her interpretation of the death; the wedding, a happy occasion, really portends some impending misfortune. The plague of birds before Sula's return to the bottom is looked upon as a portent of evil, for, like Eva, the folks have learned from their closeness to nature, to read its signs and prepare themselves for whatever is coming.

Signs and beliefs such as the wind without rain, the bride in the red dress, the plague of birds, and Eva burning the hair she combs from her head (so that enemies cannot get it and use it to direct spells toward her) might be realistic enough to have their counterparts in *The Frank C. Brown Collection of North Carolina Folklore*, or some other collection, in that there is a demonstrated present occurrence linked to some future disastrous possibility. However, the responses to Sula's birthmark form another kind of belief in the novel, one for which few historical parallels exist. Many characters believe that Sula is evil; when they view the birthmark, they project onto it features reminiscent of those assigned to boogie men. To Nel's impressionable children, Sula's birthmark is a "scary black thing"; Jude views it as a copperhead and as a rattlesnake when he sees Sula as a potentially dangerous element introduced into his home; and the people in the Bottom view it as "Hannah's ashes." Such reactions contribute to making Sula into a legend in the community. The mark becomes as distinguishing as any of those, such a blue or red eyes, limps, or warts, that Newbell Niles Puckett identified in his discussions of distinctive features of conjurers.

Through her creation of characters like Eva, Sula, Shadrack, and the deweys, and the legends and tales surrounding them, Morrison shows that folklore can be used for purposes of enhancing characterization, advancing plot, and putting forth themes. Such functions have been recognized by folklore scholars Alan Dundes and Hennig Cohen in their early studies of folklore and literature. Yet Morrison goes further in attempting to recreate the very atmosphere in which folk cultures, with all their layers and characters, blossom and grow. Like Ernest Gaines in many of his works, she makes her characters and her community the substance of a pervasive aura of folk traditions, a saturation frequently recognized more by suggestion than specifics, but that succeeds very well in showing Morrison's ties to black folk culture.

How to Become a Legend in Your Own Time

In its logic that defies syllogistic equations and in its morality that approximates amorality, if not immorality, the world Morrison has created in *Sula* shares similarities, in its interpersonal relationships, to some of the realms inhabited by the likes of Brer Rabbit and other creatures who do not adhere to the fundamentalist teachings of Protestant churches. Brer Rabbit is independent in a world where community cooperation is the norm; he frequently acts against the wishes of the community or takes advantage of their work. For example, in the tale where he steals milk or butter from the other animals during a joint farming venture, he either denies his guilt or blames Brer Possum for the offense and personally leads the act of revenge against Brer Possum. He is without compunction for shirking work as well as for leading the assault against Brer Possum. He does as he pleases, guided by what suits him rather than by any communally accepted ethical system.

The trinity of women who share the spotlight in *Sula*—Eva, Hannah, and Sula—have much in common with this world view. Their breaks from expected codes of behavior also enable them to transcend the usual depictions of black women in African-American literature, thereby debunking numerous stereotypes and myths. Eva is a slap in the face to all traditional matriarchs, for there is no God-centered morality informing her actions; yet she is paradoxically matriarchal in the power she wields as she sits "in a wagon on the third floor directing the lives of her children, friends, strays, and a constant stream of boarders." Hannah defies expectations of matronly morality by randomly sleeping with her neighbors' husbands. She also defies expectations of how a mother should feel by asserting that she loves but does not *like* her daughter. Sula, though, is the epitome of independence; she throws the community's morality back in its face by redefining behavior. She, therefore, most closely approximates the world in which Brer Rabbit lives. In her disrespect for traditional mores, in her casual use of people around her, in her refusal to feel guilty for any of her actions, Sula exhibits the folk logic and the folk amorality of the trickster.

The peculiarly moral world view of African-Americans, especially as it relates to women, has perhaps prevented the appearance of many female trickster figures. Since women essentially held the group together during difficult periods of black history in America, to depict a female who stole, robbed, or killed would have had the effect of undermining the basic survival of the group. Instead, the focus was on male tricksters, and the violence associated with Brer Rabbit became the violence traditionally identified with the male world of competition and war. Still, a few female tricksters, such as Aunt Dicy, survived, and a few women clearly adopted the survival strategies of Brer Rabbit. Black women historically could, if forced to, steal for their children—though their motives were certainly more altruistic than Brer Rabbit's; he sometimes used his children (or imaginary ones) as the excuse for amoral actions. And we know that a few women did poison their masters and that a few killed their children to prevent them from becoming slaves. Many workers in white homes wore the mask of acquiescence to cover clandestine activities designed to aid their families, such as appropriating food and clothing.

In contemporary literature, three such characters are Ellie and Vi in Douglas Turner Ward's *Happy Ending* (1964), and Mrs. Grace Love in Ted Shine's *Contribution* (1969). These women resort to role-playing characteristic of the trickster in order to acquire food and clothing for their families and to bring about the deaths of some of their white employers. Both Ward and Shine show the breakdown of traditional morality, but their characters nonetheless adhere to a logical, more flexible standard of behavior. Morrison's women similarly refuse to be bound by traditional morality or traditional roles. In their new guises, then, they exhibit the freedom, the ability to make or create themselves, that is more closely associated with black folk culture than with historical black communities.

Eva certainly starts out as a traditional mother. She tries desperately to keep her family alive after her husband's departure, but her efforts very shortly become ineffectual. Her redefinition of role begins with her depositing her three children with a neighbor and not returning for eighteen months. She chooses self over sacrifice, borders on immorality, and therefore becomes free. Her separation from people in the community and acting against their norms enable her to develop an ironic posture in relation to them; she can live with them because she is now superior to them. Her freedom, somehow tied to the loss of her leg, gives her the ability to love, hate, create, conquer, and kill, with responsibility and accountability only to herself. She is free to be moral if she wishes, amoral if it pleases her, and immoral if necessary. Her transformation is like Cholly Breedlove's when he becomes free through killing three white men; he has stretched the bonds of humanity and can now accept or discard them at will.

The first test of Eva's newfound transcendence of human bonds comes when her husband BoyBoy visits the year after Eva returns. She watches his cool, big-city ways, and his shallow arrogance in bringing his lover with him, and consciously, deliberately decides to hate him: "Knowing that she would hate him long and well filled her with pleasant anticipation, like when you know you are going to fall in love with someone and you wait for the happy signs. Hating BoyBoy, she could get on with it, and have the safety, the thrill, the consistency of that hatred as long as she wanted or needed it to define and strengthen her or protect her from routine vulnerabilities." Hatred keeps her "alive and happy." In making hate into a positive and sustaining emotion and motivation, much as Claude McKay does in his poetry, Eva inverts notions of right and wrong, thereby standing morality on its head and identifying with the folkways that defy absoluteness in behavior.

Eva has no vengeful God watching over her, ready to cast down fire and brimstone in punishment for her deviation from a traditional path. Rather, she is on her way to becoming a goddess, one whose self-creation has been inspired in part by her hatred of BoyBoy. She therefore forces other men to worship where her husband has not—literally at her feet. Such domination—sometimes subtle and sometimes not—is again one of the traits of the rebel who has destroyed human bonds and reshaped them to suit her. Eva presents the many men who visit her over the years with a tantalizing morsel that they will never have the opportunity to savor. By encouraging their presence and flirting with them, Eva assures herself of the male attention that must unwaveringly atone for BoyBoy's desertion. She manifests her hatred and scorn of men in what they see as her attraction for them, her inability to live without their attention. Her attitude toward them is not unlike that of Erzulie, the Haitian goddess of love, who demands great sacrifices of her devotees.

The provocative dynamic at work is that Eva uses the men while they believe they are bestowing their masculine attention upon her. Only a mind that has transcended mundane evaluations of the need for men in her life could effect the revenge Eva does. The freedom that has made hatred a virtue begins Eva's movement toward separation from other human bonds. Like Cross Damon in Richard Wright's *The Outsider* (1953), Eva can now assume the position of passing judgment upon others; in the process, she has put herself beyond similar judgment In the ultimate elevation to goddess, however, she appropriates the power over life and death.

In deciding that her son Plum would be better off dead, Eva recognizes no authority, no morality except herself. Plum's drug addiction offends her sense of what a man should be, especially someone she had forced to keep on living when he was a baby and for whom she had probably sacrificed her leg. To see such sacrifices thrown back into her face negates the very existence Eva has carved out for herself. In the mixture of love and revulsion surrounding her burning of Plum, Eva egotistically eliminates what offends her. No matter the motivation, her killing of Plum is just as self-centered as those murders committed by Cross Damon. Eva becomes the vengeful goddess in destroying a creature who has failed to worship in an appropriate manner at her altar. Like Satan in Mark Twain's "The Mysterious Stranger," she "blots out" what would defile her existence. If Plum were to live a healthy and drug-free life, Eva believes that would be a small price to pay in compensation for her loss of a leg and a husband, and for having suffered other indignities during those unmentionable eighteen months.

Plum's death is a blood sacrifice—whether that ritualized conception is clear in Eva's mind or not. She never considers rehabilitation for her son; the effrontery of his misuse of his life is sufficient for her to take it. She rewards those who serve her well; she casts aside those who do not. That is the distinction between her murder of Plum and her risking of her own life to save Hannah's. Hannah, Eva's oldest child, has served her mother well; after her husband's death, she had moved back into Eva's house "prepared to take care of it and her mother forever." She has also accepted the "manlove" bequeathed to her and has carried out, vicariously, the sexual activity to which Eva may allude but from which she has been restrained by infirmity and inclination. Thus shaped in the image of the goddess and responsive to her wishes, Hannah earns Eva's greatest sacrifice.

Also, in killing Plum and trying to save Hannah, Eva exhibits a preference for the woman-centered consciousness that pervades most of the novel. Perhaps Plum, in his addiction, is too sharp a reminder of the ineffectuality of BoyBoy as husband and father. Perhaps Eva sees history about to repeat itself in him. Her contemplation of "no-count" males, then, is further motivation for Eva to end a seemingly useless life. With deliberation, she murders Plum, but her attempt to save Hannah is instinctive, borne of an intuitive identification with her daughter. Since Sula has already established her tendency to otherness, Eva perhaps senses that Hannah is the last opportunity for her to perpetuate something in her own image—or at least some portions of it. She also sees that, through Hannah, more of the vengeance against men is carried out In her sexual freedom, Hannah parallels Eva in being independent of the community's mores, in finding no code of behavior except that inspired by her own desires.

In any world but the one Morrison has created, Hannah Peace would be considered a slut. However, Morrison does not allow such a moral judgment in the novel. Hannah becomes an acceptable embodiment of a pleasure principle; the women may be "exasperated" with her because she "seemed too unlike them, having no passion attached to her relationships and being wholly incapable of jealousy," but even the whores who resent her "generosity" and the church women who call her "nasty" are not inclined to believe that she is evil. Her reputation for kindness and altruism counterbalances the brief affairs she has with the husbands of her friends and neighbors. Although she has few women friends, she does not appear to be lonely or isolated. She has a secure place in the community in spite of the prevailing disapproval.

Hannah, like Eva, lives by her own set of rules. She does not equate promiscuity with immorality; it is simply a matter of getting "some touching every day," which she had determined to do after her husband's death. Still, no matter the aura of earthiness surrounding Hannah's actions, they are nonetheless antithetical to the tenets of her community. Her sexual independence makes her a disruptive force in a quiet place like the Bottom, where everybody's business is everybody's business. Hannah's disregard of expected codes of behavior makes her a rebel, albeit a tolerable one. In seeking to satisfy only herself, her desire is not far removed in kind from the likes of those trickster figures for whom sexual superiority (if not the act itself) was one of the primary motivating forces; Brer Rabbit's amoral exploits frequently involve winning the hand of a female, and he can be unscrupulous in achieving his goals. Hannah's casual attitude may be sweeter, but it certainly achieves a similar satisfaction for her.

Hannah weakens the structure of the community's morality, but she does not completely topple it. That is evident in the way the women whose husbands she has slept with take care of her body after she is burned to death: "the women who washed the body and dressed it for death wept for her burned hair and wrinkled breasts as though they themselves had been her lovers." Perhaps they are awed in the face of death, but perhaps, too, they unconsciously respect the rebel in Hannah; she has done what their ties to church and community strictures would not allow them to do. She may have thrown their morality in their faces, but she is simultaneously one of them and more than they are; she has become a legend. In taking their men, Hannah had formed an unacknowledged bond with these women in which they showed their appreciation for the same things, slightly comparable to the way in which Sula and Nel share and compare boys when they are teenagers. Hannah's attention to their men, since she is the embodiment of WOMAN, is a way of "complimenting the women" on their good taste. Her deviation from the norm, therefore, no matter how immoral, is still not as personally insulting to the women as are Sula's actions.

Sula begins her separation from the community and follows a different set of rules with the death of Chicken Little. Certainly she feels remorse for the accidental drowning of Chicken, but in her refusal to confess or ask for forgiveness from any source (even herself), the incident becomes a measure of how far an individual can live outside the dictates of a community's morality and still be "safe." Confession and acceptance of responsibility for the death would at least have been recognition of values, of a morality outside of herself, recognition that an individual has voluntary ties to the community in which she lives and must respond to those ties whether or not someone demands that she do so. The absence of "punishment" for Chicken's death signals to Sula that she can do what she wants. Life, death, responsibility, the limits of behavior—all are contained in Chicken Little's death. Once Sula ignores them and moves into a realm of her own unrestrained seeking and exploration, she is forever outside the world view of the Bottom.

When she returns after her sojourn, therefore, it is because she has exhausted the possibility for freshness of experience; she may as well be back in the Bottom if human beings she encounters elsewhere do not deviate substantially from those she has left. She returns content to continue, among the native population, whatever explorations are left. Her indifference and irresponsibility encourage the neighbors to believe that she is a witch. She is so unlike the women in her community—so young where they have aged, so thin where they are large, so complete unto herself where they need husbands and children—that they link her to extranatural forces and can never envision her sleeping with their husbands as a compliment to themselves. Instead, they view her as a sexual experimenter, someone who is picking through the men in the town the way a shopper selects tomatoes. She touches and discards each of them because none measures up to whatever undefined standard she uses for judgment.

In her indifferent and experimental behavior, there is more vengeance in Sula than in Hannah, a vengeance all the more cruel because it does not consciously identify itself as such. Sula does not respect the men enough, is not interested enough in them, to give conscious direction to her vengeance. Its very effectiveness is in its static quality, which serves to deny the manhood and nearly the humanity of the men with whom she sleeps, and it certainly denies any ties she has to the community. More so than Eva, she is the love goddess who perverts that name, who can never find a worthy mate among the puny pickings available to her. In a world in which people are tied to each other as often by their lacks (needing to borrow an egg or a cup of sugar) as by their bountifulness (giving a neighbor a mess of greens or corn), Sula's wholeness amounts to her telling the community to go to hell.

Of the three Peace women, Sula is more clearly immoral, because she sees herself as the center of the universe around which other people can revolve or not—as she needs or uses them. Eva's actions had at least been motivated by love for her children and hatred for her husband, and Hannah fulfilled a physical need in sleeping with so many men. Sula simply is—whatever she decides is convenient or desirable or pleasurable. None of her motivations comes from caring about or hating or fearing anyone. She is simply in the community; what it does or how it responds to her is of no consequence to her. The only reactions she has concerning other people are her slight remorse that Nel has responded so unexpectedly to her sleeping with Jude and feeling that she has become possessive enough of Ajax to drive him away.

If she were separated geographically from the community, as M'Dear is in The *Bluest Eye*, or like Shadrack is, Sula's difference might be more tolerable, but her placement in the center of the community, in Eva's house, makes her conspicuously a little world revolving unto itself. Still, Sula is consistent in living by the philosophy she has evolved for herself; when she becomes ill, she does not turn for assistance to the people she has ignored all along. Instead, she suffers alone. It is only upon Nel's visit that she requests medicine, and she does so with pride, not with the humility of an outsider. What Nel judges to be arrogance even in the face of death is really the logical carrying out of the philosophy Sula has adhered to all along. She has not whined or complained loudly about life, and she refuses to complain about death or the manner in which she is dying. It is all a part of the experiment that has been accountable only to itself, not to anyone or anything beyond her. That spirit, basically antithetical to the tenets of the community and to most human relationships, is what ultimately serves to make Sula a pariah. The greatest measure of her lack of status is the way people respond to her death. The do not come running to wash the body or lay it out; instead, they leave the work to the white people. We need only think of the loving way in which Aunt Jimmy is laid out in *The Bluest Eye* to understand the importance of funeral rituals and mourning to these communities. When the neighbors gather to sing at Sula's funeral, it is not out of respect for her but the contin-uation of a tradition much larger than their momentary rejection of Sula, for they are determined not to let anything "keep them from their God."

In a world in which logic is sometimes familiar and sometimes not, that which guides the actions of the Peace women and the community's response to them is similarly ambivalent, if not contradictory. In a world in which whim matters as much as premeditation, confusion results. Ultimately, we may understand and be engaged by all of the Peace women, but they are finally unacceptable except as reflections of a community that is dying. Sula carries no values that would sustain a society; Hannah would chip away at any established values; and Eva is too harsh, if not warped, in her judgments to create any but a very narrow world. While we may withhold judgment of their individual trespasses, the accumulations of their world views reflect the license-free, sometimes destructive, interactions characteristic of African-American folk culture, not their realistic counterparts for behavior.

Of Purification and Exorcism:
The Limited Powers of Fire and Water

In almost every one of the years Morrison pauses upon in *Sula*, a death occurs. The end of life becomes awesome because few of the deaths are due to natural causes or reflect a graceful demise; all of them are violent. They are also tied to fire or water, traditional symbols of purification, which become destructive when used to excess. Continuing the pattern of reversal that defines the structure of the novel, Morrison depicts deaths that negate the traditional rites associated with fire and water. Excess becomes the norm—characters are baptized into death rather than life, into stagnation rather than activity.

The fire that Eva sets to kill Plum succeeds in destroying him, but it also becomes a blot upon her soul. Plum may be removed from his misery, but his death has not brought a purification for the Peace household. The burning negates Eva's willingness to endure her son's suffering, and, from Hannah's point of view, it negates motherly affection. It creates a gap in family ties that culminates in Hannah questioning Eva about the death and in Sula accusing Eva of murder and threatening to eliminate her in the same manner. If Eva's crying explanation to Hannah can be believed, it is clear that the burning has not served as the cleansing release she desired. Rather, it has left her with an unmelting lump of grief, undissolvable and unconfessable to any comforter outside of family members.

As the sacrificial ritual plays itself out, Plum is as willing to die as Eva is to kill him. To his addict-blurred vision, Eva seems to be bestowing a blessing upon him: "He opened his eyes and saw what he imagined was the great wing of an eagle pouring a wet lightness over him. Some kind of baptism, some kind of blessing, he thought. Everything is going to be all right, it said. Knowing that it was so he closed his eyes and sank back into the bright hole of sleep." The kerosene dousing amounts to the giving of last rites before Eva lights the torch in a ritual designed to erase all traces of her son. She could just as easily have killed him with a knife, or with poison, or with an overdose of the heroin he uses. Instead, she chooses fire, with its potential for total obliteration of Plum and his drug paraphernalia. An ancient ceremony for eliminating evil or the diseased from the midst of society, Eva's use of it backfires because Plum's death only makes memory vivid. She cannot destroy what she carries in her mind without destroying herself.

The second death by fire, Hannah's burning, is also a reversal of the expected release that weather and circumstances have portended. The strange evens that Eva notices prior to Hannah's burning include a roof-rattling wind: "people waited up half the night for the first crack of lightning. Some had even uncovered barrels to catch the rain water, which they loved to drink and cook in. They waited in vain, for no lightning no thunder no rain came. The wind just swept through, took what dampness there was out of the air, messed up the yards, and went on." The expected rain turns into the fire of Hannah's burning, not the release of cooling water. Formerly consumed by passion, Hannah ironically turns into a self-contained inferno, fueled by the breeze she creates in trying to escape herself.

Eva's inability to save her daughter leads to another reversal—not the diminution of grief over time, but a sharpened focus upon it. The man who saves Eva's life boasts of "an indisputable fact which she herself admitted and for which she cursed him every day for thirty-seven years thereafter and would have cursed him for the rest of her life except by then she was already ninety years old and forgot things." There is no cleansing, no purification here; even the body of the lovely Hannah Peace is changed into a blistery, bubbly thing in respect of which the coffin remains closed at the funeral.

The death by fire also separates Eva and Sula across a chasm that can never be bridged. While Eva fought so desperately to save Hannah, she remembers seeing Sula watch her mother burn, "not because she was para-lyzed," as the neighbors tried to explain, "but because she was interested." Hannah's death burns away whatever bonds of kinship Eva and Sula have, except biologically.

Water, traditional symbol of life, is also frequently associated with death in *Sula*. It brings death and baptism into secrecy about Chicken Little's death, and it brings death to the people who make Shadrack's National Suicide Day a reality. These tunnel deaths mirror the death of the towns-people's dream that the Bottom will ever be connected to Medallion in an economically beneficial way. Their dreams of steady jobs go down under the rush of water that takes so many of their lives.

On the occasion that Chicken Little drowns, the peacefulness of the water belies its destructive capabilities—it opens up and quietly closes "over the place where Chicken Little sank." The quiet here certainly contrasts sharply with the rotting, deteriorating corpse of Chicken Little brought home a few days later, but it manifests itself in a tangible way in Sula's and Nel's minds. Repeatedly, the smoothness of the water into which Chicken Little sank is referred to as a "place," as if there is actually a marker there: "she stood looking at the closed place in the water"; "the dark closed place in the water"; "the closed place in the water spread before them"; "on the bank of a river with a closed place in the middle"; "the closed place in the water"; "water closing quickly over the place." But the marker is something that Nel and Sula carry with them in their common guilt, their common enjoyment, of what has happened to Chicken Little.

Chicken becomes a sacrifice to Sula and Nel's friendship, for there has been an accidental/intentional aura surrounding the drowning. On that day, Sula and Nel had been experiencing growing pains and were "looking for mischief." An "unspeakable restlessness and agitation held them" before Chicken arrived at their play site by the river, and they had both joined in mimicking him when he asserted that he would share his tree-climbing venture with his "brovver." Initially separated at Chicken's funeral, the girls then form an inseparable bond, one tied to Chicken's death: "They held hands and knew that only the coffin would lie in the earth; the bubbly laughter and the press of fingers in the palm would stay aboveground forever." They will be reminded of Chicken's enjoyment of Sula's swinging him as well as the responsibility that both she and Nel have for his death. The signal that they will be bonded in secrecy surfaces quickly as they walk home from the funeral; "they relaxed slowly until during the walk back home their fingers were laced in as gentle a clasp as that of any two young girl-friends trotting up the road on a summer day wondering what happened to butterflies in the winter."

The image of secrecy, grief, and sharing is realized as muddy leaves that crystallize for Nel in the little ball of fur after Jude's infidelity with Sula. Rather than a baptism or purification, the water reminds Nel and Sula of their playful killing of Chicken Little. Water that should cleanse and purify instead leads to a clogging of human emotions, a beaver's dam on the souls of the two girls. That initial blockage for Sula takes the form of not caring enough about people to be truly interested in them, an emotional constipation and superficial existence comparable to that of Avey Johnson in Paule Marshall's *Praisesong for the Widow* (1983). For Nel, the blockage is the bond she shares with Sula, which suggests that they will always be faithful to each other because of their secret; it represents a place held sacred for the entrance of only one other. When Sula sleeps with Jude, then, and breaks that bond, thereby creating a disrespect for the secret, the water imagery returns to haunt Nel in the form of muddy leaves trying to stir, which in turn are transformed into the gray ball initially described in similar muddy images: "a gray ball hovering just there. Just there. To the right. Quiet, gray, dirty. A ball of muddy strings, but without weight, fluffy but terrible in its malevolence."

The gray ball follows her for more than twenty years before she realizes that her love for Sula, what they have shared together (especially the killing of Chicken Little), takes precedence over the emotional blockage separating them. With realization comes release and the combining of the two images: "Leaves stirred; mud shifted; there was the smell of overripe green things. A soft ball of fur broke and scattered like dandelion spores in the breeze." It gives way to crying that has "circles and circles of sorrow" that evoke, in their concentric image, the place in the water where Chicken Little has drowned. Chicken Little and Jude are what both women have shared, one in the greenness of their girlhood ("overripe green things") and the other in their adulthood. Only Sula was able to realize that the basic tenet of sharing had not changed; if they could keep a secret as dark as Chicken Little's death and survive, then they should be able to survive the presumed infidelity with Jude. When Nel understands the connection, the blockage can be released—just as Avey Johnson's bowels and bladder give way on the boat to Carriacou—and the cleansing, the purification identified with water and baptism, can be effected. Assuredly, Nel is baptized into grief, but it is a grief that portends a conclusion, not one that will persist in stagnation for another twenty-five years. What began in Chicken Little's death by water eventually leads to Nel's rebirth through cleansing tears, a rebirth that at least brings an understanding of her life and of her best love.

The other deaths by water in the book are surrounded by irony, lost hope, and lost dreams. It is ironic in 1941 that Shadrack is able to get the citizens of the Bottom to follow him in his National Suicide Day ritual; never before had they been so playful or so tolerant of his obeisance to death. In following him to a wet, smothering grave, they simultaneously give meaning to his ritual and signal the death of their community. The water symbolic of life takes nearly thirty people to a denial of rebirth and regeneration except in an afterlife. Ironically, they who had intended to kill the tunnel that represented so many false promises to the town are themselves killed. Their suicide/death carries the ambivalence characteristic of this elemental force that can be beneficial if controlled or deadly in excess.

It is ironic, too, that the folks who have believed so fervently in God have one of the most potent symbols of their religion turned against them. "Shall We Gather at the River" is indicative of the assumption that they will one day reach and cross the chilly Jordan. It is the song sung at Sula's funeral in an act that is simultaneously ironic and affirming. No one believes that Sula will cross the Jordan, but they appropriately sing a song fundamental to their religion at a funeral characteristic of their beliefs. Sula gets the benefit of something in which she does not believe, and the townspeople are self-righteously able to congratulate themselves for being generous even to one of the devil's disciples.

Ironically, though, it is not the chilly Jordan at which the righteous gather; it is the chilly construction site of a tunnel of unfulfilled promises, and it is a river of their own making. The river is not symbolic of having lived and worked faithfully in God's vineyard, but of the frustration that has attended their lives in this world. The tunnel represents the "leaf-dead" promises of jobs that have been made to them and ignored, which have resulted in "the teeth unrepaired, the coal credit cut off, the chest pains unat-tended, the school shoes unbought, the rush-stuffed mattresses, the broken toilets, the leaning porches, the slurred remarks and the staggering childish malevolence of their employers. All there in blazing sunlit ice rapidly becoming water." In their effort to kill the tunnel already being overtaken by water, the people of the Bottom create the catastrophe that leaves a huge number of them dead. Their deaths by water bring the end to Shadrack's compartmentalization of death and make destructively immediate and irrev-ocable a symbolism to which they have adhered.

CAROLYN M. JONES

Sula *and* Beloved:
Images of Cain in the Novels of Toni Morrison

In *The Mark of Cain*, Ruth Mellinkoff rejects the single modern image of
Cain. She examines Hesse's *Demian* as an "intentionally distorted" treatment of the myth. In Hesse's novel, she claims:

> the interpreter has designed his interpretation to serve his own
> purpose—a self-conscious twisting to achieve personal ends.
> Clarification or elaboration of biblical texts is not the primary
> goal; rather, biblical elements are used to enhance the inter-
> preter's particular point of view about something he is critical
> of in his contemporary society.

Displacements of myth in contemporary fiction, however, are not distor-
tions but are intertextual examinations of the place and function of myth
in contemporary life. Myth as a point of reference is archetypal memory,
fixed in time and space; but as writers utilize myth, they signify on it,
displace its original meanings. This displacement, as Charles Long
explains, "gains its power of meaning from the structure of the discourse
itself without the signification being subjected to the rules of the
discourse." This allows "the community [to] undercut this legitimized
signification with a signification upon this legitimated signifying." Thus,

From *African American Review* 27, no. 4 (Winter 1993). © 1993 by Carolyn M. Jones.

the minority writer or community may emphasize a meaning or an implication of a myth that the "master narrative," the ideological script that the Western world imposes on "others," refuses to consider, and may signify the original meaning into the background, giving primary authority to the signification over the master's trope. Thinking and writing about myth in the modern world is, to use Henry Louis Gates's term, double-voiced, representing a process of both repetition and revision.

Thinking on Cain has been subject to this process of signification. Writers, working with the Biblical myth, have focused on the meaning and form of Cain's mark. Various answers for what the mark was have been offered—either a mark on Cain's forehead or a blackening of Cain's face, connecting him with Ham as a father of the black race. Cain himself has been called the mark, a pariah identifiable by his marked body—either his trembling, groaning, or incessant wandering. Yet, what strikes me about the Cain myth, reading it in a hermeneutical and intertextual relationship to Morrison's *Sula* and *Beloved* is Cain's complete refusal to remember and mourn. Cain denies responsibility both for his brother and for his act: "Am I my brother's keeper?" (Genesis 4.9). And he seeks to protect himself: "Lord, my punishment is greater than I can bear" (Genesis 4.13). Cain, concerned with self, lets sin in the door, but more importantly, he refuses to acknowledge his effect on the "other"; he refuses to remember and to mourn his brother Abel.

This refusal marks him, and tattoo becomes taboo: He is set apart as both dangerous and holy.

Sethe and Sula, both victims and victimizers, reenact the myth of Cain. Sethe is the beloved slave who is "remarked" as an animal when Schoolteacher's odious nephews drink her breast milk while Schoolteacher "remarks," writes down her reactions, using the ink that Sethe herself made. They then mark the experience on her body, whipping her and creating a chokeberry tree on her back. Sethe's mark limits her. It is the sign of her slavery, and with the return of Beloved, it traps her in 124 Bluestone. Sula, with her rose birthmark, is denied identity by her mother, and she murders a childhood friend, throwing him accidentally into the Ohio River. Yet Sula, in contrast to Sethe, claims absolute freedom, which is symbolized by her mark. Both Sethe and Sula commit Cain's act, although they do not act out of jealousy as Cain does. Sethe acts out of pure desperation, and Sula, who feels Cain's sense of rejection, kills accidentally. They also bear Cain's mark, a mark that sets each woman apart both from person identity and community, and each must undergo mourning and memory to find and define the self.

Understanding and transcending the mark has to do with coming to terms with the past. Memory is a special and essential category for Toni Morrison. To "rememory" is to make an act of the moral imagination and to shape the events of one's life into story. Even events that must be put behind one must be subjected to the formative power of memory then "disremembered," put into their proper place in the individual's life. The process of mourning is a special and essential kind of memory, because it creates a hermeneutic between the self and the "other." As Deborah E. McDowell says, "the process of mourning and remembering . . . leads to intimacy with the self, which is all that makes intimacy with others possible." Yet both Sethe and Sula forsake this intimacy. Sethe, alone at the grave of the child she murdered, trades ten minutes of sex for seven letters: Beloved. Later, at the funeral of Baby Suggs, Sethe refuses to accept the support of the community, and members of the community, in turn, abandon her. Sethe feels that she has no self, except in the role of mother. Sula, a rejected child who becomes a woman who refuses to be defined by anyone except herself, sits apart as Chicken is mourned and, later, dies alone. Both women deny themselves and are denied a sense of self and a place in the community. Sula finds her uncentered and unbounded existence is one of exile, and she seeks boundaries in herself, in the community of Medallion, and in her friend Nel; Sethe finds that motherhood is not an affirmation of her identity but another manifestation of her mark.

When Paul D, the man whose compassion is his blessedness, stands behind Sethe, holding her breasts and kissing the chokeberry tree on her back, he is affirming Sethe's whole self, though the course of the novel is run before Sethe herself can make this affirmation. Sethe's sense of her identity comes from denying the chokeberry tree, which is completely dead to feeling, and from affirming her breasts, her role as mother, having "milk enough for all." The victim becomes the victimizer as she, having enjoyed twenty-eight days of freedom, sees Schoolteacher coming to take her and her children back to Sweet Home plantation. A terrified Sethe takes her children to the coal shed at the back of 124 Bluestone Road and cuts the throat of her "almost crawling!" baby girl. The "lessons" of Sweet Home and the murder are what Sethe avoids. She, thus, traps herself in time and in space, in a house haunted by her baby's ghost, keeping the past at bay and losing the future, "not having any dreams of her own." Paul D begins to break apart this stagnation and to chase away the spirit, but he cannot do Sethe's rememory for her. Beloved, though she has many dimensions, is memory: the child that Sethe murdered comes to demand explanation, the child, that, as Mae Henderson says, Sethe must rebirth in her remarking on her own story.

Sethe thinks she is "junkheaped . . . because she loved her children," but though her individual "sin" is murder, her community sin is her pride.

Baby Suggs, Sethe's mother-in-law, begins the cycle of pride. Baby's motto is "'Good is knowing when to stop,'" but she violates that maxim when Sethe and Denver arrive safely at her house. Brought buckets of blueberries by Stamp Paid, she and Sethe make a feast for the entire community, and the satiated community becomes suspicious of the Suggs family. The animosity created by this excess is a second origin of Beloved. Baby Suggs smells the anger of the community, but behind it smells Beloved, a ghost in black shoes. The community does not warn Baby that the slavecatchers are coming to her house and, thus, participates in the murder of the child.

Sethe compounds this sin of pride and alienation when Baby Suggs dies. The community will not enter the house, so Sethe refuses to go to the funeral. At the graveside, the community does not sing for Baby and to support Sethe, so Sethe does not eat their food, and they do not eat hers. A funeral is a ritual of mourning which binds the individual and the community in an act of remembrance and which, potentially, is a point of reconciliation. Here, both Sethe and her community deny themselves this opportunity. Each refuses to engage in the rememory that will articulate Baby Suggs's place in the public sphere and that will honor her spirit as an ancestor. Thus, the individuals are denied access to her power in their private lives. There is loss on both sides. By ostracizing Sethe, the community commits a sin of pride against Baby Suggs, and Sethe, in her pride, freezes memory and makes her life stagnant. In essence, both are marked, both become images of Cain. For Sethe, this mark is deep, for it completely isolates her. Ella, for example, understands Sethe's rage but not Sethe's decision to refuse the help of the black community. Neither does she understand Sethe's act. Ella believes Sethe's rage to have been prideful and misdirected.

In Sethe's act, blood and breast milk, rage, pride, and love become one. When Sethe tells the story of her escape, she stresses that she did it alone, out of love for the children: Nobody could take care of them like she could. Nobody could nurse them like she could. Nobody else would mother them like Sethe. Like Odysseus, who cries "Nobody" and must become "Nobody," Sethe loses herself in her mother role. Morrison says that Sethe is a:

> woman [who] loved something other than herself so much [that] she had placed all of the value of her life in something outside herself . . . [This is] interesting because the best thing that is in us is also the thing that makes us sabotage ourselves, sabotage in the sense that our life is not as worthy, or our perception of the best part of ourselves . . . what is it that really compels a good woman to displace the self, her self?

For Sethe, the tree on her back is nothing compared to the fact that Schoolteacher's boys took her milk, but we realize that the two emblems are the same. The primary, destructive connection of mark and milk is illustrated as Denver, the miracle child born while Sethe is running north, from Sethe's breast right after the murder of Beloved, taking in her sister's blood with her mother's milk. Enacting her extreme and exclusive self-definition as mother, Sethe becomes what Schoolteacher defined her as: an animal without memory. Baby Suggs tells us that "'Good is knowing when to stop.'" Sethe's love, like Cain's for God, becomes one with Sethe's pride and rage. Sethe argues that, by killing her baby, she kept her safe from the dehumanization of slavery. The children are her only self, her "best things"—she claims she "wouldn't draw breath without [her] children"—and she will destroy rather than surrender them. Paul D, listening to the story thinks that more important than Sethe's act is her claim, that maybe there is some worse than slavery. And there is.

Stamp Paid tells us that whites so feared the black people they enslaved that they had to deny completely the humanity of blacks. So whites, whom Baby Suggs says have no limits, are savages, and project onto blacks that savagery:

> . . . it wasn't the jungle that blacks brought with them to this place from the other (livable) place. It was the jungle whitefolks planted in them. And it grew. It spread. In, through and after life, it spread, until it invaded the whites who had made it. Touched them every one. Changed and altered them. Made them bloody, silly, worse than even they wanted to be, so scared were they of the jungle they had made. The screaming baboon lived under their own white skin; the red gums were their own.
>
> Meantime, the secret spread of this new kind of whitefolks' jungle was hidden, silent, except once in a while you could hear its mumbling in places like 124.

The "worse sin" is to let that jungle loose. What is worse than slavery is to let the soul become so contorted that the only self you are is the self that the master defines for you. Sethe stops the Schoolteacher, but she destroys her child and nearly herself. Paul D tells Sethe that she has two legs, not four; she is human, not animal. Accepting Schoolteacher's definition of herself creates Sethe's "thick love," the love that is "safety with a handsaw" and that keeps Sethe from knowing where the world stops and where she begins. This love denies that the children are true "others." Like Schoolteacher's "thick mind," the excess of reason which allows him to deny the humanity of the human beings on whom he conducts his experiments, Sethe's "thick love" is an excessive love that allows her to destroy what she has created, to deny the humanness of her own child.

Beloved is the child that Sethe has to rebear in order to rememory the mother role and to grieve. In essence, what marks Sethe as Cain is that she refuses to acknowledge the implications of her act and to mourn properly her child. Her pride becomes a shield against her grief. Beloved shatters that defense; she takes Sethe deep into the truth that, until she mourns, she is still a slave. The three hand-holding shadows of Paul D, Sethe, and Denver which make a tentative family are replaced by Beloved, Sethe, and Denver— a mother and her children. The silent jungle speaks in 124, and Sethe is isolated in her role as mother and with her pain, denying there is a world outside her door. Eventually, even Denver is excluded, as Beloved and Sethe create anew the Cain image, the victim-victimizer/master-slave relationship. Beloved seeks "the join" to become what Sethe says she is, her best self; she draws off Sethe all that is vital until she is "pregnant" with Sethe, becoming the mother. Sethe, finally facing the memories, rejoices in the return of human feelings, yet she is as trapped in them as she was in her denial. She loses the remnants of her self and enjoys the pain.

Denver tells us that Sethe does not want to be forgiven. The relationship between the two becomes hostile, as Sethe is denied Beloved's forgiveness and as Beloved drives Sethe to self-destruction. Denver, frightened, ventures into the community. Wearing Beloved's shoes, she too makes a return from the grave that 124 has become. Denver, who was a child and innocent in Sethe's and the community's sin against Baby Suggs, can be touched by Baby's spirit. She is forced by Baby Suggs to give up her defense and face the future:

> But you said there was no defense. "There ain't." Then what do I do? "Know it, and go on out the yard. Go on."

Denver, who realizes that she has a self of her own to preserve, becomes the agent of reconciliation. She, the child who ingested blood and breast milk, is as much a symbol of Sethe's pride as is Beloved. Denver, too, has been exiled, trapped in Sethe's memories. But Baby's spirit tells Denver that life is a risk, and only through risk, relationship, and rememory is the self formed. Armed with this knowledge, Denver acts. She practices what her mother could not at the funeral—humility—and does what her mother could not—she asks for help. Her humility causes the community, especially the women, to rally around the family in 124.

Ella, taking Baby Suggs's maxim to heart, recognizes that Beloved is excess, that, though the mother killed the child, "' . . . the children can't just up and kill the mama.'" What follows this recognition is a repetition of the past—a recreation of the moment of the murder and the flooding of memory into the present so that reconciliation can take place. The women go to 124 Bluestone. They remember the feast that Baby Suggs prepared for them; they remember themselves young. They make the primal sound that they did not make for Baby at her funeral: They mourn. Meanwhile, Mr. Bodwin, the abolitionist who has helped the Suggs family, drives toward the house. Sethe believes that he is Schoolteacher, come for Beloved, and runs toward him with an ice pick. This time, she attacks the master and not the child, and this time, the child saves the mother. Denver, the flesh-and-blood child nursed on blood and milk, throws her mother to the ground, and the women of the community collapse on them like a mountain, a symbol of solidity and endurance. This action honors Baby Suggs even as it saves Sethe and affirms Denver's independence. Thus, on the level of community, rememory is accomplished.

The reenactment of Sethe's memory and that of the community exorcises Beloved, restoring the Suggs family to its place in the order of things. Still, Sethe is not yet saved. She can hate the master, but she cannot love herself. She remains in exile. Like Baby Suggs before her, she takes to her bed, feeling that, without her child, there is no future, no possibility for living and for change:

> . . . "Paul D?" "What, baby?" "She left me." "Aw, girl. Don't cry." "She was my best thing."

Paul D, who has decided that he wants to put his story next to Sethe's, affirms verbally the action he made in the beginning of the novel when he held Sethe's breasts in his hands and kissed the scar on her back:

> "Sethe," he says, "me and you, we got more yesterday than anybody. We need some kind of tomorrow."
> He leans over and takes her hand. With the other he touches her face. "You your best thing, Sethe. You are."

Sethe cries, "'Me? Me?',", a timid identification of her own self, but a bold step out of her exile. Paul D, who has made his own odyssey in the course of the novel acknowledges the link between Sethe's breasts and her back, and helps Sethe to see that they are not in opposition to one another but can be balanced if integrated into Sethe's identity. Paul D offers an alternative to the "thick love" of the victim-victimizer cycle. Thick love would rather destroy than mourn, rather face exile than put its story beside that of another. Sethe has to yield her fierce pride to become her true self. The end of the novel dramatizes Sethe's coming to wholeness, the first step in Cain's return.

Baby Suggs's spirit said to Denver, as the girl hesitated on the edge of the porch, that the life of a black person is not a battle; it is a rout. The whites have already won, and the only defense is to accept the defeat whites made on the terms of power and to claim another kind of victory. That victory comes when one takes the risk to suffer and to understand. The curse of Cain, of guilt and alienation, is broken when Sethe can mourn and when she can tell the tale with moral imagination and, thereby, find a truth different than the master's truth. The thick love, erupting from the jungle, has to be first remembered, then "disremembered," let be. The silent story, exemplified by Beloved, is "not a story to pass on"—a story neither to ignore nor to forget.

If Sethe is a woman trying to find herself, Sula Peace, at first, seems to be a complete self. Her birthmark seems to confirm this wholeness and difference, distinguishing her from other "heavy brown" girls:

> [It] spread from the middle of the lid toward the eyebrow, shaped something like a stemmed rose. It gave her otherwise plain face a broken excitement and blue-blade threat. . . . The birthmark was to grow darker as the years passed, but now it was the same shade as her gold-flecked eyes, which, to the end, were as steady and clean as rain.

As Sula develops, the birthmark on her eye changes. When she is young the rose develops a stem, and as Sula grows older, the mark grows darker.

Her mark is interpreted in various, mostly negative ways throughout the novel: Nel's children think of the mark as a "scary black thing," and Jude, Nel's husband, who gets angry when Sula will not participate in the "milk-warm commiseration" he needs to feel like a man, thinks that Sula has a copperhead over her eye. The community, indicting the evil Sula for every accident that befalls it, recognizes the mark as a sign of a murderer: They "cleared up for everybody the meaning of the birthmark over her eye; it was not a stemmed rose, or a snake, it was Hannah's [Sula's mother's] ashes marking her from the very beginning." Nel thinks that the mark gives Sula's glance "a suggestion of startled pleasure." Only Shadrack recognizes the mark as a sign of Sula's developing self: "She," he thinks, "had a tadpole over her eye."

Like Sethe, Sula is both a victim and a victimizer, becoming both at the age of twelve, when her identity is forming. Sula experiences two things that create her radical self. First, Sula overhears her mother say that she loves

Sula but does not like her. After this incident, Sula and her friend Nel go to the river and there encounter a friend, Chicken Little. While swinging him around, Sula accidentally throws him into the river:

> The water darkened and closed quickly over the place where Chicken Little sank. The pressure of his hard and tight little fingers was still in Sula's palms as she stood looking at the closed place in the water. They expected him to come back up, laughing. Both girls stared at the water.

At Chicken's funeral, we realize that something is wrong in this community. As Reverend Deal preaches, the members of the community mourn not for the dead child, but for themselves:

> They did not hear all of what he said; they heard the one word, or phrase, or inflection that was for them the connection between the event and themselves. For some it was the term "Sweet Jesus." And they saw the Lamb's eye and the truly innocent victim: themselves.

This image of individuals mourning only for themselves is intensified in Nel. She stands even more removed from the mourning process because she, afraid of being caught, separates herself from Sula and casts herself as the innocent victim: " . . . she knew that she had 'done nothing.'" Though Nel will reconcile with Sula after the funeral, during the ritual, she leaves Sula completely alone for the first time: "Nel and Sula did not touch hands or look at each other during the funeral. There was space, a separateness, between them."

Sula, alone, "simply cried." Yet, Sula's tears neither heal the great pain that she has experienced nor do they signify mourning for Chicken Little. Her inability to mourn marks her as one set apart, like Cain. The rejection by her mother and the death of Chicken, the events that Sula cannot rememory, make Sula what she is:

> As willing to feel pain as to give pain, to feel pleasure as to give pleasure, hers was an experimental life—ever since her mother's remarks sent her flying up those stairs, ever since her one major feeling of responsibility had been exorcised on the bank of a river with a closed place in the middle. The first experience taught her there was no other that you could count on; the second that there was no self to count on either. She had no center, no speck around which to grow.

With nothing to depend on, not even herself, Sula patterns her life on being unsupported and unconventional, on the free fall that requires "invention" and "a full surrender to the downward flight." Sula is, at once, all self and no self: an artist with no medium, energy without form. Refusing participation in community, Sula finds no "other," against whom she can define herself. Her energy and curiosity seek limits throughout the novel, finding the only real limit in death.

There are four temporary boundaries for Sula: the madman Shadrack and his promise, her best friend Nel, her beloved Ajax, and the community of Medallion. Shadrack's promise to Sula, along with her mother's rejection and the death of Chicken Little, becomes the basis of all her actions. Afraid that Shadrack saw Chicken Little drown, Sula runs to his house. There Shadrack makes Sula a promise: "'Always,'" answering "a question she had not asked [the promise of which] licked at her feet." Shadrack promises Sula, who comes to him in his isolation and becomes "his visitor, his company, his guest, his social life, his woman, his daughter and his friend," that he, who controls death through National Suicide Day, will keep her safe from death:

> . . . he tried to think of something to say to comfort her, some-
> thing to stop the hurt from spilling out of her eyes. So he had
> said "always," so she would not have to be afraid of the change—
> the falling away of skin, the drip and slide of blood, and the expo-
> sure of bone underneath. He had said "always" to convince her,
> assure her, of permanency.

Shadrack insures that Sula never has to mourn or remember. Hers is a life of forward movement, for Sula, there is only the moment. This sense of her permanence, of her immortality, is Sula's true mark—her blessing and her curse. It frees her to experiment, to work through the range of experi-ence, while it insures that she will find only repetition because she cannot critically evaluate what she does. For Sula, " . . . doing anything forever and ever [i]s hell." Yet in her incessant wanderings, Sula finds the same thing everywhere. The sense of her own permanence also takes away from her two essential things: fear and compassion. Lack of fear makes her hurt herself to save herself, for example, she cuts off the end of her finger to save herself and Nel—who misinterprets the act—from a group of white bullies. Lack of compassion lets her interestingly watch her mother Hannah burn and enjoy her jerking and dancing. Sula says, "'I never meant anything,'" and she is honest and right. No experience, from the most trivial—someone's chewing with his mouth open—to the most important—her mother's death—has any ultimate meaning to Sula. The darkening and spreading of the birthmark is the symbol of the tyranny of Sula's eye/I. Because Sula cannot take the perspective of the "other," she can see neither herself nor anyone else clearly.

That tyranny of the eye/I includes even Nel, Sula's best friend, who is "the closest thing to both an other and a self" that Sula finds. Sula cannot understand that, though they see together, are one eye, they are also two throats: they have different needs and are not "one and the same thing." Sula forces Nel to define herself; Sula knows Nel's name as she will not know Ajax's. Sula, however, refuses to be defined, for she feels that she knows herself intimately. She demands that Nel want nothing from her and accept all aspects of her—even her adultery with Nel's husband Jude. Sula's sleeping with Jude is not personal; it is merely another of Sula's "experiences." Sexuality, for Sula, is not the attempt to meet with an "other," but with herself. It is an attempt to find that center that she has lost:

> There, in the center of that silence was not eternity but the death of time and a loneliness so profound the word itself had no meaning. For loneliness assumed the absence of other people, and the solitude she found in that desperate terrain had never admitted the possibility of other people. She wept then . . . [in] the post coital privateness in which she met herself, welcomed herself, and joined herself in matchless harmony.

Sexuality becomes a site of memory, but not one of meeting. Sexuality is, for Sula, a place where she recovers the self that her mother took away, the self on which she can depend. It is the way to experience and to mourn the death of her dislocated self that Shadrack promised she would never experience. It is a limit, and limitation is what Sula unconsciously seeks.

Sula's desire for boundaries is best illustrated in her love for Ajax. Only Ajax, a man as strong and as free as herself, makes her desire to join the self that she finds in the sexual act with an "other," to return from her Cain-like exile in taking responsibility for another person. With Ajax, Sula feels the desires of possession and of attempting to know a person other than herself. Their lovemaking is symbolized as a tree in loam—fertile, rich, and moist— and Sula wants to look through all the layers of Ajax to find his center, to reach the source of that richness. Ajax, however, desires the Sula that is separate, complete in her solitude. He, like Sula, is a gold-eyed person, a true individual, and he leaves Sula when she wants to limit him by making him hers alone. When she says, "'Lean on me,'" Sula is asking Ajax to give up his freedom—to become bound to her, and to bind herself to him and to the community. Ajax rejects this relationship for the radical freedom that he has learned from his mother, another outsider: "He dragged [Sula] under him and made love to her with the steadiness and the intensity of a man about to leave for Dayton."

Marriage, like mourning, is a ritual that binds the self to the beloved, to the community, and to God. The loss of Ajax, and with him Sula's one attempt at joining with another in marriage and with the community of Medallion, destroys Sula. When she finds his driver's license, she realizes that, in contrast to Nel, Ajax is someone whose name she did not know. She sees that, when she "said his name involuntarily or said it meaning him, the name she was screaming and saying was not his at all." A name indicates the essence of a human being and Ajax has not given Sula that deep understanding of himself. Sula realizes that she would have had to destroy him to get it; "'It's just as well he left. Soon I would have torn the flesh from his face just to see if I was right about the gold and nobody would have understood that kind of curiosity.'" Faced with this loss, Sula becomes like the headless soldier that Shadrack sees his first day in the war. Sula's body goes on, but she has lost her head, just like her paper dolls'. Sula's headless paper dolls indicate Sula's having lost herself, having given up her name, to Ajax and her being unable to "hold her head up," to maintain herself in the face of this loss: "'I did not hold my head stiff enough when I met him and so I lost it just like the dolls.'" The image of paper dolls also suggests emptiness of body, mind, and soul, and that emptiness leads to Sula's death.

Medallion and her grandmother's room provide a final limit for the boundless energy that is Sula. Sula returns to Medallion because she has exhausted the experience of Nashville, Detroit, New Orleans, New York, Philadelphia, Macon, and San Diego. Toni Morrison has said that Sula returns because she simply cannot live anywhere else. Though Sula is recognized as evil the community more than tolerates her, and, again, we see that something is wrong in Medallion. Medallion is only a community when it has Sula for a center, when her "evil" draws its members together in fear. Bad mothers take care of their children; wives love their husbands to keep them out of Sula's bed; and every disaster, large and small, has a reason—Sula. The community is bound in hate and refuses to mourn Sula after her death. The people accept the news of her death as good and attend the funeral only "to verify [the witch's] being put away." They leave Sula to the white people, making her only "a body, a name, and an address"—denying her essence and dishonoring her. Thus, the question of the hymn "Shall We Gather at the River?" is answered affirmatively, but in a deadly way, by Sula's spirit. The destruction of the community at the end of the novel is accomplished through Sula's element—water. That ruin comes because the community's refusal to mourn marks it. The power of her spirit indicates Sula's centrality, negative or not, in Medallion. Both are

Cain, and each destroys the other. Sula takes the community with her in her return to the womb, her "sleep of water."

Medallion and her grandmother's house and room are, for Sula, the end; they represent the closure of the circle of her experience. Left by Ajax, Sula thinks, "'There aren't any more new songs and I have sung all the ones there are.'" Sula refuses to look back, and there is no future for her. In contrast to Sethe at the end of *Beloved*, Sula will not yield. Unlike Baby Suggs, who goes to bed broken, Sula is defiant to the end, as her final conversation with Nel illustrates:

> [Nel] opened the door and heard Sula's low whisper. "Hey, girl." Nel paused and turned her head but not enough to see her. "How you know?" Sula asked. "Know what?" Nel still wouldn't look at her. "About who was good. How you know it was you?" "What you mean?" "I mean maybe it wasn't you. Maybe it was me."

Sula—and we have to admire her—affirms her own mode of being in the world. All that is left for her to experience is death. Dying, she faces a sealed window—the window from which her grandmother threw herself while trying to save Hannah, Sula's mother. The boarded window soothes Sula "with its sturdy termination, its unassailable finality." The closed room represents the end of the tyranny of the eye/I, the closing off of Sula's single perspective, and the womb, the place where Sula can be completely alone, completely herself, free of distraction and curled up in water. The promise of "Always," the promise of permanence, can be fulfilled only in death, in "a sleep of water always."

For the living Sula, the mark becomes a sign of completeness that is her incompleteness—the mark of the independent self who, like Cain, refuses to acknowledge the need for and the importance of the "other." Even in dying she will not apologize to and reach out for Nel, her Abel. For the dead Sula, the mark is a sign of her permanence, her power, and her beauty. Shadrack's promise, then, is broken in one sense, but in another it is fulfilled. After her death, Sula recognizes that she needs community—specifically, that she needs Nel:

> She was dead. Sula felt her face smiling. "Well, I'll be damned," she thought, "it didn't even hurt. Wait'll I tell Nel."

This need for the "other" is confirmed after death. Sula becomes her sister's keeper; thus, Sula lives on as Nel feels the presence of her dead friend. Nel thought she never missed her husband Jude at all but that she did miss

Sula: "'We was girls together . . . O Lord, Sula, . . . girl, girl, girlgirlgirl.'" That "girl" is Nel. Shocked into seeing herself by Eva's assertion that Nel, too, is guilty and that Nel and Sula are alike, Nel realizes that Sula was right. There was no difference between them. This recognition leads Nel to mourn her other self. Doing her rememory and mourning her friend, Nel finds her own eye twitching as she takes on the mark and is reborn. After her childhood trip to New Orleans, Nel cried "me" five times, praying to be wonderful. Taking on Sula's mark, she begins to become that "me." Like Sethe at the end of *Beloved*, Nel finds that her story is bound with the story of another, and that connection, which transcends death, becomes the path to finding her identity.

Morrison has said that Sula and Nel make up one whole person: Sula is ship, the "New World Black Woman," and Nel is safe harbor, the "Traditional Black Woman." Neither is complete alone. That sense of our finitude and the necessity for contact with the "other" that is central to the Cain myth is what Toni Morrison retains in the stories of her marked women. She illustrates the sense of the risk of human life and human relationships that the Biblical myth contains, even as she signifies on the myth to affirm the healing power of memory and of ritual. She presents to us the human being, marked by oppression and/or by an act done in desperation and fear and set outside of the boundaries of community. That fallen human, however, cannot be sent "east of Eden" but must be reconciled to the self and to the community for the sake of both. In a community that has suffered through slavery and reconstruction, not a member can be lost. Cain cannot be banished forever but, somehow, must come home, lest both Cain and community be forever marked. The black community is a people in mourning, reconstructing itself through memory: This is not a story to pass on.

For Morrison, the mark must not be passed on, for it always carries possibility; it is not just a sign of alienation but one of latent beauty and wholeness. Sethe's chokeberry tree is potentially beautiful—the blood from her back makes roses on her bed—and organic—it might have cherries. When Sethe accepts her mark, she finds the true meaning of her name. She is no longer Cain, the exile, but is both Set, crucified by the tree on her back, and Seth, the son who carries on the line of Adam and Eve and who foreshadows Christ. The tree marks her as one out of Eden, yet the tree also connects her with her mother, marked with a cross, and the group of African slaves who were all marked in that way. Thus, the mark becomes a sign of community, identity, and wholeness, and Sethe, the chosen child, has to remember the stories and witness her people's history—and her own. The tree also becomes a symbol of Sethe's own power. Sethe's act, however brutal, signals individual defiance to the oppression of slavery and the beginnings of claiming and defining the self, of breaking the physical and psychological boundaries of oppression. Like the trees at Sweet Home and like Paul D's sapling, however, Sethe finally bends and, thus, survives—even prevails.

In contrast, Sula's mark is that of a self who is absolutely unbounded and free. The mark as rose and snake signifies the beauty and danger of Sula's kind of freedom. Ultimately, it symbolizes her absolute refusal to see life, to paraphrase Fitzgerald, from more than one window, from any perspective other than her own. This immense, unchecked power is destructive both for the self, as we see when Sula dies alone, and for the community, as we see when the people of Medallion refuse to recognize Sula's importance and are destroyed by the angry spirit of the dead Sula. Alone, Sula, as Morrison says, is a warning. Balanced after death, however, with the loving and stable power of Nel, who takes on the task of mourning and memory, the mark becomes tadpole and not snake. That is, it signals the development of the self and creates the compassion—the ability to be a self but also to see with the "other"—that is the basis of true community.

Both Sula and Sethe must embrace and even, finally, celebrate the mark of Cain which sets each apart but which also makes each unique—and so must their communities. Toni Morrison shows us in *Beloved* and *Sula* that we are bound together through story and through action. Memory, for the oppressed person, is a private story that must be understood, but it must also be shared. Thus, memory is also a public story made permanent as myth and reenacted through ritual—in these novels, the funeral. Myth and ritual bind the person to the group and to the sacred. Steinbeck, in *East of Eden*, says that the Cain story is "the symbol story of the [rejected, guilty] human soul." The way out of that guilt and rejection, for Toni Morrison, is to claim the mark as a symbol of the self and willingly to undergo what one has been forced to undergo in the past. The act of rememory is a private and a public act of homecoming; it is like water, forever moving, forever trying to get back to where it was.

KAREN CARMEAN

Sula

After completing *Sula* in 1973, Morrison says that she knew she was a writer. And as an indicator of talent, depth, and stylistic innovation, Sula assures Morrison's literary reputation. Superficially, the novel seems a continuation of themes and structures introduced in *The Bluest Eye*. Again, Morrison uses paired female characters; themes of identity, love, and responsibility; a vivid sense of community; shifting narrative perspectives; and rich use of irony and paradox. But *Sula* challenges readers in ways *The Bluest Eye* does not, primarily because of Morrison's presentation of evil and the structures she employs to reveal its polymorphic nature.

Divided into two roughly equal parts, with a prologue followed by chapter titles consisting of dates, *Sula* appears to move in a straightforward progression from 1919 to 1927 and then from 1937 to 1941, with "1965" as the novel's epilogue. But the events of various chapters don't necessarily occur during the dates indicated; indeed, the text spirals and laps back on itself, accruing sometimes changing or contradicting meanings as it goes. This demands the reader's concentrated effort, for Morrison here dramatizes her talent for using language as "both indicator and mask." *Sula* insists that readers put aside conventional expectations to enter a fictional world deliberately inverted to reveal a complex reality, a world in which evil may be a necessary good, where good may be exposed for its inherent evil, where

---

From *Toni Morrison's World of Fiction*. © 1993 by Karen Carmean.

murder and self-mutilation become acts of love, and where simple answers to ordinary human problems do not exist. *Sula* has drawn many critical essays that have attempted to give it a systematic, philosophically centered reading. But it defies single authoritative readings in theme and structure (also existential, Manichaen, and "other" readings come close) mainly because this is a novel about becoming and changing, sometimes in clear process, sometimes not.

Sula's prologue begins by emphasizing place, indicating that the neighborhood of the Bottom, destroyed to make room for a golf course, will play a significant role in this narrative. The Bottom is more than a setting, however. Morrison often uses community as an active character in her work. From the very start we are made immediately aware of a mythological dimension, drawn into an imaginative place where nature and people interact, as they often do in folk and fairy tales. Beginning with the end of the Bottom, Morrison introduces a pattern of inversion which she quickly succeeds with others. This includes the anecdote about the origin of the Bottom as a "nigger joke," when a white slave owner rewards his diligent slave with poor, hilly land where living will always be difficult. This "joke," based on deceit and motivated by greed, becomes an important structural and thematic thread in *Sula*, for all of its elements bear directly on the lives of the Bottom's inhabitants. Behind the scenery, as it were, is the white man, controlling the literal disposition of the land and the slave's perception of it through the manipulation of language:

> "See those hills? That's bottom land, rich and fertile."
> "But it's high up in the hills," said the slave.
> "High up from us," said the master, "but when God looks down, it's the bottom . . . of heaven—best land there is."

The "joke" effectively isolates the slave and ensures his economic failure while reinforcing the owner's sense of superiority. At the same time, however, the slave gleans some measure of success from his choice, developing a sense of humor as grimly ironic as his daily existence. Thus while the white folks hear the later inhabitants' laughter, they remain ignorant of the pain "somewhere under the eyelids."

Isolated by location, race, and economics, the Bottom develops into a neighborhood, sharing some values with nearby white Medallion and developing its own distinctive attitudes as well. Chief among them in the novel is the neighborhood's acceptance of evil, which seems a form of passive acceptance: "they let it run its course, fulfill itself, and never invented ways either to alter it, to annihilate it or to prevent its happening again. So also were they with people." This sense of endurance, superficially so stoical, perhaps even rational in the face of oppression, may also be a form of fatalistic indifference or fear. In any case, it becomes self-defeating, because it may be concluded that their "view of survival and of Nature exists only on the physical plane and is rooted in the fear of dying rather than in a desire to live." Fear leads Shadrack, most prominently, and other characters as well, to create external structures and focus on these instead of actual causes. Thus National Suicide Day, Shadrack's means of imposing order over fear, not death, becomes the structure which eventually assumes its own independent importance. This need for finding an objective correlative for fear will lead the community to focus its fear and hatred on the River Road, the tunnel, and on Sula for their perceived inherent evil while remaining blind to the mysterious and protean nature of evil.

Another character motivated by fear is Helene Wright. Here is a fear of life, suggested by her attitude toward sexuality. Raised by her grandmother in a house guarded by four Virgin Marys, Helene is cautioned against "any sign of her mother's wild blood." Helene escapes New Orleans' sultry atmosphere and her prostitute mother's shadow by marrying Wiley Wright and moving to Ohio, where she sets a standard for communal rectitude, a standard she later imposes on her daughter Nel. But Helene's existence seems more a denial of a former life than an affirmation of an improved one, especially when her veneer of dignity dissolves into a "brilliant smile" aimed at a loathsome white conductor who denigrates her at the beginning of a trip back to New Orleans. Helene's smile, a flirtatious appeal for understanding, allows Nel to see her mother in an entirely new context. No longer a woman "who could quell a roustabout with a look" but instead an image of "custard," Helene reveals an unsuspected side. The "custard" and "jelly" Nel associates with her mother suggest more than weakness. They reveal the nature of Helene's sexual fear.

Nel's trip to New Orleans gives her a glimpse of another, more complex reality rife with paradox and denial. Her grandmother's parting injunction, "Voir," is a message to see and inspect. Helene refuses to translate for her daughter. Nonetheless, Nel returns to the Bottom aware of her separate identity: "I'm me. I'm not their daughter. I'm not Nel. I'm me. Me." Contemplating her separateness, Nel wants two things out of life, to be "wonderful" and to leave Medallion. Now she is prepared to ignore her mother's objections and become best friends with Sula.

Sula's upbringing in her grandmother Eva's house is the most significant factor in developing her attitudes, her perceptions of life forming in the irregular house her grandmother designs. A microcosm of the Bottom, Eva's house contains all the elements of the larger community: love, lust, generosity, possessiveness, evasiveness, duty, tenderness, denial, and deceit. Both life-sustaining and moribund, Eva's house is a monument to her twisted sense of responsibility, a sense warped by dire circumstances.

Abandoned one November be her husband Boy Boy, Eva struggles to feed her three starving children until, sensing futility, she leaves them with a neighbor and disappears. Eighteen months later, Eva returns, with one leg missing but with notable prosperity, to reclaim her children and build her own home. Precisely how Eva loses her leg becomes the topic of speculation in the Bottom, though it is suggested that Eva sacrifices it in a train accident for an insurance settlement. Whatever the case, Eva's experience changes her from a passive victim to an active manipulator. Her motive shifts from love to hatred: "Hating Boy Boy she could get on with it, and have the safety, the thrill, the consistency of that hatred as long as she wanted or needed it to define and strengthen her and to protect her from routine vulnerabilities." Finding an embodiment of evil, a locus for her hatred, Eva participates in the community's use of fear and hatred as a defining, strengthening, and protective emotion, and her reaction brings her positive results. Later, the residents of the Bottom will hate Sula, and their reaction against her will temporarily lead to caring relationships. Eva's hatred also frees her from conventional solutions to routine problems. She becomes "creator" and "sovereign" of her home, directing the lives about her with unquestioned authority. In effect, Eva assumes godlike proportions, her removed authority indicative of emotional distance, her power over life and death unchallenged.

We see the results of Eva's authority throughout the novel, especially in relation to male characters: the deweys, Tar Baby, and Plum. All receive Eva's care and all, to some extent, become her victims. Eva's rescue of the deweys from indifferent mothers is fraught with paradox. While they doubtless benefit from whatever care they receive, these boys, originally so different in age and physical features, live down to Eva's leveling assessment: "What you need to tell them apart for? They's all deweys." As if Eva's initial dismissal of individuality arrests their development, the deweys never grow to physical or emotional maturity. Tar Baby, a white man boarding in Eva's house, receives similar treatment. Intent on drinking himself to death, he finds the shelter and indifference to his habits he requires in Eva's house.

This isn't so with Plum, Eva's only son, who grows up "floated in a constant swaddle of love and affection." Here is another verbal paradox, with "floated" and "swaddle" suggesting Plum's perpetual infancy is brought to an abrupt end with military service in World War I. A year after his return to the United States, Plum appears in the Bottom with a "sweet, sweet smile" induced by his heroin habit. Like Shadrack, Plum seems to have suffered a psychic war injury which he cannot relate. His silence and ever deeper withdrawal into drug induced euphoria finally spur Eva into action.

The scene during which Eva sets fire to Plum is suggestively political. Plum's drug habit along with military service and his discharge without adequate treatment echo Shadrack's premature release from a veteran's hospital. Both become casualties in a war which brings African-Americans no gain whatsoever. Thus the cherry pie and *Liberty* magazine assume ironic meaning and widen the significance of Plum's death. As the agent of death, Eva acts primarily out of love. Tears stream down her face as she tightly holds Plum. Grieving yet resolute, Eva's choice of death by fire echoes other mythic literary deaths and suggests purification and even rebirth, particularly with the references to "a wet light" and "some kind of baptism." But Plum neither rises from his own ashes nor does he emerge from the flame strengthened and sanctified. He is extinguished by his own mother. No one questions Eva's act, certainly not the community which never believes the rumors it circulates. Only Hannah can summon the courage to ask her mother why she killed Plum. The response Hannah hears in "two voices" suggests at least two reasons. Eva's primary motivation is to allow Plum "to die like a man" instead of retreating further into drug-induced infancy (like Tar Baby), and here Eva's motive becomes self-protective, not liberating. Dreaming that Plum is trying to reenter her womb, Eva saves herself ("Godhavemercy, I couldn't birth him twice") and her idea of what Plum should be. Her act both destroys and saves.

Doubtless, Eva's notion of manhood relates to her practice of "manlove, a love of maleness for its own sake," which she passes on to her daughters. Here, too, we trip over another paradox. Though "prejudiced about men" to the extent that she flatters their egos and criticizes wives she deems short of domestic devotion, Eva never allows herself to become the mere object of masculine attention. What can be truthfully said is that she is like Hannah in that both "exist as sexually desiring subjects rather than objects of male desire." But "manlove," the privileging of men, binds Eva to the community, cementing her to an unchallenged tradition—unchallenged, that is, until Sula reaches adulthood.

Structurally, Morrison prepares her readers for her title character through her use of inversion and paradox. Sula's delayed appearance also suggests the importance of all that precedes her in life: the Bottom, Shadrack, Helene, Eva. Thus when readers first encounter Sula savoring the "oppressive neatness" of Helene Wright's house, we know her background yet know little about her. Morrison will continue this pattern throughout the novel, removing Sula from narrative action—with calculated results.

Just as Helene is surprised by Sula's acting contrary to expectations, readers should not anticipate conventional behavior from this elusive character. Morrison created Nel and Sula to be a whole: "Each has part of the other . . . But each one lacked something that the other one had." This lack, like Sula's absences, serves to define her and is first dramatized in the novel when Sula hears her mother saying, "I love Sula. I just don't like her." Hannah's statement unwittingly severs a significant bond with Sula. Sula is conscious only of "a sting in her eye," but the event essentially points out Sula's difference from her mother. Sula and Nel immediately strengthen their union in a wordless ritual, loaded with sexual implications. But the hole they dig, both womb and grave, signals both their union and dissolution.

Chicken Little's death, which immediately follows, becomes central to the narrative because it serves to bind the girls closer together. This accident occurs at a critical age for these twelve year olds, pointing out their moral development. With Chicken's unexpected disappearance, Nel registers the first reaction: "Somebody saw." This apparent fact prompts a fearful yet determined Sula to investigate. Her discovery of Shadrack's unexpected neatness momentarily distracts Sula until she observes him in his doorway. Sula cannot voice the frightening question ("had he?"), and Shadrack gives her an answer ("always") full of ambiguity. When Sula returns to Nel, the one on whom she depends for thought, Nel denies Sula's responsibility: "It ain't your fault." Not only that, Nel seems equally distressed about Sula's missing belt, somehow equating one with the other. Nel's response suggests her own lack, a denial of her responsibility, despite the fact that she clearly represents communal responsibility throughout the novel. Her reaction seems self-contained, even detached. By contrast, Sula's soundless grief is eloquently directed at Chicken's misfortune, not her own. Absolved of responsibility, she nevertheless loses something central to her becoming whole. The test points out clearly what happened to her: "ever since her mother's remarks sent her flying up those stairs, ever since her one major feeling of responsibility had been exorcised on the bank of a river with a closed place in the middle. The first experience taught her there was no other that you could count on; the second that there was no self to count on either. She had no center, no speck around which to grow." Sula fails to see this for many years, of course. It's far too early for such sophisticated introspection. But her later actions, especially her cool observation of Hannah being burned, underscore Sula's difference, a difference later termed "evil" by the community when it watches the result of this lack.

The contrasting characters of Nel and Sula seem to retain their balance for years to come. Indeed, Sula returns after a decade's absence knowing that she has missed Nel all along. It is Nel, not Sula, who has separated, despite the fact that Sula has been physically absent. Yielding to Jude Green's need for a "hem," a someone "sweet . . . to shore him up," Nel discovers a feeling stronger than her friendship. And in marrying a man who believes that the two can make one whole and complete Jude, Nel virtually extinguishes her possibilities for developing an independent self.

The images attached to marriage in *Sula* are far from complimentary, with this social institution literally signaling the death of the female imagination and individuality. "Those with husbands," the text says, " had folded themselves into starched coffins, their sides bursting with other people's skinned dreams and bony regrets . . . Those with men had had the sweetness sucked from their breath by ovens and steam kettles." Jude's concern all along is with himself, not Nel, as he longs for confirmation of manhood denied him through racist employment restrictions. In acceding to Jude's urging, Nel joins the community's valuation of females as significant support, not independent beings. Accepting her role as wife and mother, Nel never questions the quality of her life. Any urge to examine, any incentive to leave the Bottom, or even rebel against its traditions, leaves with Sula. It does not, however, return with her.

Following Sula's return, Nel briefly rediscovers another way of seeing: "It was like getting the use of an eye back, having a cataract removed." But she is alone in celebrating Sula's reappearance. From the beginning, Sula irritates the Bottom with her individuality, her refusal to accept a woman's role. Without calling attention to the fact, Morrison gives Sula license to act as she pleases. Significantly enough, Sula can be said to behave "like a man. She's adventuresome, she trusts herself, she's not scared. And she is curious and will leave and try anything." Because of this "quality of masculinity," she is seen as a "total outrage." Thus it's not surprising for a community held together in part by traditions largely maintained by and relating to women to label Sula "devil" and "pariah." To the Bottom, she is the embodiment of evil. And what actions illustrate the nature of her evil? She places Eva in a nursing home, and she selects sexual partners from among married men. The rest is rumor.

Sula's reason for Eva's removal to a nursing home is based on self-defense. Immediately after entering Eva's house, Eva brings up two issues wholly antagonistic to Sula. She shows no gratitude (to Eva) and she has no husband or children. Their ensuing argument illustrates deeply opposed ideologies, with Eva maintaining a traditional view of Sula needing a husband and babies to "settle" her and Sula vigorously asserting her right to make herself and not be made by others. To any conforming pleasure, Sula says she's not yielding. "I'll split this town in two," she declares to Eva, "and everything in it before I'll let you put it [the fire of individuality]out!" The fire image occurs naturally enough to Sula. Knowing that Eva has burned Plum, Sula fears her. She later tells Nel about this fear, but Nel, like the rest of the community, refuses to believe the rumors of Eva's murder of her son. From Sula's perspective, putting Eva in a nursing home prevents another murder—Eva's or Sula's.

As for Sula's methods of satisfying her sexual needs, Hannah's similar acts should be recalled. Of course, Hannah's sexual acts did not antagonize the women of the Bottom. The difference stems largely from Sula's refusal to flatter male egos and thus seemingly devalue the men and, by extension, their wives. Sula's motives, however, are different from Hannah's, who simply refused to do without some "touching every day." The sexual act becomes for Sula an act of self-exploration and affirmation. Even Sula's early romantic fantasies forecast her sensual self-exploration, as she spends hours "galloping through her own mind on a gray-and-white horse tasting sugar and smelling roses in full view of someone who shared both the taste and the speed." Later, sex becomes a free fall into "a stinging awareness of the ending of things: an eye of sorrow in the midst of that hurricane rage of joy. There, in the center of that silence, was not eternity but the death of time and a lone-liness so profound the word itself had no meaning." In this state, Sula experiences her deepest feelings, deep enough to bring "tears for the deaths of the littlest things." Her sexual partner is relatively unimportant. He merely serves as the means to her end, "the postcoital privateness in which she met herself, welcomed herself, and joined herself in matchless harmony." Sula is consequently more intimate with herself than is ordinarily true of others, more knowledgeable about herself, more attuned to her own needs and desires. In the end, this inner intimacy, far from being evil, assumes a purity, signified by her association with rain.

Nel, on the other hand, has envisioned sex in terms of tangles and webs, snares for a struggling self as well as for others. Her concept of love and female sexuality is rooted in possessiveness. Thus when Sula, innocent of possessive love, takes Jude as a lover, Nel feels personally betrayed. So attached is her sexuality to her husband, Nel mistakenly believes that it departs with him. Though she grieves sexual emptiness, she fears looking at other men. Nel cannot see herself as Sula so clearly envisions her, a spider dangling by her own spittle, "more terrified of the fall than the snake's breath below." Unlike Sula, Nel fears change. She tries to hide from the fact that change is a necessary part of life. Without Sula's influence in her life, Nel's imaginativeness, her sensual enjoyment is replaced by a "little ball of fur and string and hair." By excluding Sula from her life, Nel successfully isolates her friend, but the result appears like an ironic form of suicide.

Meanwhile, Sula finally meets a man who admires female independence. Bored by clinging women, Ajax is initially drawn to Sula because he thinks that besides his mother "this was perhaps the only other woman he knew whose life was her own." Equally weary of men unable to respect her intelligence, Sula finds attractive Ajax's "refusal to baby or protect her, his assumption that she was both tough and wise." Surprisingly to Sula, Ajax prefers her in the superior sexual position during love making. In this position, Sula imaginatively mines the layers of Ajax's being to discover his essence, thinking in terms of precious metals, semi-precious stones, and life-giving loam. But their love affair ends when Sula resorts to the conventional domestic signals: a clean bathroom and table set for two. Worse, though, is Sula's invitation for Ajax to "lean on" her. Instead, he pulls her under him one last time before going to Dayton, leaving Sula stunned and empty.

Sula's thwarted affair with Ajax emphasizes the varying concepts of female love in the Bottom. She might have become, like Nel, subservient to a husband who sees his wife as someone to absorb his pain and bear his children. Or she might subscribe to Hannah's practice, which allows sexual pleasure but denies emotional ties. Before reaching adulthood Sula has rejected the former choice; otherwise she would never have left the Bottom. And after loving Ajax, she finds Hannah's approach equally unsatisfactory. Both concepts preclude mutual responsibility, the former by making women entirely responsible for domestic harmony, the latter by negating emotional connections. Sula's aborted love affair also dramatizes how her capacity for affection is constantly stifled. Looking back, she could trace a pattern of emotional connection followed by loss. Chicken dies, Nel denies her, and Ajax leaves. Looking at Ajax's drivers' license and seeing the name Albert Jacks, Sula discovers that she never knew the identity of her lover. "And if I didn't know his name," she thinks to herself, "then there is nothing I did know and I have known nothing ever at all since the one thing I wanted was to know his name. . . ." In Eva's former bedroom, facing her own as well as the evidence of her grandmother's futile expression of love, Sula might reflect on the insolvency of human relations. Unlike Nel, she doesn't expect either reward or punishment for her acts. She believes that "Being good to somebody is just like being mean to somebody. Risky. You don't get nothing for it." Still, confronting death, Sula seems satisfied that she at least lived her own life, that perhaps her way has been good.

Sula dies as she lived—alone. Alive, her impact on the Bottom had been ironically positive since in reacting to Sula's presence adults became more cherishing of their elderly parents, mothers more vigilant over their children, and wives more caring with their husbands. Their actions, however, seem generated more from spite than love. Consequently, after Sula's death, the

Bottom's residents revert to their former habits of neglect. No one claims that evil dies with Sula. The community's projection of evil on one resident and subsequently on a public works project proves ludicrous from the beginning. Signalling the fact that Sula's nature is not actually evil are her eyes, "clean as rain." What, then, is her "problem?" An omniscient observation concerning the essence of Sula's nature suggests that she was dangerous, like Cholly Breedlove, because of an "idle imagination": "Had she paints, or clay, or knew the discipline of the dance, or strings; had she anything to engage her tremendous curiosity and her gift for metaphor she might have exchanged the restlessness and preoccupation with whim for an activity that provided her with all she yearned for."

Sula's energy and intelligence go unrecognized and unemployed, ignored by a community too busy foisting its guilt and failure on her. This is distressing, as is the fact that Sula cannot overcome overwhelming odds to discover the necessary form of self-expression. Here, then, is an example of true evil in the story, coming from the waste of Sula both by herself and those around her. Without Sula upon whom to focus the blame, the people of the Bottom shift to a tunnel, part of a local federally funded road project which has raised and then frustrated resident's hope for employment. Here we see further examples of evil in the forms of sexism and racism. What may be concluded is that if the story indeed "considers the ways in which society denies women the possibility of autonomy and independence," then the tunnel suggests the larger frame of how white Medallion (and by extension the United States) denies the same to an entire race. Joining Shadrack on National Suicide Day, residents march to the tunnel and assault it with bricks and lumber. Of those who enter, many die as the tunnel collapses with Shadrack standing above " . . . ringing, ringing his bell." That the tunnel, which becomes a grave to so many, has been built by whites seems no accident.

The image of Shadrack presiding over the Bottom's death brings to mind John Donne's famous statement: "Any man's death diminishes me, because I am involved in Mankind; And therefore never send to know for whom the bell tolls; It tolls for thee." The obvious point of this image is to affirm the interrelationship of all. Throughout *Sula* we are reminded of the impersonal interest with which the white community observes occurrences in the Bottom, interest similar to that of Nel and Sula as they watch Chicken and Hannah die. As observers, all remain fascinated yet detached from the fatal activity before their eyes. These reactions emphasize their inability to empathize with and their denial of responsibility for others. Significantly, it is Nel, representing the community, who has never consciously admitted her interest and role in Chicken's death. A visit to Eva in 1965 offers her a glimmer of truth as she is forced to review her role. What bothers her is that

Eva "didn't say *see*, she said *watched*." An inner debate follows: "'I did not watch it. I just saw it.' But it was there anyway, as it had always been, the old feeling and the old question. The good feeling she had had when Chicken's hands slipped. She hadn't wondered about that in years. 'Why didn't I feel bad when it happened? How come it felt so good to see him fall?'" The more Nel ponders these questions, the closer she comes to recognizing that Sula and she are intimately bound, despite her feelings of separateness, her relief over surviving.

Morrison presents a parallel catharsis to emphasize the importance of communal responsibility. Blaming Sula and the tunnel will not improve conditions any more than personal evil can be exorcised by death because the human community's problems remains more fundamental. As she does in *The Bluest Eye*, Morrison alludes to the human soil, the conditions for growth and development critical for nurturing healthy human beings through love unblighted by possessiveness or self-sacrifice, love allowing feelings for oneself as well as for others. Seeing the painful, disfiguring effects of love, Sula creates herself in her own image, becoming totally "free." But she does not become "free" in a positive way. About personal freedom Morrison herself has said that "ideally" it means "being able to choose your responsibilities. Not not having any responsibility, but being able to choose which things you want to be responsible for." In shunning responsibility for the creation of a healthy community, white Medallion and the Bottom become culpable, not Sula. After all, she has little choice of her growing environment. Indeed, the extended neglect of children throughout the novel is a recurring reminder of communal dereliction. Chicken, the deweys, Ajax, Teapot, and Sula herself are allowed to grow with little super-vision or care. No wonder that the children who survive become as self-centered as their adult examples. Sula's solipsistic approach may seem to be more extreme than that of others. But when we see the widening rings of denial moving out from her to the Bottom to Medallion and the rest of the United States, we begin to fathom the political depth of this novel. Sula at least wholly claims her life, including its failures, while others deny their human connections in favor of simpler, safer ways.

The community of the Bottom never recognizes its moral insolvency, never sees the role it plays in its destruction. But Nel is given a belated chance for self-recognition. Her glimpse of truth is brought about first when Eva, to whom Nel has paid a duty call, confuses Nel with Sula and soon thereafter asks how Nel managed to kill Chicken. Nel's assured moral recti-tude melts as she begins to see that everyone might have been wrong about Sula, that what Sula stood for was not necessarily bad. In an exchange just prior to her death, Sula has pointed out her position to Nel:

"How do you know?" Sula asked.

"Know what?"

"About who was good. How do you know it was you?"

"What do you mean?"

"I mean maybe it wasn't you. Maybe it was me."

Years later, Nel sees that Sula might have been right. Moreover, Nel acknowledges that there was spite behind communal actions, not love or moral conviction. And when she understands this, Nel also recognizes that Eva was right to confuse her with Sula. She sees that despite their difference, they were identical in their disclaimer of responsibility.

The story ends with the beginning of Nel's painful comprehension that much of what she has believed has led her away from herself instead of leading her to truth. Morrison's dramatization of tradition's unperceived barriers to self-discovery reflects her belief in the need for experimenting with life, of breaking rules, not simply out of boredom or curiosity but because there is no other way to explore possibilities. Sula discovers the terror and thrill of the free fall into life through her own creative capacity for invention. Nel, on the other hand, values duty and tradition more than self. Taught to believe in the virtue of self-sacrifice, she denies her own possibilities and becomes dependent on others for her life's meaning, and even, as Sula points out, for her own loneliness. Trying to read Sula as an either/or proposition, that either Nel or Sula must be right, is unnecessarily simplifying and distorting of this novel, for Morrison all along intends both characters to command our attention. Like the characters, labels of "good" and "evil" become confused because "one can never really define good and evil. It depends on what uses you put it to. Evil is as useful as good is." And though what remains of the Bottom will never know that Sula was not what they thought her to be, at least Nel breaks through the barriers of traditional moral certainty to recognize a Sula she hasn't seen for a long time: "'We was girls together,' she said as though explaining something." Her reference to girlhood recalls a time of their greatest possibility, a possibility Nel rejected in favor of conventional ideas about womanhood which in turn blinded her to the truth of Sula.

Nel's grief brings the novel to a close, but like most elements of the novel, it paradoxically opens up her own possibilities. Thus in a way, the novel is open-ended. Finishing *Sula*, we have to consider carefully what we in fact do know. Our conventional expectations, after all, have been challenged through omission, contradiction, paradox, irony, and speculation, through a fusion of supernatural and realistic, and through a lean prose conjuring gothic events. By the end, we are prone to have given up any dualistic thinking in favor of the fluid, multiple process Morrison's novel gives us. The novel and the title character require imaginative exploration into the nature of life and art. Ultimately this means that, artistic structure notwithstanding, we are asked to respond to the free fall into individual consideration instead of relying upon literary conventions.

PATRICIA HUNT

War and Peace: Transfigured Categories and the Politics of Sula

In the beginning was not only the word but the contradiction of the word. In this lies the novel's flexibility and its ability to transcend the bounds of class and nation, its endless possibilities of mutation. (Ellison, "Society" 243)

I came not to send peace, but a sword. (Matthew 10:34)

. . . unless we receive full Redress and Relief from these Inhumanities we will move to renounce all Allegiance to this Nation, and will refuse, in every way, to cooperate with the Evil which is Perpetrated upon ourselves and out Communities. ("Black Declaration of Independence," The National Committee of Black Churchmen, 4 July 1970)

By comprehending the exclusion of African and African American cultural experience from the hegemonically constructed history of the United States, Toni Morrison reorients the late twentieth-century reader to a new vision which foregrounds African American participation in, and constitution of, that history. Morrison realizes her historical project in a language of scriptural allusions and figures, and thereby creates works that, like the Bible, are meditations on the interdependence of history and spirituality.

The experience of African American culture is the experience of this vital link. The Africans who underwent the horrific sea-change of the Middle

From *African American Review* 27, no. 3 (Fall 1993). © 1993 by Patricia Hunt.

Passage are simultaneously historical and spiritual presences. African religion and history in the United States were incorporated into and masked in Christian forms and figures, and the ancestral histories of the Bible (e.g., the exodus from Egypt, and the Babylonian captivity) became "the site of memory" for African Americans—the locus of both history and spirit. The coextensive ineffability and tangibility of these notions manifest themselves in Morrison's novels as a demand for parabolic interpretation; the parabolic form is at the heart of the political and theoretical status of her work. *Sula* is one such parable, and Morrison's novels are parabolic in the fullest sense: "open-ended, tensive, secular, indirect, iconoclastic, and revolutionary."

In keeping with black and feminist liberation theologies, Morrison's parables foreground the quotidian socioeconomic survival of African Americans, as well as the conflicted status—past and present—of race and racialized gender in United States culture. In Morrison's words, "The work [of art] must be political." But to label *Sula* a political text is not to say that it is programmatic or oppositional, or that its characters exemplify cultural progress. Consistent with the nature of parable, *Sula* lacks a straightforward black-and-white, good-and-evil plot. As Hortense Spillers puts it, *Sula*'s reader must "accept the corruption of absolutes and . . . the complex, alienated, transitory. . . . No Manichean analysis demanding a polarity of interest—black/white, male/female, good/bad—will work here." In this respect, Morrison is as much theorist as novelist, and her parables recall Barbara Christian's observation that ". . . people of color have always theorized, but in forms quite different from the Western form of abstract logic." Much of the criticism of *Sula* since its publication twenty years ago has focused on the "corruption of absolutes" in the novel, its movement away from what Christian calls the "Western dualistic or 'binary' frame." Morrison specifically rejects the either/or requirement that underlies what are considered classical or Western methods of reasoning, categorization, and teleology, and constantly points out the dangers inherent in a dualistic view. As Deborah McDowell puts it, "We enter a new world [in *Sula*] . . . that demands a shift from a dialectical either/or orientation to one that is dialogical or both/and, full of shifts and contradictions." The "shifts and contradictions" McDowell notices are part of the parabolic form. Moreover, the recognition of Morrison's parabolic technique draws together the major themes of her work: the anti-dualism, the historical specificity and accuracy, and the profound presence of an Africanized Christian theology.

As parable, *Sula* at every level questions easy divisions between war and peace, good and evil. At the novel's end, for example, Nel visits "the colored part of the cemetery," which contains tombstones bearing the name/word Peace, Sula's family name. "Together they read like a chant: PEACE

1895–1921, PEACE 1890–1923, PEACE 1910–1940, PEACE 1892–1959." Morrison foregrounds a number of ideas in this passage. Peace is the absence of war and, in the context of a cemetery, the absence of life (a person is said to "be at peace" when dead). But the absence of war allows for the manifestation of positive forces of growth and life, and the PEACE on the tombstone here does not signify the end of the lives of the individuals named, but the continuing cycle of life and death, of history and spirit, connected ironically and with great complexity to peace. In addition, the passage encodes an African worldview which sees a continuum, rather than a strict boundary, between the living and the dead. Here and throughout her work, Morrison does not propose a way of dividing up the world, but envisions a complex cultural universe which always already requires dismissal of a dualistic philosophical framework.

It would be incorrect, however, to read Morrison's parables as divorced from political praxis. Peace was a word of considerable, almost palpable, political significance at the time of *Sula*'s composition—during the height of the Vietnam War. *Sula* subtly interrogates the notion of war in terms of the political and social struggles of African Americans, many of which took place within the military or in terms of war-related issues such as the draft. In a sense, the Vietnam War was a testing ground for demands for equality and the end of racial oppression. Taking heed of Morrison's remark that ". . . *Sula* was begun in 1969 . . . in a period of extraordinary political activity," and in contrast to much critical work to date, I read war and men to be as central to this novel as peace and women. Of particular importance is Shadrack, whose sane insanity is his response to the horror of war and death.

The two sections in which Shadrack is the central figure—"1919," signifying the end of World War I, and "1941," signifying the beginning of World War II—frame the text. The book's epilogue-like last section, "1965," coincides with the year that the United States began regular bombing raids on North Vietnam, and was also the year of the well-known Southern California "race war," the Watts Riots. Morrison interweaves the themes of war and motherhood and probes these cultural constructs through Shadrack and his connection to Sula, and through the relationship between Eva Peace, Sula's grandmother, and Eva's son Plum. The characters of Sula and Shadrack examine and invert the societal prescriptions for women and men of mother and warrior, respectively; they are distorted mirror images of Eva and Plum. Shadrack, "blasted and permanently astonished by the events of 1917," refuses war's legacy of death. Sula refuses her grandmother's legacy of motherhood: "'I don't want to make somebody else,'" Sula says, "'I want to make myself.'" These historical references, secular figures, moral possibilities, choices, and reversals are part of the parabolic structure of the novel.

Morrison gives no unitary or univocal answer to the cultural situations and political questions drawn in her text. Instead, the parabolic structure demands moral introspection every time it is invoked: A parable teaches not a single "right answer" but constant and constantly revelatory communal and individual reflection.

Morrison's parabolic interrogation, which manifests itself as a theoretical subversion of binary categorization and a particular, historical probing of the complex relations between war and peace, is constituted through an idiosyncratic, radical, and complex biblical typology. Sula is at the center, but all characters and facets of the novel arise from the typological matrix. For example, *Sula*'s "deweys" can be seen as a disturbing fulfillment of the mystery of the Trinity (God, Christ, and the Holy Spirit):

> They spoke with one voice, thought with one mind, and maintained an annoying privacy. Stouthearted, surly, and wholly unpredictable, the deweys remained a mystery not only during all of their lives in Medallion but after as well.

However, Morrison does not use scriptural figures and stories in one-to-one correspondence to characters and subplots in *Sula,* nor does she employ traditional biblical typology, a deliberate displacement of type by anti-type. Instead, type and anti-type often inhere in a single character.

The central figures Sula and Shadrack combine and collapse a number of typologies. Among Sula's many connections to the Bible is her name: Sula is an anagram of Saul, and Sula Mae is nearly anagrammatic for Samuel; moreover, the family name Peace echoes the epithet for Jesus, Prince of Peace. Recalling that the Books of Samuel are centrally concerned with war, Sula's name incorporates, and collapses together, both war and peace. With parabolic complexity, Sula Peace, like the Prince of Peace, comes "not to send peace, but a sword" (Matthew 10:34).

As historical framework, Morrison's intricate biblical allusions are perhaps the primary way in which she constructs the "presence of the ancestor" in her novels. The Bible, as a tribal, genealogical, and oral text, has served as a typological model for African Americans as they interpret and preserve spiritual traditions and experiences, and so has become an ineluctable part of African American history and culture. "The Bible wasn't part of my reading," Morrison has said, "it was part of my life." Black theologian James Cone has written:

> Because white theologians and preachers denied any relationship between the scriptures and our struggle for freedom, we by-passed

the classic Western theological tradition and went directly to the scripture for its word regarding our black struggle.

Cone and Lawrence Levine explain that, for black Americans, Scripture has always had double meanings, speaking of freedom and emancipation as an earthly possibility and not merely a reward in the hereafter. If in *Sula* Morrison's theoretical project is to deconstruct binarism, and her political subject is African Americans in relation to war and civil rights, then the nexus of biblical allusion is the primary component of her language and specifically replicates the history and spirituality of the African American cultural experience.

As might be expected, Morrison draws on the Old Testament as much as the New Testament. Levine writes:

> The essence of slave religion cannot be fully grasped without understanding [its] Old Testament bias. It is important that Daniel and David and Joshua and Jonah and Moses and Noah, all of whom fill the lines of the spirituals, were delivered in this world and delivered in ways that struck the imagination of the slaves.

Walter Ong explains that the Bible was originally an oral text, and that its use in religious tradition of all kinds was and is "spoken": "The spoken word is always an event, a movement in time, completely lacking in the thing-like repose of the written or printed word." Sterling Stuckey has shown that black Americans have always had a distinct ethnic culture, and that it was not the case that the only culture they knew was that of their white masters and oppressors. Traditions brought from Africa, such as the ring shout, served as the foundation for the black churches which incorporate the Bible. "Culture is not a fixed condition but a process: the product of the interaction between the past and the present" Levine has said. In becoming Americans, Africans preserved the past—their spirituality and specific religiocultural traditions interwoven with Christianity. Again, Morrison's allusions in *Sula* to Samuel, Genesis, Exodus, the Gospels, and Revelation are part of her representation of the "presence of the ancestor"; they are not appropriations but constitute a facet of what Michael Awkward calls "the novel's cultural specificity." Morrison employs scriptural texts to recreate an explicit cultural topos—in *Sula*, the geography of the Bottom and Medallion, Ohio—and thus enhances historical and political understanding. Her novels re-envision the African American, and hence the American, experience in a parabolic mode, and so provide "a new way of being in the world."

Sula's first section, the only one in the novel without a year as its title, is a geography lesson on the novel's setting, the "Bottom." This section echoes the creation and destruction of the world in Genesis, but our introduction to what "was once a neighborhood" comes at its demolition, not its construction:

> . . . they tore the nightshade and blackberry patches from their roots to make room for the Medallion City Golf Course. . . . Generous funds have been allotted to level the stripped and faded buildings that clutter the road from Medallion up to the golf course. . . . There will be nothing left of the Bottom. . . .

Deborah McDowell points out that "*Sula* glories in paradox and ambiguity" and that "the Bottom [is] situated spatially at the top." The beginning of *Sula* juxtaposes the end of the neighborhood to the story of how the Bottom came to be, how "a good white farmer promised freedom and a piece of bottom land to his slave if he would perform some very difficult chores." The white farmer convinces the slave that the hilly land of the Bottom is "the bottom of heaven," recalling the meaning of the word Babylon—the gate of God. Sula contains significant allusions to the Babylonian captivity of the Israelites. Medallion, which encompasses the "neighborhood" of the Bottom, is a "little river town in Ohio," which echoes Psalm 137: "By the rivers of Babylon, there we sat down, yea, we wept, when we remembered Zion." The destruction of the hilly "Bottom," which reaches to the bottom of heaven, parallels the destruction of the Tower of Babel. Thus, at the outset of *Sula*, Morrison's theoretical collapse of binary oppositions arises from a clear, specifically parabolic, historical structure. The parable of Babel teaches not the origin of languages, but the dispersal of nations and peoples through war, greed, and oppression: "Come, let us build us a city and a tower, whose top may reach unto heaven; and let us make us a name, lest we be scattered abroad upon the face of the whole earth" (Genesis 11:4). The history of the Bottom—"the bottom of heaven"—its people, and its eventual destruction is in microcosm the history of African Americans, and the African diaspora: In the beginning, the end of the hilly Bottom, the whites have uprooted the blacks at the uncreation of the neighborhood.

There are many categorical collapses in *Sula*, such as the top/bottom pair, as well as allusions to biblical reversals entailed in Babel/Babylon, diaspora and exile. All of these collapses have theoretical, historical, political, and spiritual significance, and so constitute a parabolic structure having particular reference to the African American experience. The parabolic collapses do not annihilate themselves but exist problematically and call for constant ethical awareness, not of the collapsing categories themselves so much as the cultural superstructures in which they exist. For example, the thriving black plants torn out of the earth of the Bottom both nourish (blackberries) and poison (nightshade); categorizing living things as good or bad is irrelevant in such violent uprooting, as Morrison herself has commented in "Unspeakable Things Unspoken":

> The violence lurks in having something torn out by its roots— it will not, cannot grow again. Its consequences are that what has been destroyed is considered weeds. . . . Both plants have darkness in them: "black" and "night." One is unusual (night-shade) and has two darkness words: "night" and "shade." The other (blackberry) is common. A familiar plant and an exotic one. A harmless one and a dangerous one. One produces a nourishing juice, one delivers a toxic one. But they both thrived there together, in that place when it was a neighborhood.

Either/or categorization only reinforces the danger of dominance, the danger of violence justified by classification. Morrison provides a powerful interrogation of the moral categories of good and evil here, as well as implicitly asking what such labels do to respect and human dignity when they are confounded with race. Sula expresses the contingency and inadequacy of ethical categorization in particular, and binary categorization in general, in her last conversation with Nel:

> She opened the door and heard Sula's low whisper. "Hey, girl." Nel paused and turned her head but not enough to see her. "How you know?" Sula asked. "Know what?" Nel still wouldn't look at her. "About who was good. How you know it was you?" "What you mean?" "I mean maybe it wasn't you. Maybe it was me."

By questioning cultural categories of good and evil, Sula embodies what Morrison calls in *The Bluest Eye* "Christ's serious anarchy." When Sula returns to the Bottom after ten years which include college and living in seven cities, her presence challenges the social order of her community. As John Dominic Crossan has said of Jesus, Sula "challenges . . . civilization's eternal inclination to draw lines, invoke boundaries, establish hierarchies, and maintain discrimination."

Hortense Spillers has called the character Sula "Morrison's deliberate hypothesis." The townsfolk of the Bottom attempt to categorize her as a witch or a devil; a supernatural being in either case, but Sula continues simultaneously to reject and embrace all the categorizations placed on her. This "moral ambiguity," to use another of Spillers's phrases, is the source of Sula's integrity as a character, and what makes her the hypothesis of a reframed method of categorization. In the sense that Sula is a "hypothesis" and not an exemplar or role model, *Sula* is not a realistic novel. Catherine Rainwater calls attention to the fact that some critics see Morrison's "elusive" narrative threads as "untenable," and Morrison herself has noticed, with apparent discontent, that her work "frequently falls, in the minds of most people, into that realm of fiction called fantastic, or mythic, or magical, or unbelievable." Although Morrison's writing is not mimetic, and neither Sula nor her grandmother Eva, for example, portray "real" women, what appears fantastic or magical is always a vehicle of theoretical and political interrogation. In this way, Morrison's novels fit Sallie McFague's definition of parables of the synoptic gospels:

> . . . the outstanding features of the parables [are] the element[s] of the extraordinary, of radicalism, of surprise and reversal. They are metaphors with considerable shock value, for their intention is to upset conventional interpretations of reality. Yet . . . the parables introduce this note of extravagance in a curiously mundane, secular way: through seemingly ordinary stories about ordinary people engaged in ordinary decisions.

Sula, for all its reversals and magical extravagance, remains mundane, secular, and historically faithful.

It cannot be over-stated that Morrison's parables are rooted in history. Therefore, while some critics choose to ignore Shadrack or dismiss his significance, the fact that he is the first character Morrison introduces in *Sula* is hardly surprising. It is crucial for my reading of the subtext of men and war, history and the Bible, that following the initial geography lesson, the novel begins with "Shadrack . . . in December, 1917, running with his comrades across a field in France." He wonders why he is not feeling "something very strong"; instead he notices "the purity and whiteness of his own breath among the dirty, gray explosions." A surreal and horrifying passage follows:

> . . . [Shadrack] saw the face of a soldier near him fly off. Before he could register shock, the rest of the soldier's head disappeared under the inverted soup bowl of his helmet. But stubbornly, taking no direction from the brain, the body of the headless soldier ran on, with energy and grace, ignoring altogether the drip and slide of brain tissue down its back.

Black men participated in U.S. wars from the Revolution forward, in a military that remained segregated until after the Korean war. During World War I, nearly 400,000 black men were drafted, half of them serving in France. The black 369th Infantry were under continuous fire for a record of 191 days, for which they won the Croix de Guerre and the honor of leading the victorious Allied armies to the Rhine in 1918. The French had treated black soldiers as equals, but "the American military authorities issued orders prohibiting them from conversing with or associating with French women attending social functions, or visiting French homes."

Morrison's Shadrack survives the "fire" of the World War I battlefield, but in doing so loses his mind. As the Bottom's resident crazy man, he becomes, along with his institution of Suicide Day, "part of the fabric of life up in the Bottom of Medallion, Ohio." The horror and suddenness of death on the battlefield make the "unexpected" of it real to Shad, but for blacks in America, war was hardly the only situation in which death could be sudden and unanticipated. John Callahan has written: "The heroism of black regiments is well-known; perhaps less well-known are the humiliations and terrors these soldiers faced back home, especially in the South." Black soldiers returning from World War I were reminded that they were no longer in France, that they would no longer be treated as equals. Mary Frances Berry and John Blassingame write that, "Returning black soldiers were insulted, stripped of their uniforms, and beaten by white ruffians and police." The years 1919 and 1920 saw extraordinary violence against African Americans in the form of lynchings and beatings. Of the scores lynched in 1919, many were veterans still in uniform; Berry and Blassingame note that "police authorities gave little or no protection to black citizens." Morrison explicitly refers to such treatment in *Jazz*:

> Some said the rioters [in East Saint Louis] were disgruntled veterans who had fought in all-colored units [. . .] and came home to white violence more intense than when they enlisted and, unlike the battles they fought in Europe, stateside fighting was totally without honor.

In *Sula*'s "1920" section, we read of the "victorious swagger in the legs of white men and a dull-eyed excitement in the eyes of colored veterans," and Nel watches her mother turn to "custard" before a white conductor on a Jim Crow train headed for New Orleans. Those watching include two black soldiers "still in their shit-colored uniforms and peaked caps"; when Helene Wright becomes white before their eyes, they are "stricken."

Morrison foregrounds Shadrack, and the World War I experience, precisely to show what it was the African Americans were striving against in the 1960s. Military service for African American citizens at all historical periods has reflected their status in the culture as a whole, but during the Vietnam era the disparity between the demands placed on the African American soldier and the rights he or she was accorded was particularly conspicuous. One can hardly wonder at Shad wanting to institute a "National Suicide Day" so that ". . . the rest of the year would be safe and free."

The historical dimensions of Morrison's project include specific references to the African American experience in relation to war, as well as the historically important analogy of this experience to Judeo-Christian Scripture, which itself reflects an historical and political as well as spiritual tradition. Shadrack is a biblical name. In the book of Daniel, Hananiah, an Israelite noble, is named Shadrach by the Babylonians, who hold him and his people captive and force him to work for the King of Babylon. Hananiah and his fellow nobles Mishael and Azariah survive Nebuchadnezzar's furnace "heated seven times more than it was wont to be heated" (Daniel 3:19). In the Book of Jeremiah, another Hananiah is the prophet of peace who speaks of freedom and the fall of Nebuchadnezzar, when Jeremiah speaks of the captivity that the children of Israel have yet to endure.

Morrison is not only analogizing the Babylonian captivity of the Jews to the condition of African Americans in a racist nation. Hananiah and Jeremiah were religious prophets in dispute, but they also represented opposing political factions within captive Judah. Hananiah was one of the "anti-Babylonian 'autonomists,'" who, Norman Gottwald writes,

> equated "national survival" with the full independence of Judah under its present leadership, whereas the pro-Babylonian "coexisters" [such as Jeremiah] equated "national survival" with the socioeconomic and religiocultural preservation of the people of Judah.

Recalling the "period of extraordinary political activity" coextensive with *Sula*'s composition, we need to keep in mind the extent to which the African American cultural struggles have been, and are, rooted politically in African American churches. But the black churches were not united on the form that political activism should take, and Morrison's Shadrack may seem, like his biblical namesake in the Book of Jeremiah, as an "autonomist," a black nationalistic theologian: "The goal of Black Theology," writes James Cone, "is the destruction of everything white so that black people can be alienated from alien gods." On the other hand, the association of Shadrack with the prophet of peace Hananiah echoes the more moderate call of the Civil Rights Movement to "endure no more." In his "Letter from Birmingham City Jail," Martin Luther King said, "We have waited for more than 340 years for our constitutional and God-given rights."

In general, as part of Morrison's parabolic form, no one character in *Sula* is ever typed or categorized definitively. Morrison's Shadrack is the fictional fulfillment of both Old Testament Hananiahs. He sees people who "seemed to be smoking . . . their arms and legs curved in the breeze," just as the biblical Shadrach saw the Babylonian guards burnt to death outside Nebuchadnezzar's furnace. He is also reminiscent of the prophet Jeremiah, screaming curses at the "tetter heads" who tease him and Bottom-dwellers who but fish from him. Of the New Testament prophets, he is at once John the Baptist and John of Patmos: "His eyes were so wild, his hair so long and matted, his voice was so full of authority and thunder."

Sula first appears in the novel's fourth section, "1921." Her introduction, "Sula Peace lived in a house of many rooms. . . ," echoes Christ. "In my Father's house are many mansions. . .". The address, 7 Carpenter's Road, suggests that this is the road where Christ will be found; the number seven has great mystical significance; and Christ, of course, was not only a carpenter, but the Prince of Peace. The obvious reversal is that Sula does not live in her father's house, but in her grandmother Eva's house, with her mother Hannah and an assortment of uncategorizable people, such as the beautiful, white/black, alcoholic, angel-voiced Tar Baby and Eva's indistinguishable adopted trinity, the deweys.

Equally if not more important to Morrison's project, however, are Old Testament allusions realized in Sula and her family. *Sula* contains pervasive links to the biblical Books of Samuel, which are loci of issues of civil rights, war, motherhood, and family, and remind us of the originally political function of black churches and black theology. Joel Rosenberg comments on ancestry and history in Samuel:

> Samuel most resembles Genesis in its preoccupation with founding families and in its positioning of these representative households at the fulcrum of historical change. As in Genesis, the fate of the nation is read into the mutual dealings of spouses, parents, and children, of sibling and sibling, and of householder and servant, favored and underclass.

Sula reveals what Rosenberg calls "a complex scheme of historical causation and divine justice" in its resonance with the Books of Samuel. These books are as concerned with war as any in the Bible and, again, resemble

Genesis in their focus on familial politics of national or universal consequence.

Sula's allusions to Genesis revolve around issues of motherhood, sexuality, and gender as well as creation; J. P. Fokkelman writes of Genesis:

> The possibilities, limits, and precarious aspects of sexuality are expressly explored. . . . [there are] stories in which women struggle with each other for motherhood . . . . characters and reader are forced or invited to decide what is or is not sexually permissible. . . .

Eva, of course, is the first woman; she is, in terms of her name, "mother of all living." But Morrison's Eva is Adam in her power to name, and she is also life-taking. In *Sula*, " . . . those Peace women loved all men. It was manlove that Eva bequeathed to her daughters." Eva Peace's daughter Hannah, who is Sula's mother, possesses an extravagant love for men: "Hannah simply refused to live without the attentions of a man, and . . . had a steady sequence of lovers . . . . What she wanted . . . was some touching every day." Nancy Huston, in her essay "The Matrix of War," points out that many cultures throughout history have required "pre-war sexual abstinence," the idea being that sexual frustration would create a more aggressive and potent warrior. Hannah Peace, and Sula Peace after her, "explore their sexuality," but they don't "struggle with each other for motherhood"—Sula is Hannah's only child, and Sula never becomes a mother. And as long as Hannah and Sula make love to men in the novel, the men are not making war; that is, as long as women are not having babies, there will be no men to make war.

Sula's refuse of motherhood parallels Shadrack's refusal of war. In a sense, Shadrack is born when he has refused war and is released from the military hospital. Shadrack is the archetypal "motherless child"; his family is a mystery not only to the reader, but to other residents of the Bottom. Morrison characterizes him with complex irony, Shadrack is a "long, long way from his home," whether that home is understood to be Africa or an America that would embrace him as her child. In fact, Shadrack has no nation to defend: " . . . he didn't even know who or what he was . . . with no past, no language, no tribe, no source . . .". On the other hand, once Shadrack has affirmed his blackness, he returns to the Bottom; he has been "only twenty-two miles from his window, his river, and his soft voices just outside the door."

As Eva contrasts with Sula in terms of motherhood, Eva's son Plum contrasts with Shadrack in terms of war. Plum returns from France sane, but a hopeless junkie, a war casualty. As is she recognizes the link between motherhood and war, Eva sets fire to her son:

> He opened his eyes and saw what he imagined was the great
> wing of an eagle pouring a wet lightness over him. Some kind
> of baptism, some kind of blessing, he thought. . . . [Eva] rolled
> a bit of newspaper into a tight stick about six inches long, lit it
> and threw it onto the bed where the kerosene-soaked Plum lay
> in snug delight.

This passage is filled with allusions to Revelation:

> And when [Satan] saw that he was cast unto the earth, he
> persecuted the woman who brought forth the male child. And
> to the woman were given two wings of a great eagle, that she
> might fly into the wilderness, into her place . . . .

When Eva descends into Plum's nether room, *Sula* echoes Revelation's
"seven bowls of plagues." Compare Eva's picking up what she thinks is a
"glass of strawberry crush . . . put[ting] it to her lips and discover[ing] it is
blood-tainted water" to this passage in Revelation:

> And the second angel poured out his bowl [of the wrath of
> God] upon the sea, and it became like the blood of a dead man;
> and every living soul died in the sea. And the third angel
> poured out his bowl upon the rivers and fountains of waters,
> and they became blood.

These apocalyptic passages are prefigured in Exodus, when the Lord turns
the waters of the river to blood and later reminds the children of Israel "how
I bore you on eagles' wings and brought you unto myself." In *Sula*, deliver-
ance and apocalypse coextend, are collapsed into one. This collapse recalls
the conflicted status of African Americans in the United States: Promised the
rewards of citizenship, they continually face fire.

As with Shadrack, the Peace household fulfills more than one biblical
typology. Hannah of the Bible is the mother of the prophet Samuel. Barren
for many years, the pious Hannah dedicates Samuel's life to God, and Samuel
later anoints Saul and then David as Kings of Israel. Again, Sula's name
recalls both Saul and Samuel; in fact, the name Samuel is "an etymology of
the name Saul." Sula is not exactly Saul, nor is she exactly Samuel, although
she is a prophetic, as well as an apocalyptic character.

Readers in American culture are accustomed to employing an
"either/or" hermeneutic for all literary forms, including the Bible. But parables do not, in fact, come with the pre-determined morality associated not

only with fundamentalist Christian churches, but with certain secular misunderstandings of Christian theology. Sallie McFague defines the parabolic form:

> A parable is . . . an assault on the accepted, conventional way of viewing reality. It is an assault on the social, economic, and mythic structures people build for their own comfort and security. A parable is a story meant to invert and subvert these structures.

Not surprisingly, Morrison's critics want to identify characters precisely with a biblical namesake or as the namesake's opposite. Such a position, however, fails to take into account not only Morrison's project regarding categories but also the subversive nature of the Christian parabolic form, as well as the complexity and depth inherent in naming in the scriptural sources themselves.

In 1 Samuel Hannah's prophetic prayer, which she sings after Samuel's birth, encompasses a characteristic biblical reversal:

> The bows of the mighty men are broken, and they that stumbled are girded with strength. . . . He raiseth up the poor out of the dust, and lifteth up the beggar from the dunghill, to set them among princes, and to make them inherit the throne of glory.

As Rosenberg notes, it is a prayer in which:

> YHWH is invoked as the God of surprise, bringing down the mighty, raising up the downtrodden; impoverishing the wealthy and enriching the pauper, bereaving the fertile and making barren the fruitful—always circumventing the trappings of human vanity and the complacency of the overcontented.

The New Testament fulfillment of Hannah's song is the Magnificat of Mary. In *Sula*, it is not Sula's mother Hannah who utters yet another fulfillment of this prayer, but Sula herself. On her deathbed, Sula is speaking to her estranged and beloved Nel:

> "After all the old women have lain with the teen-agers; when all the young girls have slept with their old drunken uncles; after all the black men fuck all the white ones; when all the white women

kiss all the black ones; when the guards have raped all the jail-birds and after all the whores make love to their grannies; after all the faggots get their mothers' trim; when Lindbergh sleeps with Bessie Smith and Norma Shearer makes it with Stepin Fetchit; after all the dogs have fucked all the cats and every weather-vane on every barn flies off the roof to mount the hogs . . . then there'll be a little love left over for me. And I know just what it will feel like."

Sula's soliloquy also recalls (and inverts) the "Laws Regulating the Personal Relationships" of the Hebrews, set out in the eighteenth chapter of Leviticus. Sula has been categorized by her own people as a pariah: "Whosoever shall commit any of these abominations, even the souls that commit them shall be cut off from among their people." The laws (categories) must be broken, and abominations committed, for there to be "a little love left over" for Sula. Like the anarchic, insurrectionary Christ, Sula overturns the Law, as Jesus does in Matthew:

Think not that I am come to send peace on earth; I came not to send peace, but a sword. For I am come to set a man at variance against his father, and the daughter against her mother, and the daughter-in-law against her mother-in-law. And a man's foes shall be they of his own household. He that loveth father or mother more than me, is not worthy of me. And he that taketh not his cross and followeth me, is not worthy of me. He that findeth his life shall lose it; and he that loseth his life for my sake shall find it.

Sula's prophecy, like Christ's (and Hannah's and Mary's), describes a complete categorical collapse that entails a radical revisioning of the world. The politics of *Sula* are not programmatic; rather, the novel focuses on a social understanding that gives rise to action. Again, the historical Jesus of Nazareth constantly challenged social norms and hierarchies, law and dogma, as well as defying the complacency and acceptance of these norms by people of all social classes. Textually, such an understanding must be complex, nonbinary, encompassing and, above all historical. For example, Eva's burning of her son is a horrifying act, if we categorize *Sula* as realism. But Morrison is writing history in parabolic form, not necessarily reality, and certainly not pre-determined morality.

In terms of the interweaving of motherhood and war, Eva has removed her son from the possibility of going to war again by killing him. With historical rather than ethical reasoning, she explains to her daughter Hannah the difficulty of Plum's birth, and what the war did to him:

> "He gave me such a time. Such a time. Look like he didn't even want to be born. . . . After all that carryin' on . . . he wanted to crawl back in my womb. . . . I had room enough in my heart, but not in my womb, not no more. I birthed him once. I couldn't do it again."

Again Eva echoes Revelation, where the woman with the wings of an eagle "is nourished for a time, and times, and half a time, from the face of the serpent." The beginning and the end are joined, as with the description of the Bottom: Eva, the first woman (Genesis), is connected to the end of time, the apocalypse (Revelation). Her relation to the serpent (Satan, the dragon) is complicated: Is Eva's act of child murder evil, merciful, or a combination of both?

Sula defies any desire to categorize its events in terms of a simplistic or fundamental morality, and instead offers an historically and spiritually informed understanding of civil rights and African American military service. Morrison chooses to foreground historical and chronological events through her use of years as chapter headings (e.g., "1921," "1923," etc.). This heightens *Sula*'s departure from "reality," but not from history. As Kimberly Benston has said, "All of Afro-American literature may be seen as one vast genealogical poem that attempts to restore continuity to the ruptures or discontinuities imposed by the history of black presence in America." This is where Morrison's historical writing intersects with her theory of categorization. The fates of the Bottom-dwellers represent a political system which has enslaved people, emancipated people, enfranchised them, disenfranchised them—then simultaneously demanded their military service and denied them citizenship through civilian lives of poverty and terror. Morrison's transfigured categories fit Benston's maxim exactly because they encompass discontinuities and contradictions, which are a distinguishing characteristic of the parabolic form. Her parables accomplish connection, where before there was division, and so "restore continuity" to American history by recognizing the constitutive role of the African American experience. Morrison enriches Benston's observation in her explicit, biblical recognition of spirituality as inseparable from history.

Sula's characterization comprehends more biblical typologies than any other in *Sula*. The birthmark over her eye looks to some Bottom-dwellers like a rosebud, to others like the head of a snake. The rose is the flower of Mary, mother of Christ. Mary is the anti-type, the fulfillment, of Eve, who encounters the serpent; in Genesis, God says to the serpent, "And I will put enmity between thee and the woman, and between thy seed and her seed; he shall bruise thy head, and thou shalt bruise his heel." Sula's birthmark also recalls the seals on the foreheads of the servants of God in Revelation. Sula is Saul and Samuel and David, who is a type of Christ; she is the fulfillment of Eve (and therefore of her grandmother Eva) and Mary; and she is the prophet and the Christ, a figure of redemption and resurrection—an insurrectionary, anarchic figure, like the historical Jesus. Sula's most significant connections to other characters—to Nel, on the one hand, to Shadrack, on the other—have biblical parallels as well. Shad the fisherman is Peter to Sula's Christ, and Shadrack sees Sula's birthmark as neither a rose nor a snake but as a tadpole. Shad is both Christian apostle and African ancestral medium; thus, his "insanity" enables his transcendent vision of the tadpole: at once two animals—a frog and a fish—one in the process of becoming the other. Shadrack sees not absolute categories, either/or, but interdependence, growth, and transformation—the goal of parable.

Sula and Nel also recall David and Jonathan, biblical warriors whose greatest love was for each other. Nel's ending cry is for Sula:

> "All that time, all that time, I thought I was missing Jude. . . .
> We was girls together . . . . O Lord, Sula," she cried, "girl, girl,
> girlgirlgirl."

Her cry inverts David's lament for Jonathan, the son of Saul:

> "I am distressed for thee, my brother Jonathan; very pleasant hast
> thou been unto me. Thy love to me was wonderful passing the
> love of women."

Sula Peace represents a radical kind of love, her characterization combines Old Testament warrior/kings with the New Testament Prince of Peace. Her last question to Nel, "'About who was good. How do you know it was you?'" recalls questions posed by Jesus time and again. It is the question embedded in the inversions of the New Testament and the Hebrew Bible that allows, for example, the first to be last and the last to be first.

After Sula's death, at the end of 1940, ". . . Medallion turned silver," from "a rain [that] fell and froze," like Revelation's "sea of glass like crystal." With Sula dead, "a dislocation was taking place" for the Bottom-dwellers. Suicide Day 1941 arrives, and Shadrack becomes Moses, leading his children to the Promised Land, "as though there really was hope." At the river, the citizens of Medallion's small ghetto begin to dismantle "the tunnel they were forbidden to build," having been denied jobs on the tunnel project because of their color. But unlike the Red Sea's parting for the children of Israel, the river does not become for the folks of the Bottom "a wall unto them on their right hand, and on their left." Instead, the tunnel walls collapse: "A lot of them died there. . . [but] Mr. Buckland Reed escaped, so did Patsy and her two boys, as well as some fifteen or twenty who had not gotten close enough to fall."

Morrison's subtle theological reinterpretations no more allow for absolute categorization than does Scripture. In Exodus, "The Lord saved Israel that day out of the hand of Egyptians; and Israel saw the Egyptians dead upon the seashore," but there is no such satisfaction for Bottom-dwellers—they are the ones who die, not their oppressors. Moreover, Morrison's invocation of Exodus recalls the complexity of the chosen people's position: their relapse into worship of false idols, their forty years of wandering in the wilderness.

Morrison never forgets the inconsistencies of all human beings. In *Sula*, the dwellers of the Bottom of Medallion, Ohio, are nightshade and blackberries, both bad and good. Suffering under a social system which continues to require of African Americans their very lives, and which identifies them always as "other," the people of the Bottom are quite as capable as their white oppressors on the valley floor of invoking racism toward their own "others": "garlic-ridden hunkies, corrupt Catholics, racist Protestants, cowardly Jews," and so on. In the late sixties and early seventies, when Morrison was writing the novel, black theologians struggled to articulate a theology of liberation for their people, to repeat Morrison's words, "in a period of intense political activity." In *Sula* Morrison has given us history dependent more on spirituality than realism, something she does in her other novels as well.

The recognition of *Sula*—and I would argue that this is true of Morrison's entire cannon—as parabolic suggests that it is appropriate to characterize the novel as theological; that is, Morrison provides parabolic models for the interpretation of the kingdom of God, where the kingdom of God is always a matter of relations and communities in this world. Again, this is in keeping with Sallie McFague's understanding:

> What is stressed in parables and in Jesus' own life focuses on persons and their relationships; therefore, the dominance of the patriarchal model in the Christian tradition must be seen as a perversion in its hegemony of the field of religious models and its exclusion of other personal relational models.

Without a doubt, Morrison's political novels subvert this perverse hegemony. Christ-figures such as Sula engender social repentance and cultural reflection; their disruption of the social order inheres in the parabolic form. In turn, they evoke a desire for community and relationality, and for liberation, in the tradition of the African American Christian church.

In Morrison's historical, revisionary theology of community, the "Bottom" exists at the top, and the "fine cry—loud and long"—of woman mourning beloved woman has "no bottom and . . . no top." Of the Peace family tombstones in the Medallion graveyard we read: "They were not dead people. They were words. Not even words. Wishes, longings." In the mystical world of Morrison's Africanized Christianity, the dead remain with the living always, like Sula's "sleep of water always," and this presence and this yearning describes beauty, inscribes hope—inscribes a most significant and subversive empowerment.

PHILIP PAGE

Shocked into Separateness: Unresolved Oppositions in Sula

Like *The Bluest Eye, Sula* is based on the underlying condition that fragmentation and displacement are the fundamental barriers to the formation of African-American identities. Whereas the first novel probes the pernicious efforts of the imposition of external standards on the black community, in *Sula* Morrison more explicitly constructs a system of binary oppositions and simultaneously unravels it. Here, Morrison becomes overtly deconstructive, writing "what the French call *différance*, that feminine style that opens the closure of binary oppositions and thus subverts many of the basic assumptions of Western humanistic thought." By moving into the split, Morrison scrutinizes the ambivalent counterforces of fusion and fragmentation.

In this novel, the most important of the oppositions is between self and other. Displaced as they are by the racial dichotomy, characters in *Sula* are drawn into the traditional Western misconception that assumes the existence of a unitary self and that privileges self over other. They assume that they must have an originary self and/or that they can acquire it with or through an other. Morrison thereby directs attention to one potential response to the characters' fragmentation: fusion with another person in the attempt to solidify one's identity. Whereas the characters in *The Bluest Eye* tend to fold inward in their attempts to define themselves, the characters in *Sula* look outward to relationships with significant others. Such pairs involve parent

From *Dangerous Freedom: Fusion and Fragmentation in Toni Morrison's Novels.* © 1995 by the University Press of Mississippi.

and child, heterosexual couples, and peers—most fully the relationship between Sula and Nel.

In *Sula* Morrison depicts a rigidly bipolar world, one in which the falsifications and privileging are so extreme that the tensions between opposed terms are overwhelming, as attested by the novel's numerous deaths. As the novel documents this bipolarity and the concomitant tensions, however, it undercuts that system and privileges a fluid, open, and liberating perspective. Sula, forced to become exile and then pariah, personifies this new freedom that dares to reject the old dichotomies and to create a new kind of identity. Both the character and the novel become representative of divisions within the American and African-American cultures.

As in *The Bluest Eye* the world in *Sula* is inverted and the mode is ironic, but in *Sula*, as Deborah McDowell asserts, Morrison strikes a more elegiac chord. The dedication to Morrison's two sons looks ahead to their mother's sense of loss after their departure: "This book is for Ford and Slade, whom I miss although they have not left me." The epigraph from Tennessee Williams's *The Rose Tattoo* also evokes the pathos of loss, the loss of "glory," both for oneself and in the eyes of others: "Nobody knew my rose of the world but me. . . . I had too much glory. They don't want glory like that in nobody's heart." In the novel's first sentence, the narrator grieves for the loss of the Bottom: "there was once a neighborhood." Every chapter includes the physical or spiritual death of at least one African American, and the plot culminates with Sula's death and the tunnel disaster. As the novel spans the destructive years from World War I through the Depression to the threshold of World War II in 1941 (the year in which *The Bluest Eye* is set) to 1965 and the civil rights movement, it becomes an elegy for the victims of war, poverty, and racial violence. Morrison refers to "the nostalgia, the history, and the nostalgia for the history" in this novel, and Melissa Walker describes it in terms of "late sixties nostalgia for a lost but not so distant world." After Sula's death, the mourning becomes more poignant, first when Shadrack grieves for his lost friend: "She lay on a table there. It was surely the same one. The same little-girl face, same tadpole over the eye. So he had been wrong. Terribly wrong. No 'always' at all. Another dying away of someone whose face he knew." Then the mourning escalates further when Nel cries for her lost friendship with Sula: "We was girls together. . . . O Lord, Sula . . . girl, girl, girlgirlgirl." Like many contemporary African-American novels, *Sula* eulogizes a lost community and a lost past.

The displacements begin with the novel's setting, which begins with the first sentence: "In that place, where they tore the nightshade and blackberry patches from their roots to make room for the Medallion City Golf Course, there was once a neighborhood." As Morrison explains, this lost world is fragmented into oppositions: place/neighborhood, they/neighbors (and implicitly whites/blacks), nightshade/blackberry, roots/Medallion, houses/golf course, and past/present. The larger community is divided between town and Bottom, and the division is ironic, based on the fraud of the "nigger joke" that initiated the racial division of the land, which exemplifies Ellison's "joke at the center of the American identity."

In *Sula* many issues are depicted in terms of opposing values or terms. The present is directly contrasted with the past, and female and male roles are opposed. The Wrights, the Greenes, and the Bottom itself are studies in social conformity, which is set against the individual freedom of the Peaces. The story of Nel and Sula becomes an investigation of the meanings of good and evil, the values associated with monogamy and promiscuity, and the relevance of innocence and experience. By what it leaves out as well as by what it includes, the novel contrasts presence and absence. And, especially through Sula's meditations on her identity, the novel explores the relationship between self and other.

The novel is thus posited on a binary structure. Its setting is divided between the Bottom and Medallion, a black community and an anonymous white town, a neighborhood and a golf course. Its plot chronicles the lives of two opposed characters who grow up in two opposed houses managed under two opposed theories of child-rearing. The character pairings of Nel and Sula are doubled in the pairings of their contrasting mothers (Helene and Hannah) and grandmothers (Rochelle and Eva). As opposed to the differences in these female pairs, the men in Nel and Sula's lives are similar but also paired: each woman lacks a brother or male friend, each has an absent father, and each has her most significant heterosexual relationship with a self-doubting man who departs abruptly (Jude and Ajax). The plot opposes the highly indiviualized black characters and the nameless, featureless white characters who hover on the fringes. It opposes the sane residents of the Bottom and the insane Shadrack, whose well-ordered cabin represents a further dichotomy with his disorderly behavior. It sets children in opposition to adults, most notably in mothers' lack of love or liking for their children. It contrasts meaningful employment, such as construction work, and demeaning labor in hotels and white homes.

To reinforce this pattern of binary opposites, *Sula* is divided almost exactly into halves, a dyadic structure that is reinforced by the nearly palindromic pattern in which the introduction of characters in Part I is reversed in the dispensation of characters in Part II. In addition, the novel is split between a linear structure, implied by the inexorable march of years in the chapter titles, and a circular one, suggested by the narrator's frame that starts the discourse after the Bottom has already disappeared.

The narrative form of this novel, in contrast to *The Bluest Eye*, also reveals a binary pattern. Whereas in Morrison's first novel the conventional distinction between external narrator and character breaks down in the polyvocal narration, in *Sula*, except for two paragraphs in which Nel narrates directly, the distinction between external narrator and characters is maintained. Moreover, the narrator/character distinction is underscored by the opening section, which highlights the narrator's historical knowledge and vast distance from the characters' perspectives.

Correspondingly, the conventional distinction between an external narrator and the reader is forcefully maintained in *Sula*. This narrator, unlike Morrison's chatty narrator in *Jazz*, establishes her credentials and her distance from the reader in the opening chapter and maintains that seperation throughout. The narrator rarely permits dialogue between characters, thus retaining tight control over the telling of the story. The narrator manipulates readers, forcing the story onto them, shocking them with sudden violence, making them question their responses to such characters as Eva and Sula, delaying crucial information (such as Jude's adultery with Sula), leaving frustrating gaps between years, omitting important scenes (such as Plum's and Hannah's funerals), not reporting what happens to Eva or Sula when they leave the Bottom, and not relating what happens to Jude or Ajax after they depart. The narrator also shocks readers with mysterious beginnings of chapters (such as "It was too cool for ice cream" or "Old people were dancing with little children") and teases them by reversing the normal order of things (as when she reports the *second* strange thing before the first). Not only highly controlling, the narrator is also noticably omniscient, with access not only to many characters' thoughts but also the collective feelings of the community, for example when she describes the narrow lives of the Bottom's women or the hope that seduces everyone into the last National Suicide Day parade.

At the same time that *Sula* is constructed on a system of binary opposites, the novel subverts that structure. Perhaps the clearest example of this deconstructing is the play between linear chronology and circularity. As many commentators have noticed, the novel purports to move steadfastly forward through time, as its chapter titles suggest, but even as it does so, it moves backward and foreward, circling or spiraling through time. As Denise Heinze and Maxine Lavon Montgomery suggest, the novel's double perspective of linearity and circularity reflects a fusion of Euro-American and traditional African concepts of time.

This subversion of Western linearity represents Morrison's attack on traditional, white-imposed conceptions. Although McDowell states that "the narrative retreats from linearity," the strategy is not a retreat but the assertion of an alternative. While *The Bluest Eye* primarily laments the imposition of white, dualistic standards, *Sula* confronts such standards, loosens them, and advocates a nonlinear response. That perspective is suggested by Christian, who argues that the novel is about "the search for self . . . continually thwarted by the society from which Sula Peace comes," and by Kathryn Bond Stockton, who states that *Sula* confronts "the reign of the white gender" that "seduces blacks away from the Bottom's communal bonds into the tight configuration of the couple."

The novel's alternative position leads to its often perplexing openness. Robert Grant documents the novel's emphasis on the lack of a coherent subject and consequently on missing objects (Eva's leg and comb), absent or missed characters (Chicken Little, Ajax, Sula), and objects that evoke missing persons (Sula's belt, Jude's tie). These gaps and discontinuities create holes in the text that unhinge any straightforward narration, thereby calling into question traditional means of representation and allowing for greater reader participation. For Grant the novel thereby becomes "a prime 'postmodernist' text whose interpretational difficulties are a function of Morrison's calculated indeterminacies." Similarly, the novel raises but leaves "largely unresolved" the issue of good and evil, an issue that Morrison has said she deliberately dealt with in a non-Western, that is to say, nonoppositional, manner. Placing this alternative stance in the context of feminine writing, Barbara Rigney claims that the emphasis on absence, ambiguity, multiple perspectives, and fragmentation creates a novel that, "like all of Morrison's works, subverts concepts of textual unity and defies totalized interpretation."

The deconstructive implications of this open perspective are implied by Hortense Spillers, who contends throughout her essay for the creative openness of *Sula*, and are spelled out in detail by McDowell, who quotes Spillers ("No Manichean analysis demanding a polarity of interest— black/white, male/female, good/bad—will do"). For McDowell, "*Sula* is rife with liberating possibilities in that it transgresses all deterministic structures of opposition." "The narrative insistently blurs and confuses . . . binary oppositions" and "glories in paradox and ambiguity" as it creates "a world that demands a shift from an either/or orientation to one that is both/and, full of shifts and contradictions."

Like a jazz composition, *Sula* sounds a traditional Euro-American motif, a structure of binary oppositions. Simultaneously, it plays on that motif, modifying it, refiguring it, subverting it, fusing it with non-Western values. The result is a complex doubling, or multiplying, of perspectives, content, and form that embodies and challenges both Euro-American and African-American standpoints and that enables Morrison to fret out the fragments in a simultaneously fused and unfused whole.

Whereas *The Bluest Eye* examines isolated individuals who are split from meaningful relationships with community, family, or friend, in *Sula* characters respond to their bipolar world by attempting to create personal meaning through intimacy with another person. Such attempted dyads allow the characters temporary relief from their isolation and thus help them endure the frustrations of their marginalized and divided lives, but they also provide no lasting solution.

As this novel focuses on potential paired characters, it noticeably lacks emphasis on larger groups. There is no triad of intimate women, like the three prostitutes in *The Bluest Eye*, Pilate-Reba-Hagar in *Song of Solomon*, or Sethe-Beloved-Denver in *Beloved*. The corresponding group is Eva-Hannah-Sula, but these three women constitute a much less cohesive unit than the other triads, as evidenced by the negation in their relationships (Eva had no time to love Hannah, Hannah does not like Sula, and Sula exiles Eva to the county home). Though tied by blood in a direct matrilineal line, they are a dis-unit, a deconstructed unit. The tensions between their unity and their separateness figure the pervading tensions in *Sula* between *any* structure and its decomposition. The only united triad is the deweys, but their unity is achieved at the expense of each boy's individuality, as suggested by their namelessness. Their stunted physical and mental growth attests to the parodic and inverted nature of their relationship and thus symbolizes the lack of viability of such groups in this novel.

Pairs of characters in *Sula* frequently attempt unions—most noticeably between parent and child, in heterosexual couples, and between peers—but such unions are often short-lived and always problematic. As a result, like the frozen blades of grass during the ice storm, the characters remain "shocked into separateness." At the end of the novel, Nel senses the isolation: "Now there weren't any places left, just separate houses with separate televisions and separate telephones and less and less dropping by."

One type of attempted pair is mother and child (men are so consistently absent that no father/child relationships exist). Daughters, such as Hannah and Sula, desire closer relationships than their mothers can provide: Eva has no time or energy to love Hannah, and Hannah in turn, like her friends, expresses her dislike for her daughter. Mother/daughter relations are even more insecure in Nel's family, where Helene and her mother Rochelle are permanently estranged, where Helene's version of motherhood is to mold Nel (literally by trying to reshape her nose and figuratively by eliminating her individuality) into her own concept of white respectability, and where Nel looks upon her own children as a burden. Throughout the Bottom, except for the artificial period when people use their fear of Sula's alleged evil to rally behind each other, mothers (such as Teapot's Mamma) treat their children as difficult objects rather than as loved human beings. Nevertheless, although mother-daughter relationships appear to lack closeness and love, they do so only in comparison to a traditionally white ideal. As in *The Bluest Eye*, where imposed white standards of beauty and value are set against contrasting black standards, here white stereotypes of parent-child harmonies are implicitly contrasted with more fluid communal values. Mothers may not love or like their daughters in the ideal of the Dick-and-Jane myth, but through belief in communal values, even though such values are not ideal, mothers endure, holding their households and the community together.

Mother-son relationships are just as problematic. Like Sethe's murder of Beloved, Eva must murder Plum out of love, when the alternative for him is worse than death, in his case because he has lost his selfhood. Three Bottom sons—the deweys—are divorced from their mothers, adopted by Eva, and in the process lose their individuality and chance for maturity. Although they are fused with each other, like Plum they are isolated from themselves and society. Another Bottom son, Jude, tries to establish a motherly relationship with his wife Nel, and another son, Ajax, does love his mother, but their overpowering relationship (he "worship[s]" her) seems to prevent him from forming a lasting commitment to anything except airplanes: "This woman Ajax loved, and after her—airplanes. There was nothing in between." As Baker writes, Ajax "is properly understood . . . not as 'his own man,' but as the offspring of his mother's magic."

Characters also attempt significant relationships as heterosexual couples. Except for the marriage between Helene and Wiley (which presumably lasts because Wiley is so seldom at home), all such pairs (Eva-BoyBoy, Nel-Jude, and Sula-Ajax) are temporary. More successful are Hannah's brief, unthreatening, and mutually satisfying affairs with the Bottom's husbands. More viable is Eva's household and her role as mentor for young married couples. More enduring is the community itself, which provides an alternative form of integration to the couple.

The attempted fusion with another person is most fully exemplified in Sula and Nel's relationship. Critics agree that the two are nearly fused, the critical agreement deriving from the textual evidence of Sula and Nel's near merger into one consciousness. In her pubescent dreams each one fantasizes the presence of the other, a sympathetic female presence with whom the romantic adventure can be shared. When they actually meet, their psyches are already half-united: they are instantly like "old friends," they share "their own perceptions of things," and they are "joined in mutual admiration." Later, they have "difficulty distinguishing one's thoughts from the other's," they share one eye, and Eva alleges that "never was no difference between [them]."

Despite this near fusion, Sula and Nel are almost opposites, as suggested by their mutual fascination with the other's house and family. As Baker notes, their fantasies betray their opposing destinies: Nel passively "wait[s] for some fiery prince" who "approached but never quite arrived," whereas Sula "gallop[s] through her own mind on a gray-and-white horse tasting sugar and smelling roses." Fulfilling those early fantasies, Nel never leaves the Bottom, but Sula travels widely, and Nel becomes the model of community respectability as opposed to Sula's unconventional behavior. For Nel "Hell is change," but for Sula "doing anything forever and ever was hell." They are like the poles of two magnets, both irreconcilably repelling and absolutely attracting. After years of separation each regains a glimpse of their lost unity: in Sula's moment of afterlife consciousness she thinks of sharing her experience of death with Nel, and the final words of the novel depict Nel's epiphany of lost union with Sula.

This rich and ambivalent relationship between Sula and Nel suggests that Morrison is experimenting with alternative conceptions of selfhood and friendship. Their closeness calls into question the traditional notion of the unitary self, and their enduring yet strained relationship also questions the stereotype of undying friendship. According to Rigney, they "represent aspects of a common self, a construction of an identity *in relationship.*" Such a construction further probes the issues of unity and separateness, of self and pair.

Although Morrison in her authorial detachment can experiment with their relationship and their identities, both Sula and Nel have trouble resisting the conventional illusion that a relationship with a significant other must be total and all-consuming. Each tries unsuccessfully to find that degree of absorption with her mother and her grandmother. Then, after their momentary union as adolescents, their inevitable differences and social conventions drive them apart. Just as the momentary physical bond between Sula and Chicken Little cannot hold, Sula and Nel slip farther and farther apart. That gap begins at the moment when Chicken Little "slipped from [Sula's] hands," and the gap develops into "a space, a separateness" at Chicken's funeral. Nel then attempts to substitute an all-consuming relationship with Jude, but this attempt, in its disequilibrium, is shallow. Nel, cautious and conforming, repeats her mistake with Sula, trying to create her identity in fusion with another's. Sula, more active and nonconformist, embarks on a quest, but her quest is similar to Nel's marriage, for she seeks another Nel, a friend who will be "both an other and a self," and after her return she seeks union, first with Jude and then with Ajax. Both Sula and Nel seek totalizing unions with significant others, but when such unions do not last, their only recourse is isolation. The counterpart to symbiosis is division.

One consequence of the characters' attempts to find meaning in a relationship with another person is that they have difficulties in maintaining workable self-concepts. Their senses of self become entangled with their quests for fulfilling relationships with another, and in the process their identities, their relationships, and their communal ties all suffer.

The women of the Bottom are remarkably able to endure nearly impossible conditions, but in doing so their balance between self and other is skewed. As a result, like the characters in *The Bluest Eye*, they need "to clean themselves" on such scapegoats as Shadrack, Sula, and even their own children. Helene loses her self in her need to disassociate herself from her prostitute mother, and she endlessly repeats that loss in such acts as her self-denying smile of humiliation on the train. To compensate for such identity loss, she becomes a complete assimilationist, outdoing Pauline in her self-serving refuge in social superiority, rigid Christianity, and self-denying emulation of the white middle class. Like Geraldine and Ruth Dead, she effaces her funky self, as Helene Sabat becomes the watered-down, whitened Helene Wright, trying in her self-*right*eousness always to be considered "right." Such conforming characters, lacking a core self, disintegrate into fragments. They are examples of the black middle class whom Leroi Jones (Amiri Baraka) describes as determined "to become *citizens*": "They did not even want to be 'accepted' as *themselves*, they wanted any self which the mainstream dictated, and the mainstream *always* dictated. And this black middle class, in turn, tried always to dictate that self, or this image of a whiter Negro, to the poorer, blacker Negroes." Hannah comes closer to a healthy accommodation between self and other, meeting her own needs for male companionship without sacrificing her dignity or making unrealistic demands, but, like the other adults, she too can make no permanent relationships and is estranged from her child.

Eva is forced by her isolation and poverty to take such ultimate risks as abandoning her children and sacrificing her own leg. One-legged, she tries to stand alone, without a significant other, but in doing so, like Baby Suggs and Sethe in *Beloved*, she overdoes her independence and willfulness, assuming a goddess-like imperialism that privileges the righteousness of her self and her will at the expense of others. She "creates" the deweys, rescuing them from potentially worse fates but denying them full identity and augmenting her own selfhood at their expense. Similarly, she saves Plum from further despair, but her act of murder is also motivated by her desire to protect herself from the shame and grief of his loss of self. Eva is so busy surviving that she has no energy for the conventional (white) mother-daughter love, and that lack is also a consequence of her over-reliance on self and her lack of recognition, not to mention compassion, for others. Then, her inability to save Hannah from the fire, a reoccurrence of the fire in which she burns Plum, is part of the price she has to pay, a price she pays again when Sula, also ego-bound, rejects her.

The males in *Sula*, displaced by their inferior racial status, never achieve stable selfhood. Tar Baby, Plum, and the deweys lose their identities. They are like Shadrack, whose sense of self and other is shattered in the war. He, however, can provisionally control his fear of disintegration through his obsessively well-ordered cabin and his ritual of National Suicide Day, measures that parallel the Bottom's collective ability to control its traumas by incorporating whatever evils confront it. Other men—BoyBoy, Jude, and Ajax—are more capable of coping with life, but they never attain full integration of self and other. With no meaningful work, they lack confidence and therefore cannot remain in what they feel are half-emasculated roles. Symbolized by Ajax's fascination with planes, each of these eligible males therefore flies from the burden of a permanent role as a husband and father.

Neither Jude nor Ajax can mature fully because each remains too attached to his need for a mother. Jude does not want an equal partner in Nel but someone who will mother him. He is still a child whose selfhood is ever frail, overwhelmed by the weight of the oppressive economic and social conditions of the male work world and taking refuge in self-pity and the desire to be worshipped. He lacks the psychic resources to resist Sula or to face the consequences with Nel. Denied a complete identity by the white system's refusal of satisfying work, he wants "a someone sweet, industrious and loyal to shore him up." Unable to find or become a self, he chooses Nel in the delusion that "the two of them together would make one Jude." His choice of Nel is a displacement, a vain attempt to replace his mother, to replace his own absent identity, to find "someone to care about his hurt, to care very deeply." Ajax appears to be more secure in his selfhood: hero-like, he bears gifts of life, such as milk and butterflies, and he enjoys a temporary equality with Sula. But his close ties to his conjuring mother do not allow him to make lasting commitments to anyone else. Like Jude, his selfhood and self-confidence are frail, so at the first sign of possessiveness on Sula's part, he takes to the air, and his identity is correspondingly deflated from the heroic Ajax to the mundane Albert Jacks.

The course of Nel's efforts to establish an effective balance between self and other is more complex. Her "exhilarating" but "fearful" trip to New Orleans, including her disassociation from her mother's loss of identity on the train and her liberating encounter with her grandmother, at first enables her to find a sense of self: "'I'm me. I'm not their daughter. I'm not Nel. I'm me. Me.'" This initial spark allows her to become Sula's partner, each fulfilling the gap in the other's imagination. Her flame of independent selfhood gradually burns down, however, under the constant, distorting pressures of racial, gender, and parental influence as well as her own passivity. It falters in comparison to Sula's overwhelming, rebellious selfhood and seems to flicker out with the death of Chicken Little, after which even her relationship with Sula is not the same and for which she denies responsibility for over forty years. By the time she accepts marriage with Jude, the fire is cold, and she becomes the supportive, conforming, self-denying woman her mother tried to construct. Her attempts to fuse herself and Jude are specious, based on assimilated values, and, instead of a healthy unity, she only becomes locked in a fragmentary existence.

Nel's rejection of Sula in favor of a socially acceptable role as nurturing wife and mother leaves her with few psychic resources after that role is rendered unacceptable. Her unfulfilled self then is reflected in her inability to love her children, in which ironically she again conforms with the rest of the mothers in the community. She is unable to love or feel compassion for anyone, becoming all too much like her mother. That unfocused self is symbolized by the grey ball of fur that lurks just out of her imaginative vision. Like the white ring—also round—on Ruth Dead's table, it is the cloud in which she hides her self-knowledge and self-acceptance. Its semi-presence suggests that she at least senses that she is denying herself and therefore all others, unlike such characters as Helene, who have forgotten entirely such denial and such self-knowledge. Although it haunts Nel, the grey ball thus indicates that her quest for selfhood is not dead but merely dormant, waiting to be revived by Eva's uncanny divination of the truth of her responsibility for Chicken Little's death and therefore of her responsibility for her own life. At the end of the novel, too late for Nel to reestablish her intimacy with Sula, she dissolves the grey ball and regains a self, her relation to the other, and the deep, humanizing sorrow that accompanies the revelation.

More than any of the other characters, Sula suffers from the dislocations of self and other. The narrator is explicit: "The first experience [Hannah's denial of liking her] taught her there was no other that you could count on; the second [Chicken Little's death] that there was no self to count on either." But, unaware of any other choices, "she had clung to Nel as the closest thing to both an other and a self, only to discover that she and Nel were not one and the same thing." Neither aided by the usual models for self-development nor checked by the usual restraints, and finding that she can neither find an identity in the other nor form her own (either in conjunction with or separate from that other), she drifts into the attempt to make herself. Given the confining conditions of life in the Bottom and given the paralyzing conventions for identity in both the mainstream society and the black community, making oneself is a positive and promising choice. Pilate

Dead does achieve a healthy, self-made identity, but Sula must struggle, perhaps because, despite her aggressive self-confidence, she has "no ego," "no center, no speck around which to grow." Unlike Pilate, who knows she must guide Milkman, Sula has no defining project, no focus; she is an "artist with no art form." Along with this lack, the defining moments in Sula's development are negative. Just as Cholly's dangerous freedom and fragmented self result from the triple deaths of Aunt Jimmy, his masculinity, and his dream for a father, so Sula's undirected self follows from the triple negation of her mother's rejection, her "murder" of Chicken Little, and Nel's preference for marriage.

Part of Sula's problem is that she cannot live anywhere but the Bottom, where her only communal role is that of the pariah. She can exist only in the eyes of others, only as the nonprivileged member of another destructive opposition, but she cannot conform because that would eliminate her visibility and hence her existence. Unlike Pecola, who becomes what she perceives, Sula becomes what she is perceived to be. Thus, her birthmark continually changes shape and color, because, like Sula herself, her mark is what others see it to be. When she does lapse into conformity with the community's role of "wife," her independent selfhood, which Ajax sees and appreciates, vanishes in his eyes, and she becomes nothing to him and to herself. Sula is unable to join herself with any other, yet she is unable to exist independently. As in all of Morrison's fiction, neither fusion nor fragmentation suffices.

It is tempting to fall into the trap of praising or blaming Sula. Deborah Guth lines up previous critics into those who find Sula triumphing and those who find her failing, and Guth herself compares Sula unfavorably to Eva. But such attempts at judgment are misdirected, for, like Claudia, Sula cannot be pinned down to one reading or one value judgment. Spillers articulates the required open-endedness: "We would like to love Sula, or damn her, inasmuch as the myth of the black American woman allows only Manichean responses, but it is impossible to do either. We can only behold in an absolute suspension of final judgment." Like her birthmark, Sula remains open for interpretation.

Sula's resistance to any fixed interpretation parallels her own role in resisting the narrow formulations of self, woman, or black. She strives to remain free of convention, and correspondingly she must remain free of readers' fixed formulations. For Henderson, Sula is a representative of "the self-inscription of black womanhood," an avatar of an alternative identity and role for African-American women. In Henderson's terms, via "disruption and revision" Sula re-reads and repudiates "black male discourse," and I would add all conventional discourse, black and white, female and male. Spillers agrees in principle, arguing that Sula is "a literal and figurative *breakthrough* toward the assertion of what we may call, in relation to her literary 'relatives,' new female being," who "overthrows received moralities in a heedless quest for her own irreducible self," declaring her independence in her "radical amorality" and "radical freedom."

By this reasoning, Sula is the locus for the creativity of the novel. Like Morrison's text, Sula cannot be fully known, as Morrison creates her with unending play between interpretative possibilities. As the novel posits a world governed by binary oppositions and exerts sustained pressure against that structure, Sula personally opposes the binary world, tries to escape it, experiments with subverting it, and finally yields to it. Both novel and character, by questioning the system and by groping toward alternative responses, make themselves up and concomitantly deconstruct the status quo. *Sula* and Sula remain open, for to finalize an interpretation is to close the book and end the process. Sula thus retains her hermeneutical richness; she is the title character, inviting our interpretations, and/but she is offstage for at least half the book, again inviting but not finalizing our readings. Her birthmark is a synecdoche for this role, like her and like the novel, open for interpretation, mediating between the external object and the internal subject. It, Sula, and *Sula* are "free-floating signifier(s)."

Sula's self-created self, her role as pariah, and her confusion over self and other double Shadrack's similar status. When he sees his comrade's head blown away, Shadrack loses confidence in the stability of the other and in the order and permanence of the material world. Similarly, Sula's belief in the order of the universe is destroyed by the blank space in the water above Chicken Little's body. Each event also shatters each character's sense of self: Shadrack has to verify his own existence in the imperfect mirror of the toilet bowl, and Sula's course of self-exploration is displaced into her roles as fugitive and witch. Morrison underscores this subconscious bond between Shadrack and Sula, first in the introductory chapter and then in their encounter after the drowning. At that moment she joins him as an outcast from the social order of the community and the psychic order of integrated selves. His ambiguous word, "Always," reinforces the bond between them, implying that always life will be like this, always she and he will be pariahs. On her part she leaves her belt, which further symbolizes the subconscious ties between them. They are a peculiar dyad, linked subliminally by their mutual roles but unable to acknowledge the connection.

As Rushdy notices, just before her epiphany at the end of the novel, Nel encounters Shadrack, who "passed her by," vaguely recalling her but unable to place her. Physically, "Shadrack and Nel moved in opposite directions, each thinking separate thoughts about the past. The distance between them increased as they both remembered gone things." The novel moves from the potential and magical union of Sula and Nel, by way of the subconscious, almost telepathic empathy between Sula and Shadrack, through numerous troubled relationships including Sula and Nel's, to this state of mutual isolation. But in the next sentence "suddenly Nel stopped" because "her eye twitched and burned a little," a trace of Sula's presence in its recall of Sula's birthmark over her eye. The unspoken, unrecognized encounter with Shadrack is the catalyst for Nel's realization that she misses Sula, and Shadrack's presence thereby precipitates her belated mental reunion with Sula, which dissolves her grey fur-ball of guilt and self-denial.

As critics have noticed, Nel's cry is ambiguous. In it she finally finds her voice, but her cry is wordless, void of representational meaning. Margaret Homans contends that the cry "exemplifies the paradox of separatism in language," whereas Keith Byerman finds that the cry's lack of conventional structure makes possible the natural and human order of circles. For him Nel achieves true humanity in her cry, but for Spillers, the cry merely expresses remorse and may suggest "the onset of sickness-unto-death." Nel's cry echoes Sula's orgasmic cries—"she went down howling," during which she "met herself, welcomed herself, and joined herself in matchless harmony." Henderson argues that for Sula this "howl, signifying a prediscursive mode, thus becomes an act of self-reconstruction as well as an act of subversion or resistance to the 'network of signification' represented by the symbolic order." Each woman's undifferentiated utterance, coming at a moment of internal fusion, constitutes a cathartic release: Sula finds and accepts herself and Nel dissolves her fur-ball, a sign of her self-acceptance and internal harmony. Nel's "fine cry" places her close to Claudia MacTeer's final position—saddened, experienced, self-knowledgeable, and a potential spokesperson.

As in all of Morrison's novels, the ending resists closure. In this novel, destruction and death predominate, and the attempt to create meaning through significant pairs is always problematic. Yet characters do survive, and, strangely and inexplicable, psychic bonds do exist. Shadrack edges slowly toward emotional health through his tenuous relationship with his friend and through his grief for her. Sula, in her moment of post-death consciousness, thinks of Nel: "it didn't even hurt. Wait'll I tell Nel." Nel, after years of representation, self-hate, and isolation, is mysteriously linked to Sula by way of Shadrack, which enables her to rejoin humanity in her "fine cry—loud and long."

Conscious, direct, total union is futile and even destructive, but indirectly, without obsession or compulsiveness, meaningful relationships can endure. Just as the binary opposites are necessary, the independence of each individual must be acknowledged and preserved. The temptation is to think in terms of either/or—either I am separate or I am united, either the oppositions are opposed or they are merged—but this novel and all of Morrison's novels urge that alternative configurations are possible and necessary. Sula and Nel can't know each other's every thought, Nel and Jude can't make one Jude, Sula can't possess Ajax; but Sula's and Nel's lives do intimately affect each other's, and Shadrack can mediate between their souls. Sula, Nel, and Shadrack form a peculiar but compelling triad, subconsciously fused and necessarily fragmented.

From a social and cultural perspective, Morrison's preoccupation with divided entities in *Sula* reflects the endemic divisions within America. The gaps between pairs of characters signify the deep-seated fractures between opposed values in the larger society, particularly between blacks and whites. As with other binary pairs, Morrison juxtaposes the two races in direct confrontation, and the racial tension remains simmering, not breaking out into a race riot but contributing to the pervasive violence within the book. The two races constitute another binary pair, and the novel delineates the results of their difficulties in achieving a viable relationship.

This unfolding split is present in the tensions between the black residents of the Bottom and the whites who menacingly surround them. As opposed to *The Bluest Eye*, where the dominating white culture is present only indirectly in such forms as images of white beauty and values, in *Sula* nameless white characters repeatedly appear, always negatively with respect to blacks. The "good white farmer" tricks the gullible ex-slave into accepting infertile land in the hills, and in 1965 nameless whites reverse the trick. Other anonymous whites exert economic and political power over blacks: they withhold meaningful jobs, harass Tar Baby, arrest Ajax, and bury Sula. Enacting that power structure, the four Irish boys make sport of bullying Nel and Sula as they attempt to displace them. Whites abuse their status in their ridicule and humiliation of blacks: the white conductor treats Helene like "the bit of wax his fingernail had retrieved" from his ear as he coerces her into mortifying submission. Whites overtly consider blacks as less than human, as when the bargeman who finds Chicken Little's body wonders "will those people ever be anything but animals," and then, ironically, desecrates the corpse. The pervasiveness of his brutality is reinforced by the sheriff's opinion: "whyn't he throw it back into the water."

Another long-standing division in American culture, still present in the twentieth century, separates the idealized, agrarian past and the industrial present. The American myth promised a new beginning, an Edenic garden where the evils of urbanization and class conflict would be transcended, but the realities of slavery, the Civil War, and increasing industrialization meant the gradual fading of this Jeffersonian ideal. Racial division is fundamental to this failure: a racially segregated society intensifies rather than eliminates class hierarchy; the melting pot fails when cultural islands form. Despite the fading of the agrarian myth, it retains its force in the twentieth century in the form of nostalgia for an ideal rural past. In *Sula*, Morrison evokes this sentiment by placing the narrator in the near-present, wistfully recalling the old days when the Bottom was a neighborhood, one that, despite its problems and faults, was preferable to its obliteration. But Morrison is also ironic, for the past that the story recalls is far from idyllic: in contrast to the American agrarian dream, the African-American agrarian past is characterized by violence and hardship. In the Bottom there are no waving fields of grain, no "two chickens in every pot," and, no matter where she travels, Sula finds that "there is no promised land of freedom to look toward." Nevertheless, that agrarian past, uncomfortably close to slavery, must be remembered and reclaimed, as Morrison delineates more intensively in *Beloved* and *Jazz*.

The sense of ironic displacement, begun in the novel's preface, deepens as Morrison leads readers to the Bottom via Shadrack. Sent to serve in World War I, "when blacks as a social group were first incorporated into a modern capitalist system," Shadrack is blasted into isolation by experiencing his comrade's decapitation. The dead soldier is physically divided just as Shadrack becomes mentally divided; the soldier's physical loss of his head is transformed into Shadrack's mental loss of contact with the outside world. Together, the physical and mental displacements suggest the displaced situations of blacks: Reddy argues that Morrison's "definition by negation . . . places Shadrack the returning soldier in relationship to his enslaved ancestors." In the Bottom, Shadrack and the other residents are still on the bottom of American society, largely forgotten, and "under erasure."

The Bottom, even more thoroughly than the Ohio neighborhood in *The Bluest Eye*, inverts the American dream. As Baker claims, it symbolizes "the Afro-American Place," a place that is outside and below history, a place, in contrast to the commemorative implications of the white Medallion, that objectifies the difference between white and black. Still, it is a "place," as the novel's first sentence reminds us, a place where neighborhood is possible, where communal values at least exist and can be supportive, where one's double-consciousness becomes an essential ingredient for survival. In the narrator's present time, no amelioration of the inversion has occurred: "Things" only "seemed" "much better in 1965."

The American dream has always been inverted for African Americans: if Europeans were to be regenerated in America, Africans were exiled to it; if America meant freedom to Europeans, it meant imprisonment to Africans; if America promised unlimited mobility to white settlers, the only mobility for slaves was as fugitives; if America meant a new place for Europeans, Africans had no place of their own. R. W. B. Lewis characterizes the new American hero as emancipated from history, undefiled, and able to stand alone, none of which applies to the enslaved African American. In Fisher's terms, the existence of slaves and then of ex-slaves rendered inviable the American myth of transparency.

In addition to the double-consciousness that results from being both within and outside mainstream culture, another result of radicalization in America is that for African Americans the search for identity has been especially intense, even "desperate." The first major form of African-American writing, the slave narrative, is a response to this need. The theme is also evident in the passing novel, for example James Weldon Johnson's *The Autobiography of an Ex-Coloured Man* and Jesse Redmon Fauset's *Plum Bun*, in which the unsatisfactory choices confronting light-skinned African Americans are examined. The question of identity also dominates most African American novels of the twentieth century, such as Zora Neale Hurston's *Their Eyes Were Watching God*, Richard Wright's *Eight Men* and *Native Son*, Ellison's *Invisible Man*, and Ernest Gaines's *The Autobiography of Miss Jane Pittman*.

One form that the search for identity takes in American fiction, black and white, is the pattern of escape and return. Typically, the American hero is stifled by the community, must leave it to pursue his or her self-development, but returns to the community with his or her acquired experience. This return, however, is usually problematic, which, according to Marx, results in the often unresolved endings of American novels in which the hero is unreconciled with or even alienated from the community. Such endings are usually double endings in the sense that the departure/return cycle is fulfilled and yet a loss is inflicted. Hester Prynne is accepted by the Salem community, but in compensation the other "hero," Dimmesdale, and the "villain," Chillingworth, are exorcised. Ishmael returns to tell the tale, but Ahab and the rest of the crew must be eliminated. Huckleberry Finn is integrated into the community but, a kind of double hero, prefers perennial escape. Doubleness especially marks African-American novels. For example, the narrator of *The Autobiography of an Ex-Coloured Man* is torn between the two lives open to him; like Sula, Janie Starks returns to her community as an outcast, but internally she is fulfilled and serene; and Ellison's invisible man withdraws from the community to a questionable isolation.

Sula extends this rich tradition of white American and African-American heroes. Unwilling to subsume her identity into the mold allowed by the black community and the dominant society, she creates her own self, which gains her at least freedom and self-satisfaction ("I got my mind . . . I got me"), but which leaves her isolated and incomplete. Like the chameleon birthmark, she is an optical illusion that varies according to the observer. In Pilate, the mark of difference (the lack of a navel) becomes the germ for a true self, but Sula's birthmark, instead of making her a genuine subject, makes her always an object. Except for her childhood friendship with Nel and her ambiguous relationship with Shadrack, her interactions with other people therefore tend to be negative. She gains a self, but, unable to gain harmony with community and cosmos, she cannot achieve lasting fulfillment. A pioneer, she forges a new path, but, like so many American heroes, she cannot be absorbed by the community.

Sula's fate thus resembles that of many African Americans. African Americans are split off from mainstream American culture, and she is split off from the community and the larger society. She has the mobility of all Americans but she has only a marginal place. Neither slave nor free, she is caught in the racial enclosure of negation. Unlike Pauline, Helene, and Nel, she refuses erasure, refuses the impossible attempt to achieve transparency, but in that process, double-consciousness leads, as it does for Pecola, not to health and stability but to a mental state of morbidity and apathy similar to the condition described by Du Bois: "an almost morbid sense of personality and a moral hesitancy which is fatal to self-confidence."

Like other classic American heroes, Sula escapes and returns, and, like them, her return is problematic. She has to escape because her first attempt at an identity through companionship fails when Nel chooses the conforming role of housewife. She must return because without the negative self-definition supplied by the Bottom she has no identity, hence the anonymity of the cities she has drifted through. Upon her return, her position is more ambiguous than that of most American heroes, for her place in the community is defined only negatively. Although her self-creation represents a significant advance over Cholly, who is also "dangerously free" but cannot create his own self, Sula remains too free, too radical, too resistant to assimilation. Rejecting assimilation, she opts wholly for the other extreme of nonconformity, not realizing that this too is a bipolar opposition to be deconstructed, not accepted. She insists on absolute independence, refusing to negotiate the two extremes, refusing to bend to be absorbed within the confining limits of community, and finally accepting a fixed position in opposition to convention. But, like one-legged Eva, she cannot stand alone, so she abandons her attempt at independence when she tries to possess Ajax—in other words when she succumbs, Nel-like, to the other pole, the social pressures of domestication.

In a fictional world that emphasizes paired characters, Sula cannot survive because she finds no enduring relationship with any other character.

That she does not, and that no one else does either, suggests that the quest for identity through such relationships, while privileged by the dominant society and by the black community, is impossible in this environment. In the Bottom, external pressures overwhelm any possibility of Sula and Nel (or of any two people) working through the convoluted process of forming such a relationship. Similar pressures, plus their own internal needs, disrupt Jadine and Son's attempt at fusion, whereas Sethe and Paul D and Violet and Joe Trace are able to build satisfying relationships, even while both cases document the complex difficulties of such a process.

Like similar antisocial heroes, Sula—radical, funky, anarchistic, chaotic—must be exorcised for the community to survive. The community endures for twenty-five years but is impoverished by the loss of this energy, as Nel realizes that post-Bottom, post-Sula Medallion is spiritually weakened. Without the pariah to clean themselves on, the members of the community slip into the doldrums. Yet Sula is not entirely forgotten, as her death is connected to a strange, sad, nostalgic fruition for Shadrack and Nel.

Although the attempt to find identity through a relationship with another person is an illusion, that fundamental division between self and other must be investigated, as Morrison continues to do in her next four novels. The violence of *Sula* is necessary to loosen the rigidity of the bipolar structures. Only by questioning such structures, by accepting the inevitability of separation, and by attempting to bridge the gaps, can one understand the division and therefore one's self. Accepting the grief unblocks the repressed emotion and allows the soul to be reborn and to soar, even if it "howl[s] in a stinging awareness of the endings of things" and even if it soars in "circles and circles of sorrow." For this novel, however, the epiphany comes too late, too late to retrieve what has been lost, too late for Nel or Sula to continue her self-development. Such retrieval, development, and unification is reserved for Morrison's next hero, Milkman Dead.

BIMAN BASU

The Black Voice and the Language of the Text: *Toni Morrison's* Sula

One of the most significant developments in the African-American tradition has been the formation of a class of intellectuals (scholars, critics, writers), a formation shot through and through with conflict both within and without. The conflict, on one hand, is between African-American and American culture, and on the other, between this class of intellectuals and the "people," the "masses." The conflict, in both its productive and traumatic force, may, in fact, be seen as propelling the trajectory of the African-American intellectual and expressive enterprise. Even the terms used to understand this phenomenon offer ample evidence of the centrality of conflict in the works of African-American writers: double consciousness, dialogics of differences/dialectics of identity, simultaneity of oppression/discourse, immersion and ascent, roots and routes, anchorage and voyage, etc.

The centrality of this concern in cultural analysis cannot be elided when we shift our focus to literary studies. While this conflict is operative in practically all African-American writing, the focus here is on the tradition of black women's fiction, specifically as it appears in Toni Morrison's *Sula*. In terms of narrative strategy, black women writers have negotiated this conflict by manipulating what we have traditionally called point of view and, by extension, voice. This mobilization of voice enacts the conflict between cultures. At another level, however, African-American women's fiction has

From *College Literature* 23, no. 3 (October 1996). © 1996 by West Chester University.

produced, from within, profound philosophical reflections on language itself.

Perhaps one of the most significant, and early, contributions to the study of voice in African-American fiction is John Wideman's "Defining the Black Voice in Fiction." He calls our attention to "the colonial interface of two language cultures—one written, literary and the other oral, traditional." The former is invested with a legitimating authority in the form of a "literary frame" which functions as a legitimating device: "the literary frame was a mediator, a legitimizer." Furthermore, "The frame implies a linguistic hierarchy, the dominance of one language variety over all others."

As a result of "the colonial interface," narrative strategy in black fiction involves a negotiation with the literary frame and its linguistic hierarchy. Different writers have, of course, intervened in this hierarchy in different ways, and, as Wideman suggests, the specific modes of this intervention, in fact, provide a continuum along which African-American literature may be charted. As Henry Louis Gates has demonstrated most vigorously, Zora Neale Hurston's "oxymoronic oral hieroglyphic" constitutes her specific mode of intervention. Gayl Jones intervenes in such a way that, as Wideman asserts, "the frame has disappeared."

Although Wideman later concedes that "black speech cannot escape entirely the frame of American literary language," the significant point is that we can observe a continuum in black women's fiction in which orality ruptures the fabric of the literary text, oral syntax implodes the literary voice. And although we might also concede that strictly speaking, if somewhat fastidiously, "oral literature" is a "strictly preposterous term," black women's fiction not only contains a substratum of oral residue, but actively communicates an oral/aural and tactile experience; that is, it manipulates and redistributes the sensory configuration of the literary experience. One of the ways it does so is through its concern with voice.

The concern with voice is intimately connected in black women's fiction with the nature of language, specifically with the written word itself. Limiting ourselves to an analysis of these concerns in *Sula*, we might articulate, albeit rather schematically, two rival claims of language. The first which privileges the signifier and is perhaps best represented by Michael Foucault's method has been immensely productive in literary and cultural studies, and for specific historical reasons which we need not consider here, in minority studies generally. Foucault does not, of course, remain intractable at the level of the signifier, but in the momentum of his method, particularly in certain aspects of his archaeology, traces of which are unmistakably carried over into his genealogy, one notes the loss of agency, the sense of being inexorably determined by a set of discursive regularities. At one point of his critique of Foucault, Habermas probes into these regularities, or into their regulation, and forces us to acknowledge "'the strange notion of regularities which regulate themselves.'" While Foucault's work has unquestionably been productive, the general methodological ascendancy of discourse analysis has fostered what one critic refers to as an "exorbation of language;" and some African-American scholars have reacted against the textual orientation of African-American literary studies.

As an alternative to this textualization, different groups, have articulated different emphases, all of which aim to free literary studies from a somewhat rigid textuality. At the level of literature, the study of the relationship of the literary text to culture in general is a productive one even if, at times, the insistence on the non-textual in literary study seems to move in the direction of attempting to liberate literature from letters. At the level of language, representation may mark the epistemological limits of access, and yet representation itself seems constantly to be disfigured by unrepresentability. Even if one acknowledges that there is, at a certain level, no getting away from representation, marks of the non-representational continue to leave their traces in the text. At the same time, even if one acknowledges that there is, at a certain level, no getting away from metaphysics, tentative excursions into metaphysics run the risk of being recuperated into essentialisms; and the charge of essentialism, which in some quarters has reached a ridiculously petulant pitch, remains nevertheless, a serious one.

In *Sula* Toni Morrison doggedly pursues these possibilities of language. She has, in her non-fiction, made her intentions clear. She asserts that "in Afro-American literature itself the question of difference, of essence, is critical." She then asks, "What makes a book 'Black'? The most valuable point of entry into the question of cultural (or racial) distinction, the one most fraught, is its language—its unpoliced, seditious, confrontational, manipulative, inventive, disruptive, masked and unmasking language. Such a penetration will entail the most careful study, one in which the impact of Afro-American presence on modernity becomes clear and is no longer a well-kept secret."

Her observation about the black impact on modernity is profound, and this has been and continues to be read and demonstrated in various ways. For the purposes of this paper, however, it is her overwhelming emphasis on language that is important. Her response to the question "what makes a book black?" is tautological: what makes a book black is its black language. We may also provisionally note that her insistence that the black "difference," the black "distinction," is its "essence," its "presence" constitutes a move toward a metaphysics of race. Having observed these general directions of her comments, however, one also needs to observe that the black language of the black text, as cultural/racial index, is "the one most fraught," and the "entry," the "penetration," into this language "will entail the most careful study."

Characteristically, Morrison proceeds by exclusion and by analogy, by describing those traits that do not define black literature, or rather, by rejecting these definitions imposed by others, and by drawing an analogy with music. In an earlier interview, attempting to define "what makes a book 'black,'" she says, for example, "The only analogy I have for it is music," and a little later, "I don't have the vocabulary to explain it better." It is perhaps become all too easy to read in some of Morrison's comments a dangerous essentialism and a retrograde politics. Yet, these same comments may point toward that oral syntax that implodes the literary voice, and more generally, toward that element of the non-representational, of excess, of grotesquerie that finds its embodiment in *Sula*. In the same interview cited above, Morrison makes a pertinent remark: "There was an articulate literature before there was print. There were griots. They memorized it. People heard it. It is important that there is sound in my books—that you can hear it, that I can hear it."

The question of a defining, distinctive voice also crystallizes into a specifically technical problem of narrative strategy, that of point of view. And Morrison is heir to this concern in the tradition of black fiction. She seems, for example, altogether dissatisfied with her handling of point of view in her first novel, *The Bluest Eye*. She says she fails "to secure throughout the work the feminine subtext" and "The shambles this struggle became is most evident in the section on Pauline Breedlove where I resorted to two voices, hers and the urging narrator's, both of which are extremely unsatisfactory to me." On *Sula*, Morrison is particularly terse about the opening: she says she is "embarrassed" by it and "despises" it. She calls it the "valley man's guidance," his "door" into "the territory."

The construction of this "valley man's" door, this discursive, authenticating, introductory, "literary frame" involves the opposition between "the nightshade and blackberry patches," and "two words of darkness in 'nightshade,'" indicating "*Sula*'s double-dose of chosen blackness and biological blackness." Further, Sula is "quintessentially black, metaphysically black, if you will, which is not melanin and certainly not unquestioning fidelity to the tribe." In the next sequence of terms, Morrison moves from "metaphysically black" to "dangerously female": "She is new world black and new world woman extracting choice from choicelessness, responding inventively to found things. Improvisational. Daring, disruptive, imaginative, modern, out-of-the-house, outlawed, unpolicing, uncontained and uncontainable. And dangerously female." Sula represents "the complex, contradictory, evasive, independent, liquid modernity" which "ushers in the Jazz Age."

It is perhaps already clear that if we juxtapose what Morrison has to say about language and about Sula, or about the blackness of black language and Sula's blackness and femaleness, we find a compelling coincidence. We find direct repetition and echoes in "disruptive," "unpoliced/unpolicing," "inventive/improvisational/imaginative" and "seditious/outlawed"; the syntactically repeated closing of each sequence, "masked and unmasking" and "uncontained and uncontainable." In her descriptions of language and of Sula (i.e., in her remarks on representation and subjectivity) Morrison returns to the concept of modernity, a concept heavily sedimented with a subtext of blackness and femaleness. And, finally, she ends in both cases with the "only analogy" with music, and specifically, with "the Jazz Age."

Morrison, then, is clearly preoccupied not only with the technical considerations of point of view but also with the question of representation itself. It is as if she would have Sula become the figure of music in the text. When Morrison attempts to define the blackness of black language, she has, as we have observed, no vocabulary for it but relies on an analogy with music. So, too, when she attempts to describe Sula's blackness and femaleness. Sula, then, becomes the figure of language itself. More specifically, however, she seems to function as the figure of the semiotic in the text. She is the semiotic constituent of the symbolic, or the symbolically represented semiotic. In this sense, the collaborative effort between the narrator and Sula produces the voice of the text. This helps to explain the extreme ambivalence with which Sula is represented, the constant slippages and shifts between voices, and most importantly here, the duet enacted in the scene of Sula's "mounting to orgasm" between narrator and character, a duet, a collaboration between the unconstituted and yet inalienably constitutive semiotic and the symbolic.

Without reference to these concerns, it is not possible to understand certain key passages in *Sula*, or specifically four passages that we might arrange in a sequence. For convenience of reference, we will designate these as Sula's response to the "pathos of the black male," the "cosmic grotesque," the by now often quoted "orgasmic 'howl,'" and the "mounting to orgasm" as Sula makes love to Ajax. Critical references to these passages are generally inadequate. Some are interesting but limited; others are couched in superlatives but offer little commentary. The last passage, for example, is called "the novel's most spectacular passage" and is cited for its "stunning language of poetic metaphor"—but little else.

These passages, moreover, have not been understood in their interconnectedness, in the way they function as a specific configuration of moments which describe a specific movement in the text. These four passages function in pairs. The first two are presented in direct discourse, spoken by Sula, to Jude and Nel respectively. They are Sula's response to a black male and a black female text constructed by her two interlocutors. We might also note that while the first may convincingly be read as Sula's speech, the second is difficult to read as such. This progressive invasion of the narrator's voice into the character's speech continues in the third passage where direct quotations are abandoned and the narrator frankly describes the "orgasmic 'howl.'" The final passage, with the typographical assistance of interspersed italicized lines, enacts a collaboration of voices, a duet—a strategy that Morrison has used in her first novel and returns to at the end of *Beloved*.

These passages can be clarified by some of Bakhtin's ideas about the grotesque. Above all, and in spite of his almost unrestrained eulogization of the folk, the consistency with which he grounds his analysis in the folk offers a useful, if obvious, parallel to African-American literary theory. In fact, he asserts that the folk sense of the grotesque is not entirely recuperable in the literary text. It is born only at the "confines of languages" because "it is impossible to overcome through abstract though alone, within the system of a unique language, that deep dogmatism hidden in all forms of this system."

The intractable quality of the grotesque (which, of course, Bakhtin nevertheless tracks for some five hundred pages) leads Bakhtin into another pertinent area of our discussion, that of orality. He emphasizes the market-place form of Rabelais' language. In a remarkable resemblance to what Morrison says about her own writing, Bakhtin designates the Rabelaisian grotesque image as "a vivid and dynamic 'loud' image" a "'loud' talking image." He associates the literary text, aside from some exceptional moments when the grotesque can emerge on the "confines of languages," with an atro-phied sensuous perception of the world. This explains his assertion that "the nose and mouth play the most important part in the grotesque image of the body" and "The eyes have no part in these comic images," an assertion that we will return to.

Two specific characteristics of the Bakhtinian grotesque need to be noted: its historical continuity and its embodiment in the material, though not the individual, body. The grotesque embodies a specific conception of time, which is historical and maternalist, which defines a horizontal conti-nuity of the "ancestral body" that defeats the gloomy eschatological time of a vertically constructed medieval hierarchy. Further, this regenerative aspect of the grotesque attaches primarily to the "bodily lower stratum," but the grotesque body is also not one which is carefully demarcated and separate. It is one that stresses continuity and those parts that can be anatomically projected and penetrated: "All these convexities and orifices have a common characteristic; it is within them that the confines between bodies and between the body and the world are overcome."

If the content of the grotesque image is one of continuity and materiality, its method relies on subversion and enumeration, anatomical or otherwise. Its movement is subversive and transgressive: "Down, inside out, or vice versa, upside down, such is the direction of all these movements. All of them thrust down, turn over, push headfirst, transfer top to bottom, and bottom to top, both in the literal sense of space, and in the metaphorical meaning of the image." And the enumerations, relying on excess and hyperbolization, and close to an oral folk world, "still have something of the nature of proper nouns" which "are as yet insufficiently neutral and generalized." They are "nearer to appellations" "as yet not disciplined by the literary context and its strict lexical differentiation and selection." The language of the marketplace in Rabelais is "grammatically and semantically isolated from context and is regarded as a complete unit, something like a proverb."

The passage we have designated the "pathos of the black male," is schematic to the point of caricature:

> White men love you. They spend so much time worrying about your penis they forget their own. The only thing they want to do is cut off a nigger's privates. And if that ain't love and respect I don't know what is. And white women? They chase you all to every corner of the earth, feel for you under every bed. I knew a white woman wouldn't leave the house after 6 o'clock for fear one of you would snatch her. Now ain't that love? They think rape soon's they see you, and if they don't get the rape they looking for, they scream it anyway just so the search won't be in vain. Colored women worry themselves into bad health just trying to hang on to your cuffs. Even little children—white and black, boys and girls—spend all their childhood eating their hearts out 'cause they think you don't love them. And if that ain't enough, you love yourselves.

The passage is constructed of five units: white male, white female, black female, children, and black male. The first two images, explicitly sexual and violent, are double-faced, ambivalent. They are historical images and stereotypes recalled and submitted to a subversive gaze, turned inside out, inverted, and rendered grotesque. The first is of a lynching, of castration. The prevailing justifications behind this were attached to the sub-human, racially transgressive black phallus. The gaze of the grotesque, however, makes clear that the source of this threat lies not so much in black desire as in white fear and impotence—"so much time worrying about your penis they forget their own." The juxtaposition of the two images, passivity and dominance, evokes an unmistakable, if obsessive, homoeroticism. It is the collision of "forget their own" and "nigger's privates" within the image itself that is the condition for the emergence of Sula's grotesque: "And if that ain't love and respect."

The second image is closely related to the first. It is that of the "rape of the white woman," that vehicle of cultural purity sullied by the uncontrolled libidinal transgression of black desire. But this, too, is subverted by "the rape they looking for," in fact, "search[ing]" for. Thus the image of a racially transgressive black male sexuality collides with the white female fantasy of the erotic and prodigious superpotent black phallus. The next two images, in comparison, are truncated—one sentence each, compared to the four and five in the first and second—but they too evoke historical and social conditions meant, by Sula, to demonstrate that the black male is "the envy of the world." These images blend the historical figures of the roving black male, the abandoned black female, and the personage of the benevolent "Uncle Tom."

What is significant about these images is not only that they are drawn from a fund of historical experience, but that they have been historicized. That is, they are drawn from a specific historical and sociological body of knowledge, constructed and disseminated by the social sciences. Further, they function with "something of the nature of proper nouns"; they exert a sheer apellative force. Each image here is a "complete unit," and the serialization of such units exerts a formal pressure on content. The unit is wrenched from a disciplined and disciplinary context, is "semantically isolated," and inverted to yield a grotesque image.

The second passage, we will remind ourselves, is presented in direct quotations, spoken, or even better, delivered spectacularly by Sula, on her deathbed, presumably moments before her death:

> After all the old women have lain with the teen-agers; when all
> the young girls have slept with their old drunken uncles; after
> all the black men fuck all the white ones; when all the white
> women kiss all the black ones; when all the guards have raped
> all the jail-birds and after all the whores make love to their
> grannies; after all the faggots get their mothers' trim; when
> Lindbergh sleeps with Bessie Smith and Norma Shearer makes
> it with Stepin Fetchit; after all the dogs have fucked all the cats
> and every weathervane on every barn flies off the roof to mount
> the hogs . . . then there'll be a little love left over for me.

It is constructed of eight units, punctuated by semicolons, in one sentence. All the units begin with the subordinating "after" or "when," some packing two clauses separated by a coordinating "and," and the series leads up to the culminating "then." The subordinators thus do not introduce hierarchy into the syntax; in fact, the subordinators coordinate, linking the units in the paratactic style of oral speech.

The first two units are organized by the opposition between youth and age, the second two by that between black and white. Further, the morphology of the paired units is chiasmic, in the first, "old-teen-young-old," in the second, "black-white-white-black." The principle is that of inversion, of "inside out," which does not aggravate the oppositions but rather posits a continuity between polarities. This series of eight units does not, however, proceed in a coherently linear syntax. The first structuring principle, youth and age, for example, is already contaminated by the incestuous "girls" and "uncles." Rather, the organizing dynamic of the series is a spiraling into the anarchic grotesque. In the next two units, we have a bizarre coupling of crime and punishment, of criminals and the custodians of culture, or of law and lawlessness. These two units also transgress sexual boundaries in their movement toward homosexuality and incest. The seventh unit, maintaining a white-black polarity, makes clear the sheer appellative forces of all the units by its simple enumeration of proper nouns. But it is the last unit that is most spectacular in its embodiment of the grotesque. The weathervane that "flies off the roof to mount the hogs" is unleashed from all referential burden and strains toward an ontologically other embodied in the grotesque.

In these two passages, images function as linguistic units, or perhaps as semiotic units. While they are not entirely detached from the plot, their attachment is tangential. They are "isolated from context" and function as "complete units" in themselves. They may even, in a sense, be considered as impediments to the plot. They appear in a rupture of the text, in a semiotic convulsion that asserts the primacy of the prediscursive. They are, in Bakhtin's words, "as yet not disciplined by the literary context." And while the assertion of orality in a literary text must seem like a gross violation of "strict lexical differentiation and selection," one must note that it is precisely through these linguistic units, and their detachment from the literary context, that the images and their syntax assert the sensory matrix of an oral world.

Both passages celebrate the sheer material abundance of the body and of language, one embedded in the other, one which both threatens and impels the other. Keeping mind Bakhtin's twin emphases on the materiality of the body and the word, we can observe a tension between narrator and character, particularly in the second passage, the "cosmic grotesque." It is as if the semiotic, in rebellion, would conduct a continual raid on the symbolic function, would turn it back into itself and rupture the symbolic structuring. Embedded in the symbolic structure, the figure of the semiotic disfigures the symbolic. This is language continually invoking its other, or more specifically here, invoking the grotesque body of the community. The series of images presents a chain of signifiers, always straining toward freedom from a semantic grid, always pointing toward another chain of signifiers, an impossible chain of coupling bodies. The series, seeming to arrive at a referential point of attachment, eludes that point through a loophole in a process of continual deferral, always invoking the continuous body of the communal grotesque.

This image of the grotesque body of the community is clarified in our third passage, a passage which has received some significant critical commentary but needs to be situated in relation to the sequence of passages that is the focus here. When Sula

> began to assert herself in the [sexual] act, particles gathered in her like steel shavings drawn to a spacious magnetic center, forming a tight cluster that nothing, it seemed could break. . . . But the cluster did break, fall apart, and in her panic to hold it together she leaped from the edge into soundlessness and went down howling, howling into a stinging awareness of the endings of things: an eye of sorrow in the midst of all the hurricane rage of joy.

This passage occurs in a sequence of approximately eight dense paragraphs after Sula's break with Nel, and after the communal condemnation of Sula. In other words, it is a moment of meditative isolation. In this sequence of paragraphs, two images dominate, that in which Sula "went down howling" and that of her "free fall" into the "snake's breath," a "full surrender to the downward flight." Further, the "breath of the snake" represents the members of the community, and unlike Sula, Nel is driven back by "the flick of their little tongues." The "snake's breath," however, cannot be read as representing individual members of the community. Sula is, after all, the town pariah. If she gives herself to the community, she certainly does not do so according to any moral design.

At this point, it is useful to remind ourselves that Bakhtin is extremely careful, even to the point of what at times one senses is an anxiety-ridden redundancy, to underline throughout his study that the grotesque body is not the individual, biological body; it is not the "subjective grotesque," but the "ancestral body," "precisely the historic, progressing body of mankind." Sula, then, gives herself to the "free fall" into the "breath of the snake," that is, into the "gaping mouth" of the historic, progressing, grotesque body of the community, a mouth which, according to Bakhtin, is "the most important of all human features for the grotesque": "It dominates all else. The grotesque face is actually reduced to the gaping mouth." It may also be worth noting here that even though Bakhtin cannot entirely endorse Victor Hugo's interpretation of the grotesque, he is quite taken by Hugo's image of the grotesque, "of a serpent inside a man; 'these are his bowels.'" And Sula is, of course, in one reading (significantly Jude's), marked by "a copperhead over her eye."

That Sula does not "belong" to the community is quite clear. She cherishes her "postcoital privateness," she goes "down howling" into "soundlessness" and "the death of time and a loneliness so profound the word itself had no meaning." The community that Morrison represents here, however, is complex and ambivalent. It is both nourishing and devouring. And while the relationship between Sula and the community is marked by mutual antagonism, she is not separate from it. In fact, she is integral to it. Far from seeking nourishment from the members of the community, Sula gives herself to a collective, ritual, devouring.

In other words, the community is projected here in the terms of the grotesque. Disregarding a vertically constructed hierarchy, Sula "falls" or goes "down howling" into the grotesque space of a horizontally constructed continuity, a continuity which is not that of an abstract eternal but a historical, materialist, bodily continuity. This is also the logic of the grotesque which underlies the construction of the passage we have referred to as the "orgasmic grotesque." The linguistic units, in their paratactic syntax, uprooted from their literary context, exerting their sheer appellative force, represent this continuity. Similarly, Sula, devoured in the gaping mouth of the serpent, inhabiting an interiority, is simultaneously penetrated and inhabited by the serpent. The "breath of the snake" and the "copperhead over her eye" are integrated in the logic and syntax of the grotesque.

The last passage we will examine here has received both the least critical attention and the most uncritical appreciation. We have noted, in Bakhtinian terms, the function on one hand of appellations and proper nouns, of appellative force and pronominalizations, and on the other, of the lower bodily stratum in the three passages above. This method has underscored the materiality of the word and of the body, and these two come together in this last passage, as Sula, penetrating her lover's body, would tear into the sign, would turn it inside out in a grotesque act that is both violent and regenerative. It is an act of mutilation, dismemberment, and death, but it is also one of remembrance and regeneration.

Sula would "return to the state anterior to discourse," a state that is anterior to symbolic capacity. She would "reach out to and touch" this anteriority "with an ungloved hand." What Foucault discourages in his analysis of discourse is precisely what Sula wishes to do, "to pierce through its density [of discourse] in order to reach what remains silently anterior to it."

The passage, a lyrical representation of "the drift of her flesh toward the high silence of orgasm," follows in its entirety:

> *If I take a chamois and rub real hard on the bone, right on the ledge of your cheek bone, some of the black will disappear. It will flake away into the chamois and underneath there will be gold leaf. I can see it shining through the black. I know it is there . . .*
>
> How high she was over his wand-lean body, how slippery was his sliding sliding smile.
>
> *And if I take a nailfile or even Eva's old paring knife—that will do—and scrape away at the gold, it will fall away at the gold, it will fall away and there will be alabaster. The alabaster is what gives your face its planes, its curves. That is why your mouth smiling does not reach your eyes. Alabaster is giving it a gravity that resists a total smile.*
>
> The height and the swaying dizzied her, so she bent down and let her breasts graze his chest.
>
> *Then I can take a chisel and small tap hammer and tap away at the alabaster. It will crack then like ice under the pick, and through the breaks I will see the loam, fertile, free of pebbles and twigs. For it is the loam that is giving you that smell.*
>
> She slipped her hands under his armpits, for it seemed as though she would not be able to dam the spread of weakness she felt under her skin without holding on to something.
>
> *I will put my hand deep into your soil, life it, sift it with my fingers, feel its warm surface and dewy chill below.*
>
> She put her hand under his chin with no hope in the world of keeping anything at all at bay.
>
> *I will water your soil, keep it rich and moist. But how much? How much water to keep the loam moist? And how much loam will I need to keep my water still? And when do the two make mud?*
>
> He swallowed her mouth just as her thighs had swallowed his genitals, and the house was very, very quiet.

The passage, as we have observed, enacts a duet between narrator and character. The italicization, while keeping the voices separate, paradoxically marks their complicity. It alternates between Sula's "voice," using first and second person, with Sula "speaking" to her lover, Ajax, while reaching orgasm, and the narrator's voice using third person. The instruments she uses to reach into Ajax's anterior self, that is, a self anterior to representation, progress from a chamois to a nail file/paring knife to a chisel and tap hammer or, by metaphorical extension, an ice pick. What she uncovers, or discovers, similarly progresses from black (skin) to gold leaf to alabaster to loam. When Sula "rub[s] real hard," "scrape[s] away," and "tap[s] away," Ajax's skin "disappear[s]" or "flake[s] away," his gold "fall[s] away, and his alabaster "crack[s]" or "break[s]." In terms of sensory perception, Sula progresses from "planes" and "curves" to "smell" and "feel," that is, from visual to olfactory to tactile perception. We may represent these progressions schematically:

The moment of high literacy is marked by the sovereignty of the eye. After all the reservations and qualifications have been taken into account, the experience of literacy unequivocally privileges the sense of sight, and yet the passage, quite equivocally, moves away from sight to tactility, or from the isolation of sight to an altered sensory matrix. And while this movement need be neither nostalgic nor apocalyptic, as it often seems to be in Marshall McLuhan, for example, the trajectory of the sensory apparatus is toward the increasingly tabooed senses, a progression/retrogression that culminates in the "gaping mouth": "He swallowed her mouth just as her thighs had swallowed his genitals." Thus the body turns a cartwheel, the apparatus of speech and the abdomen, the mouth and the genitals, are rotated in a grotesque affirmation of language and the body. This entire movement, this collaboration of voices, moves toward the aphasic, the "high silence of orgasm," toward "soundlessness": "and the house was very, very quiet."

In addition to the weaving of voices, the altered sensory matrix, the rotated bodily hierarchy, the passage also establishes an ambivalence about life and death, a reciprocity between desire and death. It vigorously brings together the embodiment of death, Shadrack, and the perfect lover, Ajax. The narrator's voice observes, "How high she was over his wand-lean body, how slippery was his sliding sliding smile." Ajax's "slipping, falling smile," his "sliding sliding smile," resembles the "flake away," the "fall away," of the different layers of his being. Further, his smile and his "velvet helmet of hair" are described in the terms of Shadrack's experience on the battlefield. Shadrack watched as "the soldier's head disappeared under the inverted soup bowl of his helmet," and the body of the "headless soldier" ran on "ignoring altogether the drip and slide of brain tissue down its back." A description of sexual fulfillment is rendered in terms of death.

The metaphor of uncovering not only brings together the battlefield and the site of sexual fulfillment, but it also affirms the affinity between Shadrack and Sula in what Sula supposes is their complicity in Chicken Little's death. Shadrack had once offered Sula a word of "comfort": "he had said 'always,' so she would not be afraid of the change—the falling away of skin, the drip and slide of blood, and the exposure of bone underneath." When Sula lyrically strips away the different layers of Ajax's being, she is engaged in a potentially deadly act. These different layers "fall away" in a way resembling the headless soldier's "falling away of skin."

Death, in this passage, is a real death, not to be trivialized, but it is not a final death. It is a creative death, a "pregnant death." This is reinforced by Sula's death, immediately preceding which, the text tells us that "she might draw her legs up to her chest, close her eyes, put her thumb in her mouth and float . . . down until she met a rain scent and would know the water was near, and she would curl into its heavy softness and it would . . . wash her tired flesh always." The foetal position indicates Sula's return to infancy, to the watery womb of a prediscursive plenitude, which, as the words "curl into its heavy softness" suggest, is the plenitude of the amniotic fluid. In the passage itself, the oblique reference to Egyptian creation myths and the reference to soil, loam, and mud, on the one hand, and to water on the other, that is, Earth and Water, male and female principles, suggest creation and procreation.

In this passage, several boundaries are placed under erasure, boundaries between voices, between sensory and bodily hierarchies, between life and death. The body becomes a cipher in a matrix of signifiers, a surface that Sula would penetrate, a site where "the confines between bodies" are placed under erasure. The bodily lower stratum and the gaping mouth, the genitals and the mouth, are rotated and aligned in the topography of the grotesque body. The mouth and the womb are reciprocally and simultaneously devouring and nourishing. The boundaries between bodies begin to disintegrate as skin "falls away," as flesh is "torn" from the face, and interiority and exteriority are no longer strictly demarcated but defined in a continuity.

The figuration of death and desire in the passage denies and rejects the somber finality of death. The novel, in general, is saturated with death, and Sula herself is often participant or observer in these deaths. The text, however, seems to sustain its representation of Sula as a figure of the constitutive element of language, an element that is "uncontained and uncontainable." In this sense, in terms of its language, the text offers what is perhaps its most playful and "disruptive" amendment in Sula's death. At this point, the novel gives the slip to the grim reaper, its language offers what Bakhtin calls the "gay loophole": "Sula felt her face smiling. 'Well, I'll be damned,' she thought, 'it didn't even hurt. Wait'll I tell Nel.'" Far from a metaphysically conceived finality, or a moralistically stipulated justification, Sula's words represent an affirmation of life, irreverent, "outlawed," intractable.

Morrison's concern with orality and literacy, with interiority and exteriority, and with voice and language is certainly not anomalous, and we may turn to the work of several black women for the relevant intertextual relations. The most compelling in its uncompromising preoccupation with these concerns, however, is Zora Neale Hurston's *Their Eyes Were Watching God*. As a remarkable instance of intertextuality, one passage in particular deserves attention for its relation to the passage examined above:

> She had found a jewel down inside herself and she wanted to walk where people see her and gleam it around. But she had been set in the marketplace to sell. Been set for still bait. When God had made The Man, he made him out of stuff that sung all the time and glittered all over. Then after that some angels got jealous and chopped him into millions of pieces, but still he glittered and hummed. So they beat him down to nothing but sparks but each little spark had a shine and a song. So they covered each one over with mud. And the lonesomeness in the sparks made them hunt for one another, but the mud is deaf and dumb. Like all the other tumbling mud-balls, Janie had tried to show her shine.

The similarities between this passage and that from Sula are perhaps not immediately apparent. One may initially, however, associate the "jewel," the "glitter," the "spark" and "shine," on one hand, with the "sparkle or splutter" that is rubbed down to a "dull glow" in Nel, and on the other, with the "gold leaf" Sula can see "shining through the black." The word "mud" may also remind one of Sula's last question, "And when do the two make mud?". Missy Dehn Kubitschek, in *Claiming the Heritage*, observes that "This irreverent, edited, and conflated variation of *Paradise Lost* and several Egyptian myths emphasizes both the mud and the shine." Janie can be free, can become "an active agent," only by accepting both the shine, and the mud, only by accepting her "existential responsibility." The intertextual connection between the passages is perhaps most striking in their references to the Egyptian creation myths. We may represent this passage diagrammatically:

The process here is one which progressively diminishes the original jewel. The jewel that sung and glittered is chopped into millions of pieces which still glittered and hummed. These pieces are beaten into sparks, but they still have a shine and a song. These sparks are then covered with mud, but in their "lonesomeness," they still "hunt for one another."

The process described in *Sula* is precisely the reverse of that in *Their Eyes*. If, in *Sula*, we witness an interiorization, here we observe an exteriorization. In *Sula* we move toward uncovering or discovering; in *Their Eyes* we witness a covering. Even if the direction of the movement in both passages is different, toward an interiority and toward an exteriority, both passages deploy a method to engage the central condition of absence. The condition is one of having been plucked from a plenitude, a dislocation and diminishment, and the method deployed is one of resistance. Janie and Sula, then, are both nourished by the memory of a prediscursive universe, one that precedes the symbolic order. They both wish to recreate this universe.

In the latter, however, the "mud" is "deaf and dumb," and the human element is reduced to "sparks," which, to be sure, because of their "lonesomeness," "hunt for one another." Thus the method deployed against diminishment is relational, but it is a relation at the level of essence. In the former, in contrast, the "mud" is elemental and bodily. It is creatively constituted in a careful combination of water and soil/loam. In other words, the human element is defined in terms of existence, of the materiality and (pro)creative possibilities of the cosmic body of the grotesque.

All four passages from *Sula* that we have examined here may be exorbitant in their celebration of the signifier; they may seem to strain toward unrepresentability, to be unleashed from referentiality. But in every instance this momentum is harnessed and reined in by an insistence on the materiality of the word, the word rigorously, even strenuously, embodied. This dialectic between the abstract and the concrete, the idealist and the materialist, provides a cultural impetus for the language of the text. The word finds a local habitation in the body at the same time as the body, or, the trajectory of desire, penetrates and inhabits the word. And while the body is the historic, progressing, grotesque body of the black community, the word, here, is the oral word of black speech. This is the orality that ruptures the language of the black text.

This is also the orality that alters the sensory configuration of the literate and literary experience. The orality of black speech, by invading the language of the black text, continually resists a sterile and aestheticized textuality which, ironically enough, itself risks being recuperated into a sort of technicist essentialism—in what we have noted as a privileging of the signifier. In resisting this sort of textualization, however, the text simultaneously risks being recuperated into other types of essentialisms. This conflict between orality and textuality accounts for the uneasiness we may feel in trying to situate novels like *Sula* in contemporary critical discussions about language. This is also Toni Morrison's mode of intervention in the "linguistic hierarchy" of the "literary frame"; but more generally, African-American literature, in defining the black voice in fiction, responds to, resists, and modifies the hierarchy of the literary frame.

JAN FURMAN

Black Girlhood and Black Womanhood:
The Bluest Eye *and* Sula

From the beginning of her writing career Morrison has exercised a keen scrutiny of women's lives. *The Bluest Eye* and *Sula*, Morrison's first and second novels, are to varying extents about black girlhood and black womanhood, about women's connections to their families, their communities, to the larger social networks outside the community, to men, and to each other. Lending themselves to a reading as companion works, the novels complement one another thematically and may, in several ways, be viewed sequentially. (Morrison calls her first four novels "evolutionary. One comes out of the other." In *The Bluest Eye* she was "interested in talking about black girlhood," and in *Sula* she "wanted to move to the other part of their life." She wanted to ask, "what . . . do those feisty little girls grow up to be?") *The Bluest Eye* directs a critical gaze at the process and symbols of imprinting the self during childhood and at what happens to the self when the process is askew and the symbols are defective. In *Sula*, Morrison builds on the knowledge gained in the first novel, revisits childhood, and then moves her characters and readers a step forward into women's struggles to change delimiting symbols and take control of their lives. But excavating an identity that has been long buried beneath stereotype and convention is a wrenching endeavor, and Morrison demonstrates in *Sula* that although recasting one's role in the community is possible, there is a price to be paid for change.

From *Toni Morrison's Fiction.* © 1996 by the University of South Carolina Press.

The Bluest Eye (1970)

The opening lines of *The Bluest Eye* incorporate two signifying aspects of Morrison's fiction. The first sentence, "Quiet as it's kept, there were no marigolds in the fall of 1941," emanates from the African-American community, capturing the milieu of "black women conversing with one another; telling a story, an anecdote, gossip[ing] about some one or event within the circle, the family, the neighborhood." The line also demonstrates Morrison's urge to connect with her reader by choosing "speakerly" phrasing that has a "back fence connotation." Morrison explains:

> The intimacy I was aiming for, the intimacy between the reader and the page, could start up immediately because the secret is being shared, at best, and eavesdropped upon, at the least. Sudden familiarity or instant intimacy seemed crucial to me then, writing my first novel. I did not want the reader to have time to wonder, "What to I have to do, to give up, in order to read this? What defense do I need, what distance maintain?" Because I know (and the reader does not— he or she had to wait for the second sentence) that this is a terrible story about things one would rather not know anything about.

The line's foreboding aura charitably prepares the reader for powerful truths soon to be revealed. The pervading absence of flowers in 1941 sets that year off from all others and produces a prophetic and ominous quality which unfolds in the second line: "We thought, at the time, that it was because Pecola was having her father's baby that the marigolds did not grow." Exploiting the child speaker's naive but poignant logic, Morrison requires the reader, during this first encounter, to be accountable, to acknowledge a dreadful deed and respond to its dreadful consequences. "If the conspiracy that the opening words announce is entered into by the reader," Morrison explains, "then the book can be seen to open with its close: a speculation on the disruption of 'nature' as being a social disruption with tragic individual consequences in which the reader, as part of the population of the text, is implicated." This three-way collaboration between author, speaker, and reader is the effect for which Morrison strives in all her novels.

From this profoundly stirring beginning Morrison advances to an equally moving examination of Pecola's life—her unloving childhood, her repudiation by nearly everyone she encounters, and finally the complete disintegration of self. Through it all Morrison exposes and indicts those who promulgate standards of beauty and behavior that devalue Pecola's sensitivities and contribute to her marginalized existence.

The search for culprits is not arduous. The storekeeper who sells Mary Jane candies to Pecola avoids touching her hand when she pays and barely disguises his contempt for her: "She looks up at him and sees the vacuum where curiosity ought to lodge. . . . The total absence of human recognition—the glazed separateness. . . . It has an edge; somewhere in the bottom lid is the distaste. . . . the distaste must be for her, her blackness . . . and it is the blackness that accounts for, that creates, the vacuum edged with distance in the white eyes." The white Yacobowski is condemned for his cultural blindness, but he is not the only one responsible for Pecola's pain. Responsibility must be shared by blacks who assuage their own insults from society by oppressing those like Pecola who are vulnerable. Little black boys jeer and taunt her with "Black e mo. Black e mo. Yadaddsleepsnekked," defensively ignoring the color of their own skins. But "it was their contempt for their own blackness that gave the first insult its teeth. The seem to have taken all of their smoothly cultivated ignorance, their exquisitely learned self-hatred, their elaborately designed hopelessness and sucked it all up into a fiery cone of scorn that had burned for ages in the hollows of their minds . . ."

Teachers ignore Pecola in the classroom, giving their attention instead to a "high-yellow dream child with long brown hair" and "sloe green eyes." And when this same high-yellow Maureen Peal declares to Pecola and the MacTeer sisters "I *am* cute! And you ugly! Black and ugly black e mos," she is dangerously affirming intraracial acceptance of the world's denigration of blackness. "Respectable," "milk-brown" women like Geraldine see Pecola's torn dress and uncombed hair and are confronted with the blackness they have spent lifetimes rejecting. For Morrison these women are antithetical to the village culture she respects. They attend to the "careful development of thrift, patience, high morals and good manners" as these are defined by white society. And they fear "the dreadful funkiness of passion, the funkiness of nature, the funkiness of the wide range of human emotions" because these qualities are defined by black society. They are shamed by the "laugh that is a little too round; the gesture a little too generous. They hold their behind in for fear of a sway too free; when they wear lipstick, they never cover the entire mouth for fear of lips too thick, and they worry, worry, worry about the edges of their hair." As one of these women, Geraldine executes the tyranny of standardized beauty that enthralls some in the black community and terrorizes too many others.

When Pecola stands in Geraldine's house—tricked there by Geraldine's hateful son—she transgresses a line demarking "colored people" from "niggers," light-skinned from dark, hand-me-down whiteness from genuine culture. In her innocence Pecola does not perceive the transgression or its consequences. To her, Geraldine's world and house are beautiful. The house's ordered prettiness sharply contrasts the shabby makedo appearance of the Breedlove's storefront. Geraldine, however, does perceive Pecola's outrageous breech, and the hurting child that Pecola is becomes a "nasty little black bitch" in Geraldine's mouth. Geraldine sets her teeth against any recognition of some part of who she is in Pecola. To Pecola, Geraldine is "the pretty milk-brown lady in the pretty gold and green house." To Morrison, she is a shadow image of the Dick-and-Jane life, a sadistic approximation of the storybook people. Through her Morrison demonstrates that such a life as Geraldine's is only validated by exclusion of others.

Michael Awkward discusses this "purgative abuse" of Pecola in terms of the black community's guilt about its own inability to measure up to some external ideal of beauty and behavior. Pecola objectifies this failure (which results in self-hatred) and must be purged. She becomes the black community's shadow of evil (even as the black community is the white community's evil). "In combating the shadow . . . the group is able to rid itself ceremonially of the veil that exists within both the individual member and the community at large. To be fully successful, such exorcism requires a visibly imperfect, shadow-consumed scapegoat" like Pecola."

Even her parents, Cholly and Pauline Breedlove, relate to Pecola in this way. Ironically named since they breed not love but violence and misery, Cholly and Pauline eventually destroy their daughter, whose victimization is a bold symbol of their own despair and frustrations. In the pathos of their defeated lives, Morrison demonstrates the process by which self-hatred becomes scapegoating.

Pauline's lame foot makes her pitiable and invisible until she marries Cholly. But pleasure in marriage lasts only until she moves from Kentucky to Ohio and confronts northern standards of physical beauty and style. She is despised by snooty black women who snicker at her lameness, her unstraightened hair, and her provincial speech. In the movie theaters she seeks relief from these shortcomings through daydreams of Clark Gable and Jean Harlow. But even in high heels, makeup, and a Harlow hairstyle Pauline is a failure. "In equating physical beauty with virtue, she stripped her mind, bound it, and collected self-contempt by the heap," which she deposits on her husband and children who fail by "the scale of absolute beauty . . . she absorbed in full from the silver screen." Eventually, Pauline gives up on her own family and takes refuge in the soft beauty surrounding her in the Fisher home, where she works—the crisp linens, white towels, the little Fisher girl's yellow hair. She cannot afford such beauty and style. In the Fisher house, however, she has dominion over creditors and service people "who humiliated her when she went to them on her own behalf [but] respected her, were even intimidated by her, when she spoke for the Fishers." With the Fishers she had what she could not have at home—"power, praise, and luxury." By the time Pecola finds herself awkwardly standing in the Fisher's kitchen, responsible for the spilled remains of a freshly baked pie at her feet, Pauline is incapable of a mother's love and forgiveness. Her best response is knocking Pecola to the floor and running to console the crying Fisher child.

In substituting fierce intolerance of her family for love, Pauline refuses what she cannot transform. Her husband is an irresponsible drunk; the son and daughter are sloven. Only she has order and beauty and only in the Fisher house. Under these conditions Pauline is reborn as self-righteous martyr with no time for movies, unfulfilled dreams, and foolish notions of romantic love. "All the meaningfulness of her life was in her work . . . . She was an active church woman . . . defended herself mightily against Cholly. . . and felt she was fulfilling a mother's role conscientiously when she pointed out their father's faults to keep them from having them, or punished them when they showed any slovenliness, no matter how slight, when she worked twelve to sixteen hours a day to support them."

Like Pauline, Cholly too is driven by personal demons which he attempts to purge in violence against his family. Pauline does not see or understand Cholly's hurts, but Morrison represents them as remarkably egregious. Callously abandoned on a garbage dump by his mother, years later Cholly searches for the father who also discards him. His response to his father's angry denunciations—crying and soiling his pants—eclipses any opportunity for emotional maturity and returns him, in a sense, to the help-lessness of his abandonment in infancy. After the rejection, in a nearby river he seeks relief, even rebirth, curled for hours in the fetal position with fists in eyes. For a while he finds consolation in "the dark, the warmth, the quiet . . . [engulfing him] like the skin and flesh of an elderberry protecting its own seed." Protection is short-lived, however. There is no prelapsarian innocence available to Cholly.

In marrying Pauline, Cholly seems fully recovered from these earlier traumas. Initially, he is kind, compassionate, protective, but these feelings too are fleeting. He retreats from her emotional dependence, he is humil-iated by economic powerlessness, and he mitigates his frustrations in drink and abuse. In turning on Pauline, Cholly fights whom he can and not whom he should. This is the lesson of childhood learned when he is forced by armed white men who discover him with Darlene in the woods to continue his first act of sexual intimacy while they watch and ridicule. When the men leave in search of other prey, Cholly realizes that hating them is futile, and he decides instead to hate Darlene for witnessing his degradation. He could not protect her so he settles for despising her. Later Pauline comes to stand for Darlene in Cholly's mind: "He poured out on her the sum of all his inarticulate fury and aborted desires." Cholly, then, needs Pauline to objectify his failure.

His treatment of Pecola may also be seen in terms of scapegoating but not entirely. While Pecola's ugliness is an affront to Pauline's surreptitious creation of beauty in the Fisher house, it is a sad reminder to Cholly of not only his unhappiness but Pecola's as well. Such concern makes him a somewhat sympathetic character. He is one of Morrison's traveling men, one whose freedom to do as he pleases is jeopardized by dependent, possessive women. He has roamed around dangerously, carelessly, irresponsibly, lovingly. The appealing contradiction of his life could find expression only in black music. "Only a musician would sense, know, without even knowing that he knew, that Cholly was free. Dangerously free." After his mother's abandonment and his father's rejection, Cholly has little to lose, and his behavior is disdainful of consequences. "It was in this godlike state that he met Pauline Williams," and marriage to her threatens to conquer him.

In romanticizing Cholly, Morrison defies the unflattering orthodoxy of black maleness and makes peace with the conflict between responsibility to family and freedom to leave. Morrison respects the freedom even as she embraces the responsibility. In the freedom she sees "tremendous possibility for masculinity among black men." Sometimes such men are unemployed or in prison, but they have a spirit of adventure and a deep complexity that interests Morrison. No doubt she views their freedom as a residue of the "incredible . . . magic and feistiness in black men that nobody has been able to wipe out." Cholly exercises his freedom, but not before he commits a heinous crime against Pecola. Even his crime, however, is tempered by the author's compassion for Cholly. Coming home drunk and full of self-pity, Cholly sees Pecola and is overcome with love and regret that he has nothing to relieve her hopelessness. "Guilt and impotence rose in a bilious duct. What could he do for her—ever? What give her? What say to her? What could a burned-out black man say to the hunched back of his eleven-year-old daughter?" His answer is rape—in spite of himself. In rendering this incomprehensible instance, Morrison captures the curious mixture of hate and tenderness that consumes Cholly. "The hatred would not let him pick her up" when the violation is over; "the tenderness forced him to cover her." The awful irony of his position is overwhelming. In the end Cholly's complexity dominates the moment. Having never been parented, "he could not even comprehend what such a relationship should be." And being dangerously free, he has no restraints.

Morrison does have sympathy for Cholly (she admits that she connects "Cholly's 'rape' by the white men to his own of his daughter"), but he is not absolved; he dies soon after in a workhouse. And Morrison does not minimize his crime against his daughter. Pecola's childlike "stunned silence," "the tightness of her vagina," the painfully "gigantic thrust," her "fingers clenching," her "shocked body," and finally her unconsciousness bear witness to Morrison's aim in the novel to represent Pecola's perspective, to translate her heartbreak. "This most masculine act of aggression becomes feminized in my language," Morrison says. It is "passive," she continues, "and I think, more accurately repellent when deprived of the male 'glamor of shame' rape is (or once was) routinely given."

Feminizing language does not lead Morrison to comfortable binary oppositions of good and evil, feminine and masculine. Rather, it leads to a sensitive treatment of the complex emotions that determine character, male and female. In Morrison's writing there are no easy villains to hate; there are no predictable behaviors.

Just as Cholly is not as reprehensible as he might be, Pauline is not as sympathetic as she might be if she were stereotypically portrayed as an abused wife and as a mother. In fact, Pauline in some sense is as culpable as Cholly for Pecola's suffering. Cholly's love is corrupt and tainted, but Pauline is unloving. After the rape Morrison subtly alludes to the difference: "So when the child regained consciousness, she was lying on the kitchen floor under a heavy quilt, trying to connect the pain between her legs with the face of her mother looming over her." Is Pauline associated with the pain? She did not physically rape Pecola, but she has ravaged the child's self-worth and left her vulnerable to assaults of various proportions.

With single-minded determination Pauline survives, but Pecola withdraws into the refuge of insanity. Like the dandelions whose familiar yellow heads she thinks are pretty, Pecola is poisoned by rejection. But unlike the dandelions, she does not have the strength to persist, and in madness she simply substitutes her inchoate reality with a better one: she has blue eyes which everyone admires and envies. In pathetic conversations with an imaginary friend, Pecola repeatedly elicits confirmation that hers are "the bluest eyes in the whole world," that they are "much prettier than the sky. Prettier than Alice-and-Jerry storybook eyes."

Pecola's sad fantasy expresses Morrison's strongest criticism of a white standard of beauty that excludes most black women and that destroys those who strive to measure up but cannot. Everywhere there are reminders of this failure: the coveted blond-haired, blue-eyed dolls that arrive at Christmas, Shirley Temple movies, high-yellow dream children like Maureen Peal. And for Pecola the smiling white face of little Mary Jane on the candy wrapper, "blond hair in gentle disarray, blue eyes looking at her out of a world of clean comfort." In desperation Pecola believes that nothing bad could be viewed by such eyes. Cholly and Mrs. Breedlove (Pecola's name for her mother) would not fight; her teachers and classmates would not despise her; she would be safe. And, ironically, perhaps Pecola is right. With the blue eyes of her distorted reality comes the awful safety of oblivion.

Pecola's tragedy exposes the fallacy of happily-ever-after storybook life. Morrison repeatedly calls attention to this falseness. In the prologue and chapter headings are recounted the elementary story of Dick and Jane, mother and father:

> Here is the house. It is green and white. It has a red door. It is very pretty. Here is the family. Mother, Father, Dick, and Jane live in the green-and-white house. They are very happy. See Jane. She has a red dress. She wants to play. Who will play with Jane? See the cat. It goes meow-meow. Come and play. Come play with Jane. The kitten will not play. See Mother. Mother is very nice. Mother, will you play with Jane? Mother laughs. Laugh, Mother, laugh. See Father. He is big and strong. Father, will you play with Jane? Father is smiling. Smile, Father, smile. See the dog. Bowwow goes the dog. Do you want to play with Jane? See the dog run. Run, dog, run. Look, look. Here comes a friend. The friend will play with Jane. They will play a good game. Play, Jane, play.

In two subsequent versions Morrison distorts the Dick-and-Jane text. In bold print with no spacing between words, these latter passages take on a frenetic tone that signals perversion of communal perfection for Morrison's characters, who do not blithely run and play and live happily ever after. In removing the standard grammatical codes, symbols of Western culture, Morrison expurgates the white text as she constructs the black. Timothy Bell aptly point out that "Morrison is literally deconstructing the essential white text, removing capitalizations, punctuation, and finally the spacing until the white text is nothing more than a fragmentation of its former self at the beginning of the chapter." Home for Pecola is not the green and white picture-perfect house of the white myth. Home is a storefront where mother and father curse and fight, brother runs away from home, and sister wishes with all her soul for blue eyes. Pecola appropriates the storybook version of life because her own is too gruesome. In her life she is subject to other people's cruel whims to which she can offer no voice of protest.

Indeed, she has no voice in this text at all, a condition which loudly echoes her entire existence. She has no control over the events in her life and no authority over the narrative of those events. That authority goes to twelve-year-old Claudia, who narrates major portions of Pecola's story with compassion and understanding. Claudia and her older sister Frieda are the "we" of the opening paragraph. They witness Pecola's despair and try to save her. "Her pain agonized me," Claudia says, "I wanted to open her up, crisp her edges, ram a stick down that hunched and curving spine, force her to stand erect and spit the misery out on the streets." But the sisters fail. They do not save Pecola from her breakup. As the girls mourn their failure, Morrison chronicles the loss of their innocence. But unlike Pecola's short-circuited innocence, their loss is part of a natural ritual of growing up.

Morrison proffers Claudia and Frieda as foils to Pecola. They are strong and sturdy; Pecola is not. Claudia's independence and confidence especially throw Pecola's helplessness into stark relief. For Claudia, blue-eyed dolls at Christmas and Shirley Temple dancing with Bojangles Robinson are unappealing and even insulting. With youthful but penetrating insight, she declares her exemption from "The universal love of white dolls, Shirley Temples, and Maureen Peals."

Claudia and her sister traverse Morrison's landscape of black girlhood. Bound by a social environment that is hostile to their kind, they have "become headstrong, devious and arrogant" enough to dismiss limitations and believe that they can "change the course of events and alter a human life." With ingenious faith in themselves, Claudia and Frieda attempt to rescue Pecola and her baby. They would make beauty where only ugliness resided by planting marigolds deep in the earth and receiving the magic of their beauty as a sign of Pecola's salvation. When neither marigolds nor Pecola survive, the girls blame a community that is seduced by a white standard of beauty and that makes Pecola its scapegoat: "All of us—all who knew her—felt so wholesome after we cleaned ourselves on her. We were beautiful when we stood astride her ugliness. . . . We honed our egos on her, padded our characters with her frailty, and yawned in the fantasy of our strength."

For the most part their parents, Mr. and Mrs. MacTeer, save Claudia and Frieda from this sort of persecution. Mr. MacTeer (unlike Cholly) acts as a father should in protecting his daughter from a lecherous boarder. Mrs. MacTeer's place is not in a white family's kitchen, but in her own, where familiar smells hold sway and where her singing about "hard times, bad times and somebody-done-gone-and-left-me times" proclaims that pain is endurable, even sweet. To her daughters she bequeaths a legacy of compassion for others and defiance in the face of opposition. Her love for them was "thick and dark as Alaga syrup." The MacTeers embody the communal resiliency at the heart of black culture.

Mrs. MacTeer is not one of Morrison's ancestors—a person wise in the ways of life who transmits that wisdom and knowledge of self to the uninitiated. She is, however, one of Morrison's nurturers. Claudia remembers the feel of her mother's hands on her forehead and chest when she is sick: "I think," she says, "of somebody with hands who does not want me to die." Mrs. Macteer takes Pecola in when Cholly burns his family out. She presides over Pecola's first menses, hugging her reassuringly (the only hug the adolescent Pecola ever receives; Mrs. Breedlove's hugs and assurances are reserved for the little Fisher girl). But Mrs. MacTeer's influence in Pecola's life is short in duration. With no one else available Pecola turns to the whores who live upstairs over the storefront for instruction given lovingly. China, Marie, and Poland stand in opposition to the Geraldines in the community. They are not pretentious heirs to false puritanical values, and Morrison respects their unvarnished natures. "Three merry gargoyles. Three merry harridans," they are quick to laugh or sing. Defying all stereotypes of pitiable women gone wrong, they make no apologies for themselves and seek no sympathy. "They were not young girls in whores' clothing, or whores regretting their loss of innocence. They were whores in whore' clothes, whores who had never been young and had no word for innocence." Pecola loves these women, and they are more than willing to share the lessons they've learned, but their lessons are wrong for Pecola. They can tell her stories that are breezy and rough about lawless men and audacious women. But they cannot teach her what she wants most to know: how to be loved by a mother and a father, by a community, and by a society.

For that she turns in the end to Soaphead Church, the itinerant spiritualist and flawed human being. A pedophile and a con man, Soaphead has not transcended the pain of life's humiliations and is deeply scarred. Morrison describes him as "that kind of black" for whom blackness is a burden to be borne with self-righteous indignation. Of West Indian and colonial English ancestry that has long been in social decline, Soaphead, existing at the bottom of the descent, is "wholly convinced that if black people were more like white people they would be better off." He, therefore, appreciates Pecola's yearning for blue eyes. But Soaphead's powers are fraudulent as are his claims to have helped Pecola by "giving" her blue eyes; he does little more than use her in his own schemes of revenge against God and man. With no one to help her counteract the love of white dolls with blue eyes, Pecola cannot help herself, and she is obliged to be the victim—always.

Indeed the effects of Pecola's devastation are unrelenting as measured in the passing of time in the novel—season after season: Morrison names each of the novel's sections after a season of the year, beginning with autumn and ending with summer. The headings are ironically prophetic preludes to the story segments. They stand out as perverse contradictions of Pecola's experiences: thematic progression is not from dormancy to renewal for Pecola. In spring she is violated; by summer she is annihilated. Morrison uses this disruption of nature to signal the cosmic proportion of Pecola's injury.

Sula (1973)

The Bluest Eye was not commercially successful at the time of its publication (its popularity has risen in tandem with Morrison's reputation). Yet, it did inaugurate its author's public literary life. After writing it, Morrison became a frequent reviewer in the *New York Times* and an authoritative commentator on black culture and women's concerns. Three years later *Sula* was both a commercial and critical triumph. It was excerpted in *Redbook* and widely reviewed. The Book-of-the-Month Club selected it as an alternate, and in 1975 it was nominated for the National Book Award.

If *The Bluest Eye* chronicles to some extent an annihilation of self, *Sula*, on the contrary, validates resiliency in the human spirit and celebrates the self. In *Sula* Morrison returns to the concerns of girlhood explored in her first novel, but this time she approaches her subject in celebration, as if to see what miracles love and friendship may accomplish for Sula and Nel that they could not for Pecola, Claudia, and Frieda.

Sula Peace and Nel Wright are each the only daughter of mothers whose distance leaves the young girls alone with dreams of someone to ease the solitude. When they first met, "they felt the ease and comfort of old friends." Indeed "their meeting was fortunate, for it let them use each other to grown on." Sula's spontaneous intensity is relieved by Nel's passive reserve. Sula loves the ordered neatness of Nel's home and her life, and Nel likes Sula's "household of throbbing disorder constantly awry with things, people, voices and the slamming of doors . . ." Over the years "they found relief in each other's personality."

In examining their friendship, Morrison tests its endurance. As she says, not much had been done with women as friends; men's relationships are often the subject of fiction, but what about women's strongest bonds? As perfect complements, one incomplete without the other, Sula and Nel together face life, death, and marriage, and eventually they also must face separation. Throughout, Morrison affirms the necessity of their collaboration.

Adolescence for Nel and Sula is marked not by individuation, but by merger, as a single, provocative play scene illustrates. In the summer of their twelfth year, with thoughts of boys and with "their small breasts just now beginning to create some pleasant discomfort when they were lying on their stomachs," the girls escape to the park. In silence and without looking at each other, they begin to play in the grass, stroking the blades. "Nel found a thick twig and, with her thumbnail, pulled away its bark until it was stripped to a smooth, creamy innocence." Sula does the same. Soon they begin poking "rhythmically and intensely into the earth," making small neat holes. "Nel began a more strenuous digging and, rising to her knee, was careful to scoop out the dirt as she made her hole deeper. Together they worked until the two holes were one and the same." In their symbolic sexual play, Nel and Sula, unlike Pecola, have absolute control in this necessary right of passage (without the intrusion of a masculine presence) which conjoins them until, like the holes, they are one and the same.

Two other significant moments define their intimacy as well. The first is Sula's cutting off the tip of her finger in response to a threat by a group of white boys whose menacing bodies block the girl's route home. If she could do that to herself, what would she do to them, Sula asks the shocked boys. The second is the death of Chicken Little, the little boy whose body Sula swings around and around in play until her hands slip, and he flies out over the river and drowns. Nel watches, and no one discovers their culpability. At the graveside they hold hands. "At first, as they stood there, their hands were clenched together. They relaxed slowly until during the walk back home their fingers were laced in as gentle a clasp as that of any two young girl-friends trotting up the road on a summer day wondering what happened to butterflies in winter."

Not even Nel's marriage dissolves their "friendship [that] was so close, they themselves had difficulty distinguishing one's thoughts from the other's." They are both happy; Nel becomes a wife, and Sula goes to college. Ten years later Sula's return imparts a magic to Nel's days that marriage had not. "Her old friend had come home. . . . Sula, whose past she had lived through and with whom the present was a constant sharing of perceptions. Talking to Sula had always been a conversation with herself." Their lives resume an easy rhythm until Nel walks into her bedroom and finds her husband and Sula naked. Not surprisingly, this episode supersedes the women's friendship. Jude leaves town, Nel, and their children, and Nel blames Sula. Three years later, when Nel visits a dying Sula, she asks, "Why you didn't love me enough to leave him alone. To let him love me. You had to take him away." Sula replies, "What you mean take him away? . . . If we were such good friends, how come you couldn't get over it?"

With Sula's question Morrison calls into doubt the primacy of Nel's marriage over women's friendship, intimating that their friendship may even supplant the marriage. Years after Sula's death, Nel comes to this realization at her friend's grave. "All that time, all that time, I thought I was missing Jude. . . . We was girls together. . . .O Lord, Sula . . . girl, girl, girlgirlgirl."

Nel and Sula's estrangement offers Morrison an opportunity to examine women's lives in and out of marriage. As girls Nel and Sula had cunningly authored the dimensions of their own existence without the permission or approval of their families or the community. "Because each had discovered years before that they were neither white nor male and that all freedom and triumph was forbidden to them, they had set about creating something else to be." Morrison does not elaborate further on the specific nature of their creation, but clearly each positions herself just outside the village perspective, thinking and behaving with a certain independence. "In the safe harbor of each other's company they could afford to abandon the ways of other people and concentrate on their own perceptions of things."

The experience that determines Nel's perspective is a train ride with her mother. The two travel for days from Ohio to New Orleans for Nel's great-grandmother's funeral. Her mother's shuffling acquiescence in the face of the white conductor's hostility during the trip, the sullen black male passengers whose refusal to help her mother reflects their own helpless humiliation, the indignity of squatting to relieve themselves in the brush in full view of the train, her mother's stiff shame of her own creole mother's life as a prostitute—all these experiences teach Nel lessons about other people's vulnerabilities. Back home in the safety of her bedroom she resolves to develop her strengths. Looking in the mirror, she whispers to herself "I'm me. . . . I'm me. I'm not their daughter. I'm not Nel. I'm me. Me . . ." Adopting me-ness as her mantra, Nel gathers power and joy, and the "strength to cultivate a friend [Sula] in spite of her mother." Nel's daring is eclipsed, however, by marriage to Jude. For Helene Wright, Nel's mother, marriage is one of the neat conditions of living that defines a woman's place, and Nel accepts a similar arrangement for herself. Nel does not choose Jude; she accepts his choosing her as a way of completing himself. Without Nel, Jude is an enraged "waiter hanging around a kitchen like a woman" because bigotry keeps him from doing better. "With her he was head of a household pinned to an unsatisfactory job out of necessity. The two of them together would make one Jude." In marrying Jude, Nel gives up her youthful dreams (before she met Sula) of being "wonderful" and of "trips she would take, alone . . . to faraway places." In marrying Jude, she gives up her me-ness.

Predictably, when Jude leaves, after his betrayal with Sula, Nel suffers psychic disintegration, and later, after a necessary recovery, she endures shrinkage of the self. She considers the release that may come with death, but that will have to wait because she has three children to raise. In this condition Nel wraps herself in the conventional mantle of sacrifice and martyrdom and takes her place with the rest of the women in the community. Although Nel does not discover it until after Sula's death and she is old, the real loss in her life is that of Sula and not Jude. And the real tragedy is that she has allowed herself to become less than she was.

Sula is different from Nel. It is Sula's rebellious spirit that fuels the intermittent moments of originality that Nel manages to have. In Sula's presence Nel has "sparkle or sputter." Sula resists any authority or controls, and

Morrison offers her as one of the lawless individuals whose life she is so fond of examining. From Sula's days in childhood when she retreated to the attic, she rebels against conventionality. She is surprised and saddened by Nel's rejection of her over Jude. She had not expected Nel to behave "the way the others would have." But nothing, not even her closest and only friend's censures will force Sula to abridge herself.

Even near death, Sula will have none of Nel's limitations. To the end she proclaims, "I sure did live in this world. . . . I got my mind. And what goes on in it. Which is to say, I got me." Sula's me-ness remains intact; she has not betrayed herself as Nel has, and any loneliness she feels is a price she is willing to pay for freedom.

By and large, Sula's assessment of her past is credible. Only once has she come close to subsuming herself to some other, named Ajax. Shortly after Ajax shows up at her door with a quart of milk tucked under each arm, Sula begins to think of settling down with him. All of the men in her past had, over the years, "merged into one large personality" of sameness. "She had been looking . . . for a friend, and it took her a while to discover that a lover was not a comrade and could never be—for a woman." But those thoughts exist before she meets Ajax; he is different in some ways. He brings her beautiful and impractical gifts: "clusters of black berries still on their branches, four meal-fried porgies wrapped in a salmon-covered sheet of the Pittsburgh *Courier*, a handful of jacks, two boxes of lime Jell-Well, a hunk of ice-wagon ice . . . " Sula is most interested in him, however, because he talks to her and is never condescending in conversation. "His refusal to baby or protect her, his assumption that she was both tough and wise—all that coupled with a wide generosity of spirit . . . sustained Sula's interest and enthusiasm."

Their interlude ends when Ajax discovers Sula's possessiveness. For the first time Sula wants to be responsible for a man and to protect him from the dangers of life. Giving in to a nesting instinct that is new for her, she is on the verge of making his life her own. But before that happens Ajax leaves, and Sula has only his driver's license as proof of his ever having been there. Sula's sorrow is intense, but short-lived, unlike Nel's enduring suffering for Jude. In the end, when Nel accuses her of never being able to keep a man, Sula counters that she would never waste life trying to keep a man: "They ain't worth more than me. And besides, I never loved no man because he was worth it. Worth didn't have nothing to do with it. . . . My mind did. That's all." Sula had needed Nel, but she had never needed a man to extend herself. Even in lovemaking she had manufactured her own satisfaction, "in the postcoital privateness in which she met herself, welcomed herself, and joined herself in matchless harmony." With Ajax those private moments had not been necessary, but without him Sula abides. The self, Morrison instructs, should not be liable in its own betrayal.

Sula is, without a doubt, a manifesto of freedom, and that fact in large part accounts for its popularity with readers and critics who champion its triumphant chronicle of a black woman's heroism. That does not mean, however, that the novel approximates the ideal or that Sula's character is not flawed. Morrison describes her as an artist without a medium. "Her strangeness . . . was the consequence of an idle imagination. Had she paints, or clay, or knew the discipline of the dance, or strings; had she anything to engage her tremendous curiosity and her gift for metaphor, she might have exchanged the restlessness and preoccupation with whim for an activity that provided her with all she yearned for." An art form augments life by giving it purpose; perhaps it teaches the individual compassion, but without it someone like Sula is, as Morrison describes her, strange, naive, and dangerous.

In this view Sula is without an essential quality of humanity. She has taken little from others, but more important she has *given* little. She does not mean others harm: "She had no thought at all of causing Nel pain when she bedded down with Jude," but without the moderating and mediating influence of her own humanity, Sula is unthinking and childlike. It is as if some crucial element of consciousness had been arrested in childhood when she heard her mother say to a friend that she loved Sula but did not like her or when "her major feeling of responsibility [for Chicken Little's death] had been exorcised." After that, "she had no center, no speck around which to grow." The most bizarre episodes of her conduct may be understood in this context: feeling no emotion but curiosity while watching her mother burn to death, putting her grandmother in a nursing home for no good reason, and, of course, having sex with her best friend's husband.

Imperfect as she is, however, Sula does escape the falseness and emptiness of Nel's life. As Nel takes her place beside the other women in the community, she and they are identified with spiders, whose limitations keep them dangling "in the dark dry places . . . terrified of the free fall." And if they do fall, they envision themselves as victims of someone else's evil. Sula, on the other hand, is one of Morrison's characters who is associated with flight, the metaphor for freedom. Sula is not afraid to use her wings fully to "surrender to the downward flight." She is unafraid of the free fall.

Flight in Morrison is usually associated with men and not with women, who are more often than not Morrison's nurturers. Of course, Morrison offers neither quality by itself as the archetypal model; in the best scenarios the individual is capable of both nurturance and flight. Indeed, Nel and Sula are incomplete without each other. As Morrison says, "Nel knows and believes in all the laws of that community. She is the community. She believes in its values. Sula does not. She does not believe in any of those laws and breaks them all. Or ignores them." But both positions are problematic, Morrison continues: "Nel does not make that 'leap'—she doesn't know about herself [she does not discover until too late, for example that she had watched Chicken Little's drowning with excitement]. . . . Sula, on the other hand, knows all there is to know about herself. . . . But she has trouble making a connection with other people and just feeling that lovely sense of accomplishment of being very close in a very strong way." Nurturance without invention and imagination is analogous to flight without responsibility. Ajax is the only other character in the novel who is identified with flying. He loves airplanes, and he thinks often of airplanes, pilots, "and the deep sky that held them both." When he takes long trips to big cities, other people imagine him pursuing some exotic fun that is unavailable to them; in truth, he is indulging his obsession with flying by standing around airports watching planes take off.

Metaphorically, Ajax is always in flight—from conventionality. Without work, but willing to be responsible for himself, Ajax does not take cover in domesticity. Unlike Jude, who is only half a man without Nel as his refuge from life's injustices, Ajax does not need Sula to kiss his hurts and make them better. Unlike Jude, Ajax has self-esteem that is not diminished by white men's refusal of work, and unlike Jude, he does not run away and leave behind a wife and children. Ajax does leave Sula, but his action is not a betrayal. Ajax and Sula had come together, not as fractional individuals in need of the other to be complete, but as whole people, and when that equation is threatened by Sula's possessiveness, Ajax leaves Dayton and airplanes. Of men like Ajax Morrison writes:

> They are the misunderstood people in the world. There's a wildness that they have, a nice wildness. It has bad effects in a society such as the one in which we live. It's pre-Christ in the best sense. It's Eve. When I see this wildness gone in a person, it's sad. This special lack of restraint, which is a part of human life and is best typified in certain black males, is of particular interest to me. . . . Everybody knows who "that man" is, and they may give him bad manes and call him a "street nigger"; but when you take away the vocabulary of denigration, what you have is somebody who is fearless and who is comfortable with that fearlessness. It's not about meanness. It's a kind of self-flagellant resistance to certain kinds of control, which is fascinating. Opposed to accepted notions of progress, the lock step life, they live in the world unreconstructed and that's it."

As characters in flight both Ajax and Sula stand in opposition to the community that is firmly rooted in ritual and tradition. As the devoted son of "an evil conjure woman," whom most regarded as a neglectful mother, Ajax is accustomed to rebuffing public opinion, and as a man he is given a license to do so. As a woman Sula must *take* that license, and in the fray she alienates the community. Sula returns to town after ten years and refuses to honor the town's ceremonies: "She came to their church suppers without underwear, bought their steaming platters of food and merely picked at it—relishing nothing, exclaiming over no one's ribs or cobbler. They believed that she was laughing at their God." Soon the town names her a devil and prepares to live with its discovery. In fact, Morrison says, the town's toleration of Sula is in some way a measure of their generosity: "She would have been destroyed by any other place; she was permitted to 'be' only in that context, and no one stoned her or threw her out."

Clearly, however, the town needs Sula as much as or perhaps more than she needs it. In giving the novel an extraordinary sense of place, Morrison builds the community's character around its defense against this internal threat. Sula is not the only danger, but for a time she is the most compelling. Her defiance unifies the community by objectifying its danger. Women protected their husbands; husbands embraced their wives and children. "In general [everyone] band[ed] together against the devil in their midst." No one considered destroying Sula or running her out of town. They had lived with evil and misfortune all of their lives; it "was something to be first recognized, then dealt with, survived, outwitted, triumphed over."

The predominant evil in their lives, more pervasive and enduring than Sula, is the external force of oppression. Morrison's characteristic treatment of bigotry is not to delineate the defining episodes of white hatred but instead to direct attention to the black community's ingenious methods of coping: using humor, garnering strength from folk traditions, and perversely refusing to be surprised or defeated by experience. Residents of the Bottom waste little time complaining and get on with the business of their lives. Morrison captures here, as she does elsewhere, the rhythms of the black community: men on the street corner, in pool halls; women shelling peas, cooking dinner, at the beauty parlor, in church, interpreting dreams, and playing the numbers, working roots.

Yet, Morrison says, the music and dance belie the pain of men without work and of families living on the frayed edges of the prosperous white town below. Each contact with life beyond the borders of the Bottom recalls the isolating constraints of race prejudice: Helene's brutal reminder by the train conductor that her place is in the car with the other blacks; Sula and Nel's encounter with the four white teenagers who determine the physical boundaries of the girl's world by forcing them to walk in round-about circuitous routes home from school; Shadrack's arrest by police who find him "wandering" in the white part of town. Even dead Chicken Little's space is designated by the bargeman who drays the child's body from the river, dumps it into a burlap sack, and tosses it in a corner. The sheriff's reports that "they didn't have no niggers in their county," but that some lived in those hills "cross the river, up above medallion," underscores the expectation that black life will not spill out of the hills. Morrison acknowledges the destructiveness of this enforced separation, but she also treats the isolation ironically by converting its negative meaning into a positive one. Cordoned off as they are, the people are self-sufficient; they create a neighborhood within those hills "which they could not break" because it gives continuity to their past and present.

In assigning character to the Bottom, Morrison establishes worth in terms of human relationships. As she says:

> there was this life-giving very, very strong sustenance that people got from the neighborhood. . . . All the responsibilities of the neighborhood. So that people were taken care of, or locked up or whatever. If they were sick, other people took care of them; if they were old, other people took care of them; if they needed something to eat, other people took care of them; if they were mad, other people provided a small space for them, or related to their madness or tried to find out the limits of their madness.

Shadrack's presence in the Bottom is evidence of the community's willingness to absorb the most bizarre of its own. When Shadrack returns from World War I and does not know "who or what he was . . . with no past, no language, no tribe," he struggles "to order and focus experience" and to conquer his fear of death. The result is National Suicide Day, which Shadrack establishes as the third of January, believing "that if one day a year were devoted to it [death] everybody could get it out of the way and the rest of the year would be safe and free." At first frightened of him, in time people embrace him and his day. Once they "understood the boundaries and nature of his madness, they could fit him, so to speak into the scheme of things." That is, according to Morrison, the black community's way.

Sula's mother, Hannah, and grandmother Eva had borne their share of these community responsibilities in the big house where youth, old age, disease, and insanity kept company. (Eva takes the life of her son, Plum, but Morrison treats it as an act of compassion, not of selfishness.) Sula is different, however. In refusing to become a part of the community, she refuses a part of her cultural and personal history. Her determination to define herself and to redefine a woman's role places her at odds with the community. And yet, the community makes room for her in a way perhaps that no other place would. There are both variety and cohesiveness in the Bottom, where characters as unlike as Sula, Nel, Ajax, and Shadrack coexist. "There are hundreds of small towns" like Medallion, Morrison explains, "and that's where most black people live. . . . And that's where the juices came from and that's where we *made it*, not made it in terms of success but made who we are."

Morrison suggests that this quality of neighborhood life is endangered. As the buildings and trees are leveled in the Bottom to make room for a new golf course and as blacks leave the hills to occupy spaces vacated by whites in the valley below, Morrison wonders if economic and social gains are worth the sacrifice of community, because without community the cultural traditions that inform character are lost to future generations.

Chronology

<table>
<tr><td>1931</td><td>Born Chloe Anthony Wofford on February 18 in Lorain, Ohio, second child to Romah (Willis) and George Wofford.</td></tr>
<tr><td>1953</td><td>Graduates with B.A. in English from Howard University. Changes name to Toni during years at Howard.</td></tr>
<tr><td>1955</td><td>Receives M.A. in English from Cornell University for thesis on theme of suicide in William Faulkner and Virginia Woolf.</td></tr>
<tr><td>1955–57</td><td>Instructor of English at Texas Southern University.</td></tr>
<tr><td>1957–64</td><td>Instructor of English at Howard University.</td></tr>
<tr><td>1958</td><td>Marries Harold Morrison, a Jamaican architect.</td></tr>
<tr><td>1964</td><td>Divorces Morrison and returns with two sons to Lorain.</td></tr>
<tr><td>1970</td><td>Publishes her first novel, *The Bluest Eye*. Takes editorial position at Random House in New York City, where she becomes a senior editor and remains until 1983.</td></tr>
<tr><td>1971–72</td><td>Associate Professor of English at the State University of New York at Purchase.</td></tr>
</table>

1974   Publishes *Sula* and an edition of Middleton Harris's *The Black Book*.

1975   *Sula* nominated for the National Book Award.

1976–77   Visiting Lecturer at Yale University.

1977   Publishes *Song of Solomon*, which receives the National Book Critics Circle Award and the American Academy and Institute of Arts and Letters Award.

1981   Publishes *Tar Baby*.

1984–89   Albert Schweitzer Professor of the Humanities at the State University of New York at Albany.

1986   Receives the New York State Governor's Art Award.

1986–88   Visiting Lecturer at Bard College.

1987   Publishes *Beloved*, which is nominated for the National Book Award and the National Book Critics Circle Award.

1988   Receives Pulitzer Prize in fiction and the Robert F. Kennedy Award for *Beloved*.

1989   Appointed Robert F. Gohen Professor at Princeton University.

1992   Publishes *Jazz* and two collections of essays, *Playing in the Dark: Whiteness and the Literary Imagination* and *Race-ing Justice, En-gendering Power: Essays on Anita Hill, Clarence Thomas, and the Construction of Social Reality*.

1993   Wins Nobel Prize for Literature and publishes lecture and acceptance speech delivered at the ceremony in Stockholm, Sweden.

1996   Publishes *The Dancing Mind*, her National Book Foundation Medal acceptance speech.

1998   Publishes *Paradise*.

Contributors

HAROLD BLOOM is Sterling Professor of Humanities at Yale University and Professor of English at the New York University Graduate School. His works include *The Anxiety of Influence* (1973), *Agon: Toward a Theory of Revisionism* (1982), *The American Religion* (1992), *The Western Canon* (1994), and *Shakespeare: The Invention of the Human* (1998). Professor Bloom is a 1985 MacArthur Foundation Award recipient and served as the Charles Eliot Norton Professor of Poetry at Harvard University in 1987–88. He is the editor of more than 30 anthologies, and general editor of several series of literary criticism published by Chelsea House.

RITA A. BERGENHOLTZ has recently completed a dissertation on twentieth-century satire and holds a Ph.D. from the University of South Florida. She has published articles on Swift, Conrad, Nabokov, and Garcia Marquez. She teaches expositor/writing and literature at Florida Tech in Melbourne, Florida.

MARIE NIGRO teaches courses in composition, linguistics, and modern fiction at Lincoln University in Pennsylvania. She coauthored and has directed the Writing Across the Curriculum program there since its inception. In addition to numerous articles and presentations on writing, linguistics, and responses to reading literature, Dr. Nigro has recently completed two instructional videos for the PBS series, *A Writer's Exchange*.

BARBARA CHRISTIAN is Associate Professor of Afro-American Studies at the University of California, Berkeley. Her articles have appeared in such journals as *Women's Studies*, *Blackworld*, and *Journal of Ethnic Studies*.

HORTENSE J. SPILLERS is Professor of English at Haverford College. She is coeditor (with Marjorie Pryce) of *Conjuring: Black Women, Fiction and Literary Tradition* (1985).

STEPHANIE A. DEMETRAKOPOULOS is Professor of English at Western Michigan University, and author of *Listening to Our Bodies: The Rebirth of Feminine Wisdom*.

MELVIN DIXON is Professor of English at Queens College, CUNY. His essays on black literature and criticism have appeared in scholarly journals and anthologies, including the collection edited by Robert B. Stepto and Michael S. Harper, *Chant of Saints: A Gathering of Afro-American Literature, Art and Scholarship*.

TRUDIER HARRIS is J. Carlyle Sitterson Professor of English and Chair of the Curriculum in African and Afro-American Studies at the University of North Carolina at Chapel Hill.

CAROLYN M. JONES is assistant professor of Religious Studies and English at Louisiana State University, where she also teaches in the university's honor's program.

KAREN CARMEAN is Associate Professor of English at Converse College and former editor at *The Washington Post Book Review*. She has published essays on literature and film in such scholarly journals as *Critique, CLA Journal, New Orleans Review*, and *Round Table*.

PATRICIA HUNT, an affiliated scholar at the Beatrice M. Bain Research Group at the University of California at Berkeley, holds a Ph.D. from CUNY, where she studied scripture and history in Toni Morrison's fiction.

PHILIP PAGE is Professor of English at California State University at San Bernadino.

BIMAN BASU is Assistant Professor of English at the Illinois Institute of Technology.

JAN FURMAN, Assistant Professor of English at the University of Michigan, Flint, has published widely on nineteenth-century slave narratives and on contemporary African American literature.

Bibliography

Bjork, Patrick. *The Novels of Toni Morrison: The Search for Self and Place Within the Community*. New York: Lang, 1992.

Bloom, Harold, ed. *Toni Morrison*. Philadelphia: Chelsea House, 1990.

Carmean, Karen. *Toni Morrison's World of Fiction*. Troy, NY: Whitston Publishers, 1993.

Century, Douglas. *Toni Morrison*. Philadelphia: Chelsea House, 1994.

Christian, Barbara. *Black Women Novelists: The Development of a Tradition, 1892–1976*. Westport, CT: Greenwood Press, 1980.

Coser, Stelamaris. *Bridging the Americas: The Literature of Paule Marshall, Toni Morrison, and Gayl Jones*. Philadelphia: Temple University Press, 1994.

Furman, Jan. *Toni Morrison's Fiction*. Columbia: University of South Carolina Press, 1997.

Gates, Henry Louis, Jr. and K. A. Appiah, eds. *Toni Morrison: Critical Perspectives Past and Present*. New York: Amistad, 1993.

Harris, Trudier. *Fiction and Folklore: The Novels of Toni Morrison*. Knoxville: University of Tennessee Press, 1991.

Heinz, Denise. *The Dilemma of "Double-Consciousness": Toni Morrison's Novels*. Athens: University of Georgia Press, 1993.

Holloway, Karla F. C. and Stephanie A. Demetrakopoulous. *New Dimensions of Spirituality: A Biracial and Bicultural Reading of the Novels of Toni Morrison*. Westport, CT: Greenwood Press, 1987.

Kramer, Barbara. *Toni Morrison, Nobel Prize-winning Author*. Springfield: Enslow Publishers, 1996.

Mbalia, Doreatha Drummond. *Toni Morrison's Developing Class Consciousness.* Selinsgrove, PA: Susquehanna University Press, 1991.

McKay, Nellie, ed. *Critical Essays on Toni Morrison.* Columbus: University of Missouri Press, 1989.

Middleton, David L. *Toni Morrison: An Annotated Bibliography.* New York: Garland, 1987.

Mobley, Marilyn Sanders. *Folk Roots and Mythic Wings in Sarah Orne Jewett and Toni Morrison: The Cultural Function of Narrative.* Baton Rouge: Louisiana State University Press, 1991.

Morrison, Toni. *The Dancing Mind: Speech upon Acceptance of the National Book Foundation Medal for Distinguished Contribution to American Letters on the Sixth of November, 1996.* New York: Alfred A. Knopf, 1996.

————. *Conversations with Toni Morrison.* Jackson: University of Mississippi Press, 1994.

Peach, Linden. *Toni Morrison.* New York: St. Martin's Press, 1995.

Rigney, Barbara Hill. *The Voices of Toni Morrison.* Columbus: Ohio State University Press, 1991.

Samuels, Wilfred D. and Clenora Hudson-Weems. *Toni Morrison.* Boston: Twayne Publishers, 1990.

Smith, Jeanne Rosier. *Writing Tricksters: Mythic Gambols in American Ethnic Literature.* Berkeley: University of California Press, 1997.

Weinstein, Philip M. *What Else but Love? The Ordeal of Race in Faulkner and Morrison.* New York: Columbia University Press, 1996.

Acknowledgments

"Toni Morrison's 'Sula': A Satire on Binary Thinking" by Rita A. Bergenholtz from *African American Review* 30, no. 1 (Spring 1996). © 1996 by Rita A. Bergenholtz. Reprinted with permission.

"In Search of Self: Frustration and Denial in Toni Morrison's *Sula*" by Marie Nigro from *Journal of Black Studies* 28, no. 6 (July 1998). © 1998 by Sage Publications Inc. Reprinted with permission.

"The Contemporary Fables of Toni Morrison" by Barbara Christian from *Black Women Novelists: The Development of a Tradition, 1892–1976* by Barbara Christian (Westport, Conn.: Greenwood Press, 1980). © 1980 by Barbara Christian. Reprinted with permission.

"A Hateful Passion, A Lost Love" by Hortense J. Spillers from *Feminist Studies* 9, no. 2 (Summer 1983). © 1983 by *Feminist Studies*. Reprinted with permission.

"Sula and the Primacy of Woman-to-Woman Bonds" by Stephanie A. Demetrakopoulos from *New Dimensions of Spirituality* by Karla F. C. Holloway and Stephanie A. Demetrakopoulos (Westport, Conn.: Greenwood Press, 1987). © 1987 by Karla F. C. Holloway and Stephanie A. Demetrakopoulos. Reprinted with permission.

"Like an Eagle in the Air: Toni Morrison" by Melvin Dixon from *Ride Out the Wilderness: Geography and Identity in Afro-American Literature* (Urbana,

Ill.: University of Illinois Press, 1987). © 1987 by the Board of Trustees of the University of Illinois. Reprinted with permission.

"Sula: Within and Beyond the African-American Folk Tradition" by Trudier Harris from *Fiction and Folklore: The Novels of Toni Morrison* by Trudier Harris (Knoxville, Tenn.: The University of Tennessee Press, 1991). © 1991 by Trudier Harris. Reprinted with permission.

"*Sula* and *Beloved*: Images of Cain in the Novels of Toni Morrison" by Carolyn M. Jones from *African American Review* 27, no. 4 (Winter 1993). © 1993 by Carolyn M. Jones. Reprinted with permission.

"*Sula*" by Karen Carmean from *Toni Morrison's World of Fiction* by Karen Carmean (Troy, N.Y.: Whitston Publishing Company, 1993). © 1993 by Karen Carmean. Reprinted with permission.

"War and Peace: Transfigured Categories and the Politics of *Sula*" by Patricia Hunt from *African American Review* 27, no. 3 (Fall 1993). © 1993 by Patricia Hunt. Reprinted with permission.

"Shocked into Separateness: Unresolved Oppositions in *Sula*" by Philip Page from *Dangerous Freedom: Fusion and Fragmentation in Toni Morrison's Novels* by Philip Page (Jackson, Miss.: University Press of Mississippi, 1995). © 1995 by the University Press of Mississippi. Reprinted with permission.

"The Black Voice and the Language of the Text: Toni Morrison's *Sula*" by Biman Basu from *College Literature* 23, no. 3 (October 1996). © 1996 by West Chester University. Reprinted with permission.

"Black Girlhood and Black Womanhood: *The Bluest Eye* and *Sula*" by Marva Jannett Furman from *Toni Morrison's Fiction* by Marva Jannett Furman (Columbia, S.C.: University of South Carolina Press, 1996). © 1996 by the University of South Carolina. Reprinted with permission.

Index